International African Library 24
General Editors: J. D. Y. Peel, David Parkin and Colin Murray

SERVING CLASS

The *International African Library* is a major monograph series from the International African Institute and complements its quarterly periodical *Africa*, the premier journal in the field of African studies. Theoretically informed ethnographies, studies of social relations 'on the ground' which are sensitive to local cultural forms, have long been central to the Institute's publications programme. The *IAL* maintains this strength but extends it into new areas of contemporary concern, both practical and intellectual. It includes works focused on problems of development, especially on the linkages between the local and national levels of society; studies along the interface between the social and environmental sciences; and historical studies, especially those of a social, cultural or interdisciplinary character.

International African Library

General Editors

J. D. Y. Peel, David Parkin *and* Colin Murray

Mzee Salum at work: Tanga 1986

This book is dedicated to:
Dalail, Nana and Theo Sabri
And to the memory of Emmeline Tattersall
who died in 1974
and Mzee Salum who died in 1994

SERVING CLASS

MASCULINITY AND THE FEMINISATION OF DOMESTIC SERVICE IN TANZANIA

JANET BUJRA

EDINBURGH UNIVERSITY PRESS
for the International African Institute, London

© Janet Bujra, 2000

Edinburgh University Press Ltd
22 George Square, Edinburgh

Transferred to digital print 2005

Typeset in Plantin
by Koinonia, Bury, and
Printed and bound in Great Britain by
Marston Book Services Limited, Oxford

A CIP record for this book is available
from the British Library

ISBN 0 7486 1484 2

CONTENTS

ACKNOWLEDGEMENTS

For a variety of reasons this study has been long in the making. It might never have been completed were it not for two key considerations. No other study of the occupation of domestic service in Tanzania has yet been written so I owed it as a token of respect to all those whose time, enthusiasm and ideas were given so unsparingly to fulfil my promise to disclose its economic and political significance. My commitment has been to uncover the paths trodden by the poor into domestic work in Tanzania and to understand the terms and conditions of their employment, but also to hear how they survive in a world of hardship, how they weave together the strands of work and family into a fragile web, of their resilience, their sorrows, their ingenuity and warmth. If I have worked to make sense of their lives, it is in the end their lives of work which have made this book. I am particularly indebted to Sesilia Vinsenti, Bakari Mtangi, Amina Hemedi, Mzee Salum and Ayoub Mtangi whose first-hand experience of domestic toil taught me more than I can say.

Since the late 1980s when the bulk of the material for this book was collected Tanzania has experienced a sea-change in political and economic terms, with socialism now effectively abandoned along with the one-party system of government, and a pragmatic commitment to economic liberalisation and multi-party democracy taking its place. As this began to happen my research data seemed to be overtaken by events, though I continued to visit and observe and soon became caught up in another project altogether. This involved research in the area from which most of the servants with whom I had worked earlier originated. I realised that far from being rendered obsolescent, the original data of 1986, backed up by return visits in 1989, 1992, and annually from 1994, enabled me to view the institution of domestic service from the vantage point of a longer historical perspective, in which whilst much else had changed, domestic work persisted and continued to occupy large numbers of men and women.

This research would not have been possible without a grant from the Economic and Social Research Council of Great Britain which funded the initial study, and the generosity of the Department of Peace Studies at Bradford which gave me sabbatical leave to write it up. I want to thank also the many others, without whose encouragement, stimulus and productive criticism I would never have kept going: to Pat Caplan and Caroline Ramazanoglu for their shining examples; to Laurel Brake, Fatma Bujra, Anita Carr, Graham Day, Marie Macey, Russell Murray, Gill Seidel and Moira Vincentelli for their warm and unstinting support; to Issa Shivji whose insistence on the relevance of class perspectives to political struggles in Tanzania first drew me into the topic; to Karen Tranberg Hansen for helping me to publish the first account of this material; to Azmina, Bibiye (Fatma Ahmed), Mama Luis and Esther Mbughuni, Davina and Ciriaco Pereira, Kassim Siagi and Jane Tame for their kindness, caring and hospitality whilst I was in Tanga, as well as for their willing help and stimulating curiosity. Finally I thank all the students and colleagues who, over the years, have been drawn into my enthusiasm and excitement to untangle what it is about domestic labour and who does it that matters so much to us all.

1

SIGNS OF THE TIMES

A group of women sat in the kitchen house preparing vegetables. They were laughing and joking, and the servant of the house, a boy of 14 or 15, was laughing with them and joining in the animated and uninhibited conversation. Heads uncovered, bodies relaxed and comfortable, low cut bodices exposing generous bosoms, they peeled and kneaded and talked. Suddenly one made a sign to listen and they fell silent. The unmistakable sound of the old man of the house was heard, his wooden sandals clopping on the path as he approached. Quickly the women pulled their wrappers over hair and breasts and upper arms and sat more formally, lowering their eyes to their work. The boy resumed his task with a will and everyone was subdued. The old man paused at the door, barking out a question to his wife, which she answered quickly as he passed on. Everyone relaxed again.

It was this incident which first set me thinking about domestic service in Africa. It happened in Kenya in the 1970s, in an Arab family into which I was married. The rigid rules of gender separation to which women here were expected to conform with men of their own race and class, were apparently suspended when it came to African male servants. True, this male was only a youngster like most of the servants working in that area – they were young lads from the hinterland of this small town. But elsewhere in East Africa many older men were to be found working as servants, and their employers were Europeans, Asians, Arabs and Africans. Why were men found doing a job which in Europe was 'women's work'? How did they feel about being at a woman's beck and call? Whilst evidently badly used in terms of wages and conditions of work, did they find any consolation in the human relations of domestic service? How did their female employers handle these relationships?

In Africa poets and novelists have often drawn on the dramatic contradictions of domestic work. In 1970 Frederick Oyono saw the occupation of 'houseboy' as encapsulating the personal degradation wrought by colonialism in Africa. But independence did not sweep it away – as Ngugi wa Thiong'o angrily affirms, it became a class phenomenon:

> It's the children of the poor
> Who look after rich people's homes

In postcolonial Kenya, he asserts, its explosive mixture of sexual and class exploitation had not changed, nor even the nomenclature of dominance:

> A housemaid!
> To be collecting all the shit in somebody else's house?
> And when the memsahib is out of sight
> The husband wants the maid to act the wife![1]

In her story about the cook-steward, 'For whom things did not change', the Ghanaian author, Ama Ata Aidoo, muses on the tensions in postcolonial Africa: 'When a black man is with his wife who cooks and chores for him, he is a man. When he is with white folk for whom he cooks and chores, he is a woman. Dear Lord, what then is a black man who cooks and chores for black men?' (1970:17). As the cook-steward himself puts it: 'My young master, what does "independence" mean?' (29).

My own grandmother had worked as a skivvy in the home of the local vicar to enable my mother to attend secondary school (at a time when British working class children did not go automatically). I resisted being placed in the role of 'mistress' in Kenya – at least until it became clear how arduous housework was in a situation lacking any labour-saving devices, and that local custom and practice did not permit of men lifting a finger in their own homes. Finally, the constant stream of men and women begging for work at my door became irresistable. I engaged a woman in her forties, unable to feel comfortable with the idea of working with a strange man in the house.

Back in Britain in the mid-1970s, by now a single parent, the domestic labour debate became a matter of daily struggle, as well as an issue of theoretical concern. The question of the terms and conditions under which labour power is created, and the way in which specialised personnel are designated to perform this task is a central one for society, even though it so often gets dealt with behind the scenes, in the privacy of the family. Feminism brought these processes out into the open for public scrutiny, and found them wanting. Not only did this have a salutory effect on sociological theory, it also had political reverberations around the world – mostly mere 'interpersonal contestations' perhaps, as Seccombe (1974) termed them – but none the less threatening to established arrangements for all that.

This book documents the on-going struggles which ensue when the vital work of manual and emotional labour within households is turned into wage work. This has happened and is happening in the most diverse times and conditions: my focus here is on developing countries where, for many people, there is no parallel to the specialised role of the 'housewife', and where domestic labour at higher class levels is performed by servants (who at least get 'wages for housework'). In Latin America, where these servants are mainly women, it seemed to be a simple case of women transferring skills learnt at home to the marketplace. But what if the servants were male (as was the case in Tanzania and many other parts of Africa)?

It would not be the first time, nor the last, that men displaced women when work is transferred from home to the marketplace (baking, brewing, healing, spinning, had all suffered this fate during Britain's industrial revolution). But when this displacement involved an occupation markedly redolent of womanhood, and entailed transfer to another setting of domestic servitude rather than to a factory or workshop, it raised compelling questions. The study of domestic service is not a trivial sideshow to the grander subjects of social analysis. It is one which demands reflection on the great debates of social theory: on theories of development, of gender and class and of the metanarratives through which these used to be addressed.

In the early 1980s, when I first planned to do the research on which this book is based, very little had been written about domestic service in Africa, other than Jacklyn Cock's classic work *Maids and Madams* (1980) and Van Onselen's more historical study *New Ninevah* (1982), both dealing with South Africa. Since then there has been an explosion of interest in the subject of domestic service throughout the world, exploring the highly contested themes of class, race, gender and capitalist transformation with which it reverberates and debating the theoretical terms in which it could best be understood. Marxism and feminism have been challenged by world systems theory, interpretivism and postmodernist approaches in the attempt to make sense of domestic service.

Even the very terminology has been subject to debate. Sanjek and Colen (1990:1) deliberately eschew 'stigmatised terms such as "servant", "domestic" or "domestic worker"' to engage with this phenomenon, and insist on their substitution by 'household worker'. I have chosen not to do this, not least because today's politically correct language can be tomorrow's embarrassing gaffe. Domestic chores are 'work' even when performed by family members (usually women), and for me, the key feature of domestic service is that it is *wage*-labour. More important is that the contested nature of the nomenclature is central to the lived experience: domestic workers fight about what they should be called, in the effort to snatch some self-respect in a demeaning situation. How they are termed by their employers is not always the name they give themselves. At any one time a range of terms are in use, some as put-downs, others tolerated, others proudly claimed. In the analytical literature the most common usage is 'domestic service' and I have employed this term, along with others which seemed appropriate.

The book is called *Serving Class* to emphasise that domestic service is not a matter simply of service to particular class-defined employers. It is an institution which both expresses and facilitates the reproduction of class as a set of social relations. I argue that the study of domestic service can cast a novel light on processes of class formation and consolidation in a postcolonial setting. 'Class' is here understood not only as a matter of emergent structures of material inequality, but also of agency and subjectivity in the making of history. There are class projects tied in with the employment of domestic servants – for those who employ them as much as for those who are employed.

As an independent African country, Tanzania offered a contrasting setting to apartheid South Africa. Moreover this was a postcolonial society in which, for a time, socialist rhetoric and a discourse of equality might have put the institution of domestic service into question. The setting for the study was a large town (Tanga) where marked industrial development might have been expected to generate alternative employment, leaving employers with a 'servant problem'. It did not. The major focus of the book is on the mid-1980s when a series of economic and social crises undercut Tanzania's economic base, a process which, rather than undermining domestic service, paradoxically promoted its class value.

But the book traverses a longer historical perspective. As wage-labour, domestic service is a product of the colonial period with its racialised social order. It might not have been expected to survive into the postcolonial era, or at least to have taken on quite different meanings, once the white and Asian employing class began to give way to a new stratum of African employers. Postcolonial domestic service could not be understood without some exploration of these shifts in meaning. The chapter on the supply of domestic labour could not have been written with confidence until a later (1995) visit to the area where most domestic servants originate. Repeated visits to Tanzania through the 1990s allowed me to track the story through the collapse of the socialist experiment and into the era of a new market-oriented economy, and to assess the continuing reliance on domestic work as service to the better-off and as employment for the poor. Along the way there has been a gradual feminisation of the occupation, but one delayed by the failure of industrial growth and the determination of men to hold on to jobs which they considered worth having. In the mid-1980s men were still predominant in the domestic workforce and this prompted an investigation of the way that domestic service was crafted as a man's job in Tanzania.

By focusing on the social relations of domestic service in the mid-eighties (when their enactment was at its most problematic in terms of the political economy) but putting this period in historical perspective, I aim to illuminate the enduring features which explain the persistence of domestic service through considerable transformations in political and economic conditions and extensive reworkings of the discourse of servitude.

DOMESTIC SERVICE IN COLONIAL AND POSTCOLONIAL TANZANIA

Domestic service as wage labour – a colonial institution – has survived into the postcolonial phase everywhere in Africa. The irony of its persistence in postcolonial Tanzania is that although this occupation depends on, and expands with, class divisions in society, it went unchallenged in a period (1967–80s) when the Tanzanian government declared its objective to be the achievement of an egalitarian socialism, aimed at preventing the growth of class divisions in society.[2] Servants toiled unnoticed throughout this period and they continued to be in demand as the 1990s marked the effective abandonment of any claim to socialism.

Whereas in the colonial period the employment of domestic servants was a matter of public discourse and the subject of official concern (see Chapter 4), in the postcolonial period they have generally been invisible. Socialist rhetoric encouraged only occasional challenge to the persistence of such a class-bound institution. At the highest level, it was students who drew attention to the fact that, since 1972, there had been government reimbursement for the salaries of domestic servants employed at the residences of Regional Commissioners (Peter and Mvungi 1985:191). At the lowest level, the discovery of childminders being employed by workers at the Urafiki Textile Mill led Mgaya to comment that 'the present practice among the working class to employ ayas [childminders] is exploitative and incompatible with the socialist aspirations of our country' (1976:149). Mascarenhas and Mbilinyi (1983) note the class as well as the gendered nature of domestic service, though only in passing.

As socialist egalitarianism faded, these critical voices were stifled. Amongst local feminists, some continued to recognise the contradiction of female employers 'mistreating other women', but they were also caught up in other dilemmas as 'career-oriented women with houses, husbands and small children to take care of'. They now identified themselves as employers, 'at the mercy of [the] housegirl' with her petty pilfering, unreliability and lack of gratitude (Sheikh-Hashim 1988:10).

The pioneering feminist magazine *Sauti ya Siti* (Women's Voice), in which Sheikh-Hashim's article appeared, has campaigned tirelessly for the rights of poor and disadvantaged women. In later issues (1989, 1991, 1995) the involvement of child labour in domestic work is remarked upon in articles on 'street children'. What is notable in these later articles is that a new discourse of 'children's rights' (backed by the ILO and other international bodies) has obliterated any discussion of the exploitative terms of domestic work in general – it is no longer seen as a class issue.

Otherwise the cheapness of servants as an aid to gracious living may be remarked by outsiders – as reported by a local newspaper in 1988: 'With four domestic servants (US$40 per month), lunch for four people at

US$20, a fully-furnished four bedroom bungalow at US$500 per month and combined water and power bill of US$10, Tanzania has become a paradise for expatriates and diplomats' (*Sunday News* 10 July 1988). The quotation is notable also for exposing the ratio of costs to each other, with four servants costing less per month than one meal out! The continuing necessity of servants as a bulwark against the unreliability of modern domestic arrangements may also occasionally be noted by locals – as in the comment by a washerman in Zanzibar in 1994 that his handwashing and 'charcoal battleship' (charcoal iron) were still in demand as electricity supplies were so poor and irregular (*Africa Events* September 1994).

But in general servants are unseen, with none of the issues that their employment seemed to raise in colonial times remarked upon in public discourse, even though their presence and their due fulfilment of duties is so vital to many – and frequently a matter for private concern.

ACCOUNTING FOR DOMESTIC SERVICE

Any researcher aiming to discover the true dimensions of the occupation of domestic service from official records or from census data is soon disappointed. Since independence official labour force statistics no longer allow even for an estimate of the numbers in domestic work.[3] Domestic servants are specifically excluded from many counts.[4]

Colonial records, by contrast, yield a mine of 'data'. Archival work reveals that domestic service was unexpectedly relevant to the key relations with which colonial officials were concerned and to their presentation of these in ideological terms. However, even though officials claimed to need statistical information to justify their advice in the context of policy formation, very little reliance can be put on the numbers quoted – they were generally the broadest kind of estimate.

At one level this was a definitional problem of who was to count as a domestic servant. Domestic service was not invented by European immigrants: in the precolonial period some Africans, as well as Arabs and Indians, had domestic slaves and household skivvies,[5] whilst in colonial times non-Europeans continued to form part of the employing class.[6] Nevertheless, when colonial officials made estimates of the numbers employed in domestic service they generally counted only those employed by fellow Europeans and Asians, and sometimes only the former. In 1949, for example, an estimate by the Labour Commissioner of the number of domestic servants in Dar es Salaam was based on the number of Europeans in the town, 'allowing three [servants] per male and one per female of the European population'. Although a pencilled note queries the estimate of servants per head as 'Excessive?' the omission of other employers is not questioned.[7]

This exclusive focus on European and Asian practice and the invisibility of African employers requires its own explanation. It spoke both of self-

Table 1.1: Colonial and postcolonial estimates of domestic wage labour

Date	Estimated No.	Men	Women	Juveniles	Source[8]
1926	20,000	–	–	–	Annual Blue Books
1936	20,000	–	–	–	Annual Blue Books
1940	30,000	–	–	–	Annual Blue Books
1942	35,000	–	–	–	Annual Blue Books
1947	25,500	–	–	–	Census of Native Labour
1948-50	30–40,000	–	–	–	Labour Department
1951	15,342	13,631 (89%)	653 (4%)	1058 (7%)	Tanganyika Statistical Abstract
1952	20,430	–	–	–	East African Statistical Abstract
1971		86%	14%		NUMEIST Survey

interest (since any policy changes would impact on Europeans as employers) and instrumentality (since the distinctive inclusion of 'Asiatic' employers offered the opportunity to contrast their practice unfavourably with that of Europeans). It would also seem that the racialised distinctiveness of employer and employee defined domestic service for colonial officals. Was there a (justifiable?) presumption that such difference induced an element of formality into the relationship, confirming its status as employment rather than kinship or mutual help? Did racialised distinctiveness facilitate accounting procedures? What is evident is that to bring Africans into focus as fellow employers would have been at odds with their stereotypical colonial representation merely as workers/subjects.

Given these distorting perceptions (to be further explored in Chapter 4), the 'statistics' must be viewed with scepticism.

In 1926 it was estimated that 20,000 were employed as domestic workers, constituting 7% of all wage employees. Thereafter estimates varied between 20,000 and 40,000 and from 4.6% of the wage labour force up to as high as 13%. It is likely that these were underestimates even of those more formally employed, but there is some relative significance to be gained from them. The wage labour force in colonial Tanganyika was never large (most Africans remained peasant farmers and industrial development was in its infancy) but within it, domestic service employed more workers than manufacturing or mining throughout this period, and was dwarfed only by agricultural labour, the construction industry and transport.[9]

If there was little precise accounting of the numbers in domestic service through the colonial period and usually no gender disaggregation, one thing is clear. Throughout the colonial archive they were almost always referred to as men. Indeed this was taken to be so self-evident as to require no comment and can thus be taken as a form of negative evidence. The only specific statistical reference to women is in 1951, when it was calculated that 653 females were in domestic employment throughout the country (see Table 1 above). Again the issue of who was counted and who was invisible renders the apparent exactitude questionable, but it suggests that women formed only a tiny minority amongst domestic servants at the end of the colonial period (4.5% of adults).

Frustratingly inadequate as these colonial estimates were, they render the silence of the postcolonial phase doubly disappointing. The only source for any postcolonial calculation lies in a large sample survey (NUMEIST) carried out ten years after independence in 1971 by researchers at the University of Dar es Salaam (Bienefeld and Sabot 1972; Sabot 1979). The value of this survey was that it encompassed both men and women. Based on a random sample of 5523 urban residents (52% male; 48% female) in the seven largest Tanzanian towns, it reported that 40% (2190) were engaged in wage labour (85% of them men). One hundred and forty-four of these were domestic workers (6.6%) of whom 86% were men amd 14% women. Men and women in wage employment were equally likely to become domestic servants, with 6.6% of men and 6.5% of women having done so (Bienefeld and Sabot vol. 3, 1972:26–7).

The proportion of domestic workers amongst wage employees revealed here is not so very different from some of the earlier colonial estimates, even though it is quite probable that this survey uncovered a broader range of domestic servants – working for employers of all ethnic groups and across the spectrum of income levels – than colonial estimates. The NUMEIST survey also shows that whilst men remain in the overwhelming majority amongst domestic workers, the proportion of women is three times higher than was estimated for 1951. Bienefeld and Sabot particularly remark upon the shifting sex composition of migrant labour moving into urban areas in the late 1960s and early '70s. A sharp rise in the proportion of women amongst the recent migrant population was noted, with women now in the majority. Moreover, a third of the women who had arrived most recently were unmarried, as compared to only 13% of women arriving in earlier periods. This suggested a sharply rising rate of independent migration by women (Sabot 1979:94). From other sources there was continuing evidence of narrowing urban sex ratios and an increasing proportion of women in wage employment.[10]

I assumed that by the mid-1980s women would have ousted men from the lowly occupation of domestic worker and my study would uncover the inside story of the 'feminisation' of domestic service. In the event, my own data from Tanga indicated that the majority of these jobs were still monopolised by men, though women held 28% of them. A vital first step towards understanding this limited change is through consideration of economic and political transformations in Tanzania.

ECONOMY, MIGRATION AND POLITICAL CHANGE: FROM TANGANYIKA TO TANZANIA

Tanganyika was originally a Trust Territory, mandated to Britain by the League of Nations in the aftermath of the First World War. German rule and German administrators and settlers were succeeded by British officials, planters, missionaries, entrepreneurs and their families. Asians and Arabs played a mainly commercial role, though Asians were also found in government service, and a few became plantation owners. All of these incomers became employers of domestic servants, drawn from a pool of African labour. Tanganyika was a colony dominated by African peasant production but with a small European-dominated plantation sector (the most important crop, sisal, became Tanganyika's major export) and some small-scale semi-capitalist production of coffee by Africans. The wage labour force remained small – employed for the most part in sisal production and infrastructural activities. There was little industrialisation. Wage workers were semi-proletarianised migrants from rural areas, almost exclusively men.

With Independence in 1961, political dominance passed into the hands of Africans, and a new ruling class emerged (Shivji terms them the 'state/ bureaucratic bourgeoisie': 1976, 1986). These were men (and a few women) occupying positions of political dominance linked to the administration of state assets – a role enlarged by the extensive programme of nationalisations carried out in Tanzania after the Arusha Declaration of socialism in 1967. Despite the state ideology of socialism and equality, the employment of domestic servants by this class was not discouraged; as we have seen, it was built into the conditions of service of some of its members. Nor did revolutionary language diminish the pool of migrants seeking domestic work; indeed socialist policies seemed to increase the flow.

The NUMEIST survey was carried out at a time when Tanzanian industry was beginning to expand and the economy was showing modest improvements in growth year on year. Despite this, Sabot notes in 1971 that 'one of the most striking features of the Tanzanian labour market over the past 25 years [i.e. since 1948] has been the absolute decline in the total number of wage employment opportunities' (Sabot 1979:64).[11] This was also the year when Tanzania's 'socialist experiment' in the countryside, designed on paper to draw rural people into collective forms of production, went sour and became an involuntaristic drive for 'villagisation' (Von Freyhold 1979; Coulson 1982; Yeager 1989). Men and women continued to migrate into urban areas looking for work but there were fewer openings, and those who were least educated or without skills were increasingly excluded from production or white collar jobs (Bienefeld and Sabot 1972:29). So despite the fact that domestic servants were the lowest paid of all workers and their hours 'notoriously long', the supply of labour for such work remained high.

By the mid-1980s wage employment was increasing, but this was accounted for not by economic growth but by expansion of the class of state functionaries.[12] The '80s were a period of severe economic stagnation and decline, with inflation at record levels and a drastic fall in real wage levels (65% between 1979 and 1984: Maliyamkono and Bagachwa 1990:40). Even at the highest executive level, salary earners could not support their families from the incomes they received. Nor were rural producers faring better: official prices for agricultural commodities (especially export crops) fell in real terms, though food crops could be sold unofficially (and to some extent illegally) in 'parallel' markets where prices were rising fast (ibid.:75, 82, 149). In 1983 the government introduced harsh penalties for those seen as economic saboteurs. An Economic Crackdown focused on hoarders, foreign currency smugglers and illicit traders. Asian entrepreneurs and members of the newly powerful African state functionary class were particularly suspect (ibid.:ix–xix).

With potential employers strapped for cash, and with official socialist rhetoric rendering both ostentatious living and petty accumulation problematic, a decline in the demand for domestic servants might have been the outcome. Paradoxically the opposite seemed to be happening in the 1980s: loyal domestic servants were more in demand precisely to facilitate the operation of a 'second' (unoffical) economy without which many people could not have survived. Domestic help was sought for a variety of reasons: to support the wage employment of both spouses where this could be achieved; to facilitate the private entrepreneurial activities of state employees – officially prohibited under the Leadership Code section of the Arusha Declaration of 1967[13] (but unofficially rife); and where assistance in augmenting, hiding or destroying illicit goods and property was required. Meanwhile the supply of those desperately seeking work did not diminish. Annual urban growth rates, largely fuelled by migration from the rural areas, remained at over 11.5% during the whole period from 1965–88 – during this period Tanzania had the second highest rate of urban growth in the world (World Bank 1990:238).[14]

The early 1980s saw the Tanzanian government applying its own medicine of structural adjustment prior to an accommodation with the IMF in the mid-1980s (after a protracted period of local opposition and ideological soul-searching). By the 1990s the main consequences of economic 'liberalisation' could be seen in dramatic and punishing cut-backs in state employment and public services, some sluggish signs of economic growth as officially measured, but also a burgeoning of the informal/unofficial economy and apparent rises in rates of consumption despite declining real official wage levels. The Leadership Code was officially abandoned in 1991; it had been unofficially breached for a decade before this at least. The door was now open – for all those who could – to enrich themselves.

By the 1990s then, another set of circumstances, with a play of equally contradictory pressures, characterised the market for domestic service. Profit-making was now acceptable – indeed it was officially approved as a way of generating employment opportunities (*Bulletin of Tanzanian Affairs*, 39, 1991:12) – and income disparities are now marked.[15] Displays of wealth, whilst still limited compared to many African countries, are now not disallowed (the most potent symbol the Pajero or other highly expensive four-wheel drive vehicle).[16]

Conspicuous consumption in the form of establishments of domestic servants would now appear to be on the increase, whilst those struggling to get in on the new order are still employing domestic workers to facilitate petty entrepreurial ventures. At the same time more rural women and younger people are migrating independently than ever before and constituting a flow of 'green labour' available to those seeking domestic workers.

TANGA : THE FIELDWORK SITE

Tanga was chosen as the site for field research because, as Tanzania's second largest city (with a population of around 120,000 in 1986 when the research began: TIRDEP:1985) and one with a long history of industrial development and political activism it seemed a promising place to look at domestic service as an index of class relations. Since early colonial times the town had been an important administrative centre and site for the industrial processing of export crops grown in the region. It was a focal point in the country's transport system, with its docks and railhead serving the sisal plantations established in the early years of the twentieth century. Missionary and settler influence in the surrounding region was stronger here than in any other part of Tanzania.

By the end of the colonial period Tanga Region accounted for around 30% of national employment (both in surrounding plantations and in the town itself: Shivji 1986:17) and the concentration of wage employees in the town expanded in the years immediately after independence with the establishment of textiles, fertilisers, pharmaceuticals and a steel rolling mill. For some time after independence Tanga continued to have the highest percentage of wage employees in urban Tanzania and the largest number of non-Africans in any Tanzanian town.[17]

In this setting there had evidently long been people who would expect to employ domestic help. In 1952, the region of which Tanga is the head had the second largest number of domestic servants (2739) after the capital, Dar es Salaam.[18] There had also been a continuous expansion of the pool of potential workers through migration into Tanga town of temporary workers (Sabot estimated the proportion of migrants as 79 per cent in the early 1970s: Table 2.2, 1979:49).

Migrant workers did not come to Tanga primarily to seek domestic work.

During the colonial period large numbers found work in the docks, on public works and the railways, and thousands were contracted to work on the sisal estates in the rural district around Tanga – some of these coming from as far afield as Northern Rhodesia and Malawi. Although the overwhelming majority of these sisal workers were men, women and juveniles were also employed on a small scale. By 1947, although women constituted only 3.4% of the national wage labour force, the majority of these were in sisal and half of these employed in Tanga district.[19] Many sisal workers stayed on in the area after they had completed their contracts.

Both sisal and dock workers were organised and sometimes militant (Iliffe 1979a; Shivji 1986). The colonial archives refer to frequent 'disturbances' at sisal estates in the district, and in 1937 there were stoppages at the docks and amongst labourers employed by a company supplying coal to the railways. In 1939 there was a major dock strike accompanied by violent altercations with police which led to a Commission of Enquiry.[20]

In colonial records frequent contrasts are drawn between this work and that of domestic service in Tanga. When the employment of juveniles in sisal estates was questioned it drew attention to their work as domestic servants (indeed local sisal estate owners pointed this out!); when the 1937 dock strike took place it was noted that apart from the railways and public works, domestic service was the only other major occupation open to workers in the town, and unfavourable comparisons were made between dockworkers' wages and conditions and those of domestic servants: whilst the latter were paid less (Sh20–30 per month as compared to Sh1.50 a day for work in the docks) their work was on a monthly rather than daily casual basis.[21]

Domestic servants were regarded as a more manageable workforce than men working in large organisations. Whilst there was a 'daily stream of domestic "boy" shauris' [problems/complaints] dealt with by the Labour Officer, labour control was at first largely in the hands of female employers. By the 1940s the Women's Service League of Tanganyika had set up an Employment Bureau in Tanga which worked to 'improve servants' standard of work and their attitude ...' as well as to place them with employers.[22] But it was not long before servants began to organise themselves, and a more militant trend began which led to the establishment of a branch of the African Cooks, Washermen and Houseservants' Association in Tanga.[23]

The implications of all this are dealt with in Chapter 9; the point here is that Tanga's history and social conditions throw up some challenging questions about the development of domestic service and the behaviour of domestic workers.

Tanga has always been a sharply demarcated town in class and ethnic terms. The railway line which runs from north to south, parallel to the sea, created a dividing line between those who were wealthy and favoured and those who were not. In German times a curfew operated; 'after 4pm anyone in the "European" part of the town was liable to arrest' (Mbughuni 1991:18). On the coast side lay leafy suburbs such as Nguvumali and Ras Kazone, where all the official buildings, yacht club and the residences of officers were built in colonial times. The commercial centre of banks, large shops and main market were also sited on this favoured side of the line.

On the other side of the tracks was the 'native quarter' of Ngamiani (literally 'the place of camels', reminding us that Tanga used to be a departure point for slave trading caravans plying into the interior). Here in the colonial period streets were laid out on a grid system and numbered – by 1986 they had reached more than twenty. During the colonial period Ngamiani was a source of pride to officials and residents and described as 'easily the finest laid out town in East Africa' (*The Tanga Post* 22 Jan. 1921). A later European observer was more critical: 'the non-native area has had all the plums ... while south of the line [in Ngamiani] a couple of paltry water kiosks and a public lavatory are all that can be seen' (1945).[24]

Europeans invariably lived on the right side of the tracks, whilst Indian owners of shops and small businesses tended to live above or aside them, with a concentration of Asians in the town centre, but a scattering into Ngamiani and wherever else trade and commerce led them. Chumbageni, between the town centre and Nguvumali, had a more mixed population of Arabs, Goans and Indians. Africans lived almost exclusively in the Native Quarter or in servants' quarters behind their employers.

By the 1980s the town was more diverse, though colonial class/ethnic divisions had left a deep mark. By now Ngamiani was bustling and crowded, it had two major markets, schools, bus station, mosques and churches, dispensaries and clinics, water works, and rather more water kiosks and public latrines than in the 1940s. On the better side of the tracks there had also been changes. New suburban settlement was evident, along the same axis as in colonial times, but curving round now into Usagara. In these areas wealthier people of all origins were to be found, though with more Africans in Usagara, Europeans more often in Old Nguvumali or Ras Kazone, and houses built with new 'Arab money' (from workers of Arab origin in the Gulf) strung along the roads out of town towards Ras Kazone. There was also an area of municipal and largely African housing in Kisosora between the town centre and Old Nguvumali. Industrial development was marked but the larger establishments were concentrated in areas such as Gofu Chini.

This was the setting in which I carried out field research in 1986 and 1989, with several briefer return visits between 1991 and 1997 (for a discussion of the methodology employed see Appendix). At the time of my first visit Tanga was in economic decline, reflecting both the national crisis as well as more localised misfortune, namely the collapse of the sisal industry (brought about both by the withdrawal of foreign capital in fear of political unrest after independence as well as a slump in world prices which accompanied the shift to synthetic fibres). All the infrastructure which had supported the export of sisal was collapsing – railways, roads and docks. This was a period of severe shortages accompanied by the retreat of many labour migrants back into subsistence agriculture, at precisely the same time that others arrived as agriculture failed to supply their needs. By the early 1990s Tanga was beginning to revive economically, but by the time of my latest visits in the late 1990s, the town had again fallen on hard times. The closure of the fertiliser factory (in consequence of pollution) was followed by collapse of the previously thriving textile industry, killed off by the importation of second hand clothing.[25]

2

BRIEF LIVES: A TALE OF TWO SERVANTS

I begin with the telling stories of two long-term servants.[1] The institution of domestic service is woven out of experience, individual as well as collective. Life histories, though partial, idiosyncratic and passionate, offer a vivid immediacy to set against drier accounts of social structures and practices. They are also suggestive of the extent to which men and women, in conditions not of their own choosing, may nevertheless 'make their own history'. Such accounts do not restrict themselves to the vicissitudes of work, for these take on varied meanings within the context of whole lives. There are many strands in these two lives which are taken up in later chapters – how a domestic wage labour force is created and maintained out of rural transformation, what difference gender makes to the experience, what kind of subjectivity emerges from class exploitation and what strategies are devised to further the interests of domestic workers and outwit employers.

Historians – and especially those who have worked to uncover the lives and stories of the dispossessed, the 'hidden from history'– have struggled to find ways of relating to their data and their 'subjects' which both critically interrogate them as sources as well as giving them the space to speak for themselves.[2] A relevant illustration is Stanley's account of Hannah Culwick, nineteenth-century servant and later mistress of her employer. Stanley agonises over the extent to which Hannah, in a diary written at her 'massa's' bidding, might have edited out some of her true feelings and views as both servant and mistress, and she struggles as a feminist with Hannah's willingness to abase herself for her master (1984:12–15). Burnett, drawing on the diaries of working men and women in the 1820s–1920s, comments on 'one of the most remarkable characteristics in much of the writing ... [i.e.] the uncomplaining acceptance of conditions of life and work which to the modern reader seem brutal, degrading and almost unimaginable' (1974:14). Stanley's view is that it is inappropriate to impose on the past 'images and constructions drawn from the present' – though she is far from an uncritical cipher and engages avidly with Hannah's position.

Oral history offers a better prospect for intellectual dialogue, but does not erase the differences in perspective and experience between researcher and narrator. Mbilinyi, writing of her attempt to recover the history of Rebeka

Kalindile of Rungwe in Tanzania, describes the painful confrontations which occurred when her own 'feminist' reading of aspects of Kalindile's life was challenged by the narrator herself. She also describes the way she had to come to terms with this: 'we must learn to understand and respect the contradictory ways in which women have coped with oppression' (1987:36). Stanley insists that 'one of the first tasks of feminism is to listen to *and to hear* what other people provide as their own explanations of their behaviours' (1984:15).

In this chapter I want to listen to the voices of two of those for whom domestic toil was one element in lives of hardship and struggle. In these stories I discern themes, and note contradictions and questions, which were not always taken up or fully explored with the narrators. Much of the material was disclosed in 'ordinary conversation' (rather than as a separate activity labelled 'research') and in which reminiscences were exchanged by all parties including myself.

Abu was a man in his late thirties when I knew him first. He had been a servant for over a decade but was then working as a shoemaker. He came to visit us at home and there began a friendship in which explaining himself and his life was an important dimension. Sara was my own 'househelper', a woman of about fifty. She was a great talker: reminiscences, rather than being drawn from her, were foisted upon me unbidden and with infectious enthusiasm. At times I experienced this as intrusion – it threatened to interrupt my 'real work' of writing up notes or reading, or her 'real work' of washing clothes or sweeping up. More commonly it helped to pass the time companionably as we cooked or ate together, cleared the table or went to the market. Her story did not emerge as a tidy chronological account, but as a series of fragments not always consistent with each other. It was pressed upon me in the course of everyday life, generally stimulated by the events or material props of our household and always with a purpose (at first definitely her own).

The accounts I had in my notes were elaborated over time as the relationships matured and as unfolding developments in their own lives spurred them to reconsider their destinies. This continued in the form of correspondence after I left Tanga – particularly in the case of Abu who was an assiduous letter writer, and in return visits including stays in Abu's home area of Lushoto some years later. Three years after my initial research I asked each of them if I might tape-record an account of their lives. Although both tapes contained material that was new – particularly the responses of Abu and Sara to my own questions – in another sense they were flat and formal compared with the lively and anchored nature of ordinary conversation. I draw on both sources here.

Abu's account of his life was in no sense extraordinary, compared to those of other men to whom I talked, though I came to know more of it. Like many servants he was a migrant from the Usambara area and maintained strong links there. Sara's story was also not atypical, except that she was one of a minority of women who had made a lifetime 'career' out of domestic service and were still employed in it. She too was born in a rural area, though from a village nearer to Tanga. Unlike Abu she maintained no crucial material ties to her rural birthplace.

THEMES AND QUESTIONS

This tale of two servants allows us some insight into important dimensions of domestic service in Tanzania: in particular the salience of gender and class power seen from the perspective of individual actors.

Although Sara and Abu shared similar circumstances and experiences – of rural origin, migration and urban poverty, and while their paths had converged in their mode of livelihood as domestic servants, what they did not share was gender. We shall see that both were stubborn fighters in the battle for survival, but that being a man gave Abu an occasional edge, even though his occupation was at odds with his manhood, whereas Sara's hardships were compounded by being a woman. I explore here the extent to which their gender is consciously part of their own life-view.

These two life histories speak of the struggle to survive in a difficult world where negotiation with, and accommodation to the class power of others is integral to the daily battle. They disclose 'a strategic knowledge' of how power works (Foucault 1980:145), raising questions about agency as well as structure. These two people reflect on what happens when servants attempt to assert or empower themselves, how they assess their own chances of betterment, and how they compare individual with collective means to improve their lives, and whether gender power can erase class power. One feature is very striking, and that is the way in which the 'great events' of Tanzanian history – key phases in socioeconomic development such as independence or the adoption of socialism, all developments intended to empower the people – either passed these two people by or had contradictory or unintended conseqences of which they became the victims.

SARA'S STORY

Sara was born in the mid-1930s, the middle daughter of seven children. She was born in Mlingano, a sisal area of mixed population about fifteen miles outside Tanga, her father a Sambaa (whose mother was Bondei), her mother a Zigua. Her father was a sisal worker who became a clerk in the sisal factory, and they acquired land which her mother cultivated. Her maternal grandfather had been a cook for Germans, her mother's brother a servant for Europeans and Asians.

Like other children in that area Sara began work on the sisal estates – first as a water-carrier for a European, later employed to do weeding and clearing with other children for a wage of Sh6 a month. She eventually went to a Catholic mission school in the late 1940s when she was twelve. She completed her primary education, but did not continue as her parents expected her to marry and needed to send her younger brother to school. Soon after this she was married off to a rich old cattle dealer and moved into Tanga to live with him. The marriage was an unhappy one, childless for more than ten years.

Sara was offered some assistance by the Catholic church to which she belonged, and in 1964 she was given a job as a cleaner in a school run by Catholic Sisters. That job ended four years later when the Sisters (Europeans) left Tanzania, and Sara sought other work, at first in factories machining sacks and clothes. Her marriage was finally terminated by her husband's death in 1971, by which time she had two young children. For various reasons she did not inherit any of her husband's wealth, and was forced to support herself. From that time on she worked as a servant, for Goans, Indians and Europeans. She never remarried, but had at least one relationship with a Kenyan migrant worker, the father of her last child, which ended when the border between Kenya and Tanzania was closed in 1976.

What is telling about Sara's account is partly the vivid illustrations it offers of the lives of poor women, partly the way in which she herself recreates and harvests the past to make sense of the present. Each fragment of the past, culled from memory, is marshalled to back up a view of life, every tale has its moral.

One story, about her relationship with the Kenyan, ended as follows: 'He was already married in Kenya, so I didn't want to marry him. I had my work, and if you have work then no man can oppress you'. Sara saw herself as a worker, and as a survivor: 'I never stay without work, mama ... It just goes on like that – I never lack for work. I leave this job, I start another'. But she also has a view of herself as a woman, and it is a perception beset by contradictions. I look at this first, and then relate it to how she survives as a worker.

I remembered her telling me the following story, which in my memory had been translated as illustrating her pride in the value of women. I had it near verbatim in my notes: 'It's like the story of the cat, mama. The cat decided that it would live with the most powerful animal, so first it was attracted by the swift gazelle, but when the gazelle was killed by a lion it followed the lion; and when the lion was killed by an elephant it transferred its allegiance again. Then one day a man came along and shot the elephant with his gun, so the cat followed the man. When the man reached his door his wife was waiting there, and he gave her his gun and she took it into the kitchen. And then the cat knew that the woman was the most powerful animal in all the world, and it has lived with her in the kitchen ever since'.

When I recovered this story from my notes I discovered that what I had forgotten was its context – and it was nothing to do with gender! I had mentioned Muslims, and Sara suddenly announced that she herself had been born a Muslim, to Muslim parents. Her father and mother, she claimed, had been forcibly converted to Protestantism by the Germans. After the Germans left they reverted to Islam. But when their children were young they decided to convert to Catholicism: 'My mother saw where the greatest help came from – it was the Mission which brought the most help' – medicine, clothes for the poor and so on. So they were all baptised as Catholics. Sara chuckled delightedly as she told me this – and, 'it was like the story of the cat, mama'. The identification which was being made here, in other words, was with the cat, exercising its animal cunning, rather than the woman! And anyway, what kind of power could be conferred by being the keeper of a gun for someone else (a man)? It is the limited and circumscribed nature of the woman's 'place' (the kitchen, waiting at the door) which is evident here, rather than any real 'power'. So maybe the cat misunderstood the situation? In any case the history of instrumental conversion is one which Sara shared with many others – it was yet one more ploy for survival in a world of more powerful others.

Rather than confidence in the power of women, it was an overwhelming sense of powerlessness which characterised many of Sara's stories of her past – albeit disguised by the cheerful and wry manner in which they were told. This was particularly true of her account of her marriage, retailed to me on two separate occasions. When she had completed Standard 7, the Sisters pleaded that she be allowed to continue to secondary level, but 'my father insisted that I marry an old man who had asked for me. In those days you were just told – this is the one'. He was over sixty and she was just twenty. On a later occasion she expanded this account. The old man sent intermediaries to negotiate the size of the bridewealth with her father and mother: 'it's like trading'. She did not see the old man until after this, and then her response was one of revulsion: 'he had a huge fat belly, mama, and when he went through a door he had to go sideways! I told mama, "I can't", but mama said, "tell your father". And Baba said, "Refuse him, but then I will disown you"'. Then the padre became involved. 'He looked at me and he asked me, "Do you love this man, Sara?" I hung my head and answered him in a low voice: "I love him". He didn't believe me. He asked me, "Where did you meet this man to make friends with him?" I said I saw him in Tanga. "Oh", said the padre, "It is your father who wants this and not you". I was afraid, mama, and I just stayed silent'.

It would appear that the padre did not take the matter further. The tone of the next part of the story was different: for the first time in her life Sara became the centre of attention, and she recalled this with excitement and pleasure, telling me how the Sisters at the mission helped her to get the wedding clothes together – they ordered a dress, head dress and gloves from Kenya. 'The gloves were long, mama, white and lacy with little red flowers'. This was spoken with joy and satisfaction, but then her memory of the occasion as one of horror and distress, overlaid by anger, once again predominated: 'But the bridegroom! An old man like that! A noisy big mouth, drunk all the time!'. When the priest asked her if she would have this man to be her husband she remained silent and started weeping. They asked her a second time, 'and still I didn't answer'. Then the best man, who was her brother, told her off in Kisambaa (rather than Swahili which the priest would have understood). 'He told me, "If you refuse to answer the third time the whole thing will be off, and our father will be severely reprimanded. He will murder you – he has laid on a huge reception ...!" So there I was, kneeling at the altar, tears streaming down my face, and I had to say: "I accept"'.

What comes over in this account is Sara's overwhelming sense of isolation, as a young girl subject to her father's will. There was no support from anyone: her mother is shown as deferring to her husband, her brother to his father; the padre, whilst recognising the true state of affairs does not intervene, the Sisters conspire in the pretence that this is a happy occasion. Patriarchy is forcefully exemplified.

Sara's memory of her marriage was as bitter as that of the wedding. 'He beat me without reason ... He injured me ... He used to come home drunk with his trousers all dirtied, and I had to wash them ...'. And then there was her failure to conceive for over ten years. Sara told me about this in a matter of fact way – did she experience it as shame and humiliation or, given her feelings towards her husband, was she indifferent? Was it an added justification for her husband's brutality towards her? I cannot say, for trying to stop Sara in full flow was never easy! And the point of all these stories was not so much her memory of being victimised by her husband's behaviour, but of having found allies to checkmate him.

What is very striking in Sara's account is the absence of any mention of support from other women, or any perception of women as natural allies. Instead she turned to those whose active promotion or connivance had landed her in her predicament in the first place, in a clearly instrumental endeavour to transform patriarchal relations into patron–client relations with herself as supplicant and recipient of favours.

The most significant of these was the Church. First the Fathers intervened and told her husband off for 'drinking like a pig – but mama, ah! He didn't change'. Then the Sisters helped her out by finding her a job as a cleaner in the Catholic school. It was even one of the Fathers who sent Sara to a gynaecologist, and organised for her to have an operation (after which she became pregnant at last).

Sara's second key source of support was her younger brother, James, away at the time Sara married. On his return he too lived in Tanga working for the electricity supply company. 'He was horrified to discover how this old man was mistreating me ... James told him: "You can't treat my sister like this! She left school so that I could go on"'. The old man ignored him. 'So James had another idea. He saved up the money to pay back the bridewealth – at home we marry with money – and he went and returned it. Ah! Mama! I was so afraid of what my husband would do! I ran away to my brother's house. I did not go back'.

On another occasion Sara told me a story which appeared at variance with the account of James's intervention. When her husband died, she told me, he was still a wealthy man, with three houses and 280 head of cattle. 'It was I who should have inherited – I was still married to him. But his brothers came along and sold two of the houses and all the cattle [and pocketed the proceeds]. The third house was in Tanga – it was virtually a ruin – but they sold the plot too'. Whilst the thesis that 'I was still married to him' seems to contradict the account of James returning the bridewealth, in the eyes of the Catholic church of course she was still married.

Again, although there was bitterness and anger in her tale of disinheritance (which affected the two children whom she had borne to the old man as well as herself), the point of the story was to show how she had rescued something from this setback. This time she approached her employer (the Sisters having left, she was now working for a Goan family) and took a loan, with which she was able to purchase the Tanga plot. Over the years she tried to save enough to rebuild the house, constructing three rooms and a kitchen, before the money dried up: 'and then we didn't even have enough money to eat, never mind to build'. With each year's rains the house was gradually undermined and eventually collapsed back into a ruin.

Women are rightly celebrated for their capacity to 'get by', 'make ends meet', struggle on against impossible odds. All over the world this tends to be taken for granted by those in power, if it is not altogether ignored. How do they do it? Sara presented this as a lonely struggle in which one lived off one's wits in a largely unfeeling world. It was not simply that she needed to find ways of earning an income, and that in this she was in competition with others, but that despite being an 'independent woman' she was never able to escape from family responsibilities. This was not just a matter of providing for her own children, it was also that others in the family 'took advantage' of her, and she lacked the power to say no, because women are expected to shoulder such burdens uncomplainingly.

During 1986 there were periods when she shared her tiny house with a sick sister, the sister's husband and three children, her own mother, another niece, and five children of her brother whose marriage was breaking down. Her own daughter and the niece were as capable of finding work as Sara herself, but they were unwilling. Sara said: 'If there was a man in my house, those girls would be working'. 'But there is you!' I exclaimed. 'Ah! me! I can't do anything, I have no voice, they don't listen – they are thinking "ah! what can she do to us?"'. And later it was a man, her cousin, who finally told her visitors that they had over-stayed their welcome. Her account of this was telling: 'He told them: "Why are you people still here, and Sara has no means?" … They were all so offended and angry! but I was grateful to him for speaking out, although I hid my feelings. But it's true – just because I have a job everyone comes, and then because they are at home they welcome even more people. I just want to be alone with my children'.

Even this could be a problem, for who was to care for those children whilst Sara was working? Sara found herself, as a servant paid a pittance, hiring some even more needy person. In the early 1970s she employed a girl of thirteen from a village on the Mombasa road to live in with them. Every month her mother and brother came to stay with Sara for a few days, returning home with the girl's wages, a fraction of her own. After two years the girl was called home, and Sara found a sixteen year old boy to take her place. Again he was a village boy, and his wages were collected monthly by his father. When she did not need him any more she found him a position as an apprentice to a mechanic: 'and he is grown up now and married – and still thanking me'.

If Sara sees herself as weak because she is a woman, she also sees herself as a survivor, facing and surmounting problems with which few men have to contend. She presents herself not as a victim but as one who actively devises strategies to manipulate more powerful others (generally male) into assisting her. She knew that men often won in this game. She recounted to me how once, looking for work, she had left a glowing testimonial of her abilities with a fellow African, a man who promised, on her behalf, to approach newly-arrived Europeans who were taking up posts in the Cement factory where he worked as a supervisor. 'So I waited and waited and I sent one of the children to ask, and he said not yet … And I waited and waited and he said not yet … he had used my testimonial to get other people jobs! They said they were Sara! There are so many Saras there now!' She laughed heartily at this memory. But at the time, 'I felt so bitter'.

Getting work was an essential element in Sara's game-plan. Remember her insistence that: 'If you have a job then no man can oppress you'. Her account of her life as a worker provided her own evidence of this firmly held belief – for had she not survived, bringing up three children without a man? To what extent did her narrative highlight the particular experience of being a woman worker?

Altogether Sara had spent about eighteen years working as a servant when I came to know her. Two jobs were of long duration, testifying to her ability to please her employers (this is how she saw it) and they came to an end through no fault of her own. Other briefer jobs were terminated by her, usually through devious means as I shall describe. She had also worked for short periods in factories – grinding work, long hours spent in sometimes dangerous and always exhausting conditions ('choking dust everywhere … the machines drive you'). And to supplement meagre wages and to eke out an existence between jobs there were what Burnett calls the 'multiplicity of little contrivances' (1974, pxviii): retailing salt, making coconut oil for sale, collecting firewood for cooking, cultivating a small plot on the outskirts of town where she grew beans and maize for family use, brewing local beer ('but that is bad work. People get drunk, quarrel, pull out knives …').

Her account of selling salt was a vivid one, and illustrates the cultural barriers that limit women. Children – nearly always boys – are sent out to do hawking. A grown person is reluctant: 'I would feel ashamed', and girls may be 'badly used by hooligans'. So it was Sara's two young sons who went out to sell the salt. They were in desperate straits at the time and she felt the boys were not making the profit fast enough, so one day she insisted on accompanying them. Her older son was embarrassed to be seen selling salt with his mother and she agreed that they split up. 'I tried to call out "Salt!", but only a croak came out. Eventually there was a woman who bought Sh2 worth but I was too generous with the measure. I felt such a fool! Soon I gave up and went home. The boys came back with Sh180, and I had only earned Sh2! "We told you, mama", they said. I never went again'.

Wage labour produces a more certain and regular income, and Sara thinks of herself primarily as a domestic worker, one who is, moreover, good at her work, and adept in assessing what will please and satisfy employers. She is proud of these skills, learnt, she informed me, from the Sisters, who were very particular about standards of cleanliness and good behaviour: 'polishing, scrubbing … honesty'. I noted that in telling me of her apprenticeship she assimilated herself to a child – and would appear to have been treated like one! On one occasion, she told me, one of the Sisters had struck her for not doing her work properly, although afterwards 'she pretended she had mistaken me for one of the schoolchildren'.

She was proud of her acquisition of knowledge, which she felt would equip her to work for Europeans again. In describing her experience of a later job as servant to a German couple she said: 'The woman herself was a housewife. So all the time she was interested in "show" [she used the English word here]. I realised that what was expected here was like when I was with the Sisters … I didn't disappoint her in anything. When it reached midday, they went around to admire, saying: "Nice, nice, Sara"'.

This was no mere pride in skill; it was also quite instrumental – Sara was transparently aware of the value of pleasing the employer. The rewards might appear meagre, but for her they were literally a lifeline. And hence, the above account continues: 'And then there was the bread. She told me, eat half, take the rest. When two weeks had passed she told me to take flour: "take flour, Sara, take sugar". And so it went on …'. Longer term stratagems could then be devised: 'I knew that if I stayed two years I could ask this employer [the husband] to lend me some money. I could get something out of him. That's the reason I like Europeans, mama – they really help'.

This perspective was not one specific to women. Male servants were also proud of their domestic skills and conscious of the need to please. A complicated set of tactics is required to make this endeavour fruitful – the employer is artfully flattered, and the servant's problems are impressed upon her so that (hopefully) her heart is moved by compassion. Sara was explicit about this, comparing servant work favourably with other jobs for its 'inside advantages'. 'Let's say I work for you now, I get loans ... I might get a skirt; the milk which is left over you may say "Sara, take this for the children"'. Even if the wages for other jobs were better, it could not make up for the 'inside advantages': 'I would be blessed because the whole time you'd be seeing what condition I was in : "Sara is in difficulties, let me help her. Take a little bit of sugar, you can put it aside for the children ..."'

Employers of course join in the game – they have their own ways of inhibiting such moral pressure, as we shall see in Chapter 8. Sara was fully aware of the ways in which servants are put in their place, kept at arm's length. In almost every place she had worked, she told me, the servant had her own separate plate, cup, knife and fork, to be used by her alone. And she had almost always eaten separately from the family. She was taken aback to be asked by one employer: '"Sara why do you use the same plate all the time?" I said, "It's what I've been used to"'. She was amazed to be told that she could take any plate, 'those people did not discriminate' – but it was the exception which confirmed the more usual practice.

Sara did not generalise about employers – there were those with whom you could work, and who were sympathetic to your needs, and there were others who took advantage. In the case of the former, Sara worked long and hard, and stayed as long as she was able. In the latter case she looked for ways of getting out. In one case an employer tried to make her work longer hours than agreed. 'There was no end to it [literally "the employer had no 'time'"]. She would say: "You can leave at 3pm, and then, just before you are due to go she finds other work – ten fish will arrive to be cleaned! And me, I have problems at home, there are the children. When I eventually arrived home I would be too tired to do any work on the farm [see below]. So I left. I didn't tell her the reason. I said, "Mama, I have to go to Pangani" [a small town twenty miles or so from Tanga]. And she said, "Oh Sara, hurry back and work for us again – I haven't had such a good worker as you before, so agreeable ..."' Sara did not go to Pangani, but after a few days sent another woman who was seeking work to go to the employer's house. She was taken on.

Both men and women face employers who stretch their hours of work. But men are unlikely to face situations of sexual harassment. In one job Sara was approached by the man of the house: 'he suggested wrong things to me, and he said he would look after me, and that I would have all I wanted. I told him I couldn't do that because his wife had treated me with with kindness and respect ... No, there was no question of force: ah! wouldn't I have made a lot of noise! Soon after this I asked for leave to go back to Tanga. I told them my mother needed me, and they gave me so many presents. I knew I could not go back'.

In another house Sara left because her European employer took an African mistress, who frequently got drunk, broke things and blamed Sara: 'She was an evil woman, that one, mama. Oh yes, mind you, she was educated ... she spoke English as if it were her mother tongue ... I thought it would be better if I left this job ... that woman could really hurt me'. Her employer believed his mistress rather than Sara. He called Sara a 'stupid woman' and, 'he was bigger than me'. Whilst denying that the breakages were her fault she told him that the work was too hard for her. For female servants, male employers can also be physically threatening.

In both these jobs she would have preferred to stay because there were benefits – left-over food, cast-off clothes, occasional gifts. But the problems were too difficult to handle. Occasionally Sara lost good jobs through no fault of her own. The cleaning work at the Catholic school came to an end, not just because the European Sisters went back home, but also because, as part of its adoption of socialism, Tanzania encouraged schoolchildren to be self-reliant, and not to despise manual labour. Sara and another cleaner found themselves without work when the children were told to sweep amd clean out the lavatories.

Sara neither joined nor ever considered approaching the union for support against employers. Her response was blunt: 'Never! I didn't need them. There is CCM [then the ruling single party] and the Youth League and JUWATA [the state-sponsored union], but we people who don't get much can't afford them. I have a CCM card because without that you can't receive money through the post office ...' This suggests instrumentality and a lack of awareness of the value of collective action, but as I shall show in Chapter 9, Sara's assessment of the union was not unjust. She was cynical of collectivism, as she did not think it had done anything to help her. For example, she told me that she had managed to get a small plot on the outskirts of Tanga through her ten-cell leader (then the basic political unit), and that the arrangement was conditional on her offering labour on the collective farm once a week: 'the government has decreed it. But we don't see any benefits. The big ones eat it all'.

There is little in Sara's story which touches on the great national events of this turbulent period (1950s–80s). Independence – a watershed in all historical accounts – had passed her by without making its mark. The arrival of socialism was hardly noted – or rather, its appearance in her story is as a trigger for her dismissal from employment, rather than as the advent of a new dawn. Towards the great institutions of socialist Tanzania – the party, the government, the union – she maintained an attitude of scepticism.

ABU'S STORY

Although Sara had been widowed for fifteen years before I first met her, she was still scarred by the brutal experience of her marriage. It overshadowed all else in her narrative of life's events. To that fact she was able to attribute much of her present condition – her driving determination to work, her poverty, and her weakness – but also, paradoxically, her strength and resilience.

In Abu's story his wife was a shadowy figure, clearly a central prop of his existence, but one to which he gave no definitive force. I did not learn her name until I met her several years later: in his account he avoided even the phrase 'my wife', speaking rather of 'she' or occasionally using the circumlocution 'the mother of children' (*mama watoto*). Nor did he name his children, until I specifically asked him, although they were evidently very dear to him. Very forthcoming about his public life, Abu was reticent about the private.

If the contrast between Abu and Sara was striking in this respect, so too was the meaning which he gave to work. There is no male equivalent for 'if you have work, then no man can oppress you'. Abu saw his working life as being more than mere survival – it represented, in his terms, a conscious striving for betterment. Despite the fact that he too had suffered disappointments, and had not progressed very far, he was a contented man: 'To be honest, I don't see my life as the usual one of a lower class person [*mtu wa chini*] – not at all – I know that I have a good life. It's different from that of other people at home in the village – completely different'. But whilst he saw himself as having improved his situation relative to others in his village, he identified himself always as a countryman, not a townsman.

A key feature in his sense of having improved himself was that he was no longer a servant. Unlike Sara, and despite the fact that his main experience of service had, in his eyes, been a good one, he did not value this occupation or see it as a source of opportunities. To him it was 'lowly work' (*kazi ya chini*), a job which people did not choose, but were forced to do because there was no other work.

Abu was born around 1950 in a village in the heart of the Usambara mountains not far from the district capital, Lushoto. Both his parents were Sambaa. His father had two wives and each wife had several children. There was a tanning factory in the area and his father worked for many years as a packer in the factory, whilst his wives cultivated. Abu was the fourth child, but the first to go to school. Despite suspicion amongst Muslims against mission schools, it was a Catholic school to which he was sent. It was a blow to him when he was withdrawn in Standard 5. His father claimed the fees were too much for him, but then it transpired that his younger brother (the son of a co-wife) was eager to go in his place. 'But I was the only one who took to studying'. After leaving school he helped out on his father's land for several years, earning a small income for himself on the side by working as a woodcutter. Then his father set up a small shop in the village, using the pension money he received when he retired from work. 'There wasn't anyone who could do accounts except me, so he put me in the shop to look after things'. But his younger brother's jealousy hindered his progress there too, and he left him to it, and began to cultivate on his own.

It was not until he was twenty that he first left home to seek work. He was insistent that his departure was not in response to hardship or family problems, but rather because it was the usual thing: 'there were hardly any young men of my age who hadn't been away ... I didn't have any urge to leave as I was quite satisfied where I was – I wore good clothes and I was used to life at home'. He went to join his father's brother's son, who was now working in Korogwe, a small town half way to Tanga. There he got a job as a servant for an Asian family, staying for two years until there was a quarrel, and he left and came to Tanga.

This was in the early 1970s. In Tanga he stayed with another cousin. At first he could only find work as a 'turnboy' (driver's mate) delivering and collecting building materials. Later he had a job as a builder's mate, but left when he managed to find domestic work, first with an Indian bachelor, and then with another Asian family, through the intercession of his mother's sister's husband who was also working in Tanga. He stayed for eight years with this large family, more than contented, until the young people began to leave to get education in Britain. Eventually his employer went too. Before leaving, the family arranged for Abu to go into their cobbler's shop to learn shoemaking and repair. This is where he was working when I came to know him, and it was a job he found very satisfying.

Later the shop was seized by the government as the owner did not return, and all the workers were laid off. Abu then went into partnership with another cousin: a government servant who was not formally allowed to own a business. They set up a shop together with Abu as the front. But the cousin cheated him out of the profits, and so he decided to return home to Lushoto, and to combine trading with agriculture, or perhaps the establishment of a shoemaking business. He soon discovered that his capital was insufficient for anything but the most petty of trading operations (e.g. buying salt in Tanga to sell in Lushoto) and by the early 1990s he had become almost a full time farmer again. By the mid-1990s he was working as an overseer on a local road project; when this folded he opened a small teahouse. But the essential base of these income-earning activities was agriculture.

My interest in Abu's story was especially in the relationship between his work as a servant and his perception of himself as a man. His assessment of domestic work was and is an ambivalent one. At one point in the tape he said: 'To be honest I have found servant work to be good work and that is why I continued with it'. But he also told me then that even if his previous employer came back he would not agree to be a servant again. In the mid-1990s he looked back on the job as one 'without status' (*siyo ya sifa*), but when I exclaimed at his ability to make hundreds of delicious breadcakes for selling in his teahouse, he told me proudly that this did not faze him; he had learnt whilst with his last employer to provide food for feasts.

Abu found many aspects of domestic service demeaning to him as a human being. It is instructive to see the way he dealt with this and to compare it with Sara's responses to employer oppression. For example, his first employer in Korogwe, finding him a very willing worker, said to him after a while: 'Oh, you are finishing your work very quickly, I must find you something else to do'. The Indian had an unmarried sister living with him, and his idea was that she should make breadcakes and Abu should go out and sell them. Abu said that his heart sank when he heard this: 'it would be so embarrassing, shouting out "*maandazi! maandazi!*" in the streets like a small child' (this clearly echoes Sara's feelings about selling salt). But Abu did not protest; he felt he had no choice but to agree: 'I will try'. His employer took advantage of his compliance, and every day increased the number of cakes he had to sell, blaming him if he returned with any. Then his employer bought a refrigerator on hire purchase so that his sister could make ice cream to sell. 'They told me: "You must work hard so that we can pay off the debt". And they got a bicycle to take the ice cream around – one with a horn which made a silly sound – and they told me to go to the bus station and sell. What could I do? I went for two days ... and then I said I couldn't go any more because people were laughing at me. Then they said, "go to the school" and I didn't mind that ... But all they time they increased the amount to be sold, and were angry if I didn't sell it'.

Not only was Abu, a grown man, being sent out to sell 'like a small child', he was also not paid extra for the additional work. Eventually he complained about his low wage (Sh55 a month), but they said that since he was given tea in the morning and a midday meal he was not entitled to more. He therefore decided not to eat their food any more. When they asked why, he invented a wife whom he had just married, and who expected him to eat at home. But at the end of the month they still paid him Sh55. Now he protested: '"But I am no longer eating with you! I have a wife now, and I can't live on what you are giving me". The boss was annoyed: "Why are you starting to make trouble? All this time we have got on well, why start to be difficult? But if it's more money you want, how much more is it?"'. Abu suggested Sh100 would be more reasonable, and the man said he would pay it, but he would also cut from his wages the cost of a flask which Abu had broken. A quarrel ensued and Abu lost his job.

Employers can withold both work and wages. This power makes workers hesitant to confront them, given their own isolated position and lack of any contractual rights. So Sara invented a journey, and an anxious mother; Abu invented a wife: both adopted stratagems of guile to defend themselves against exploitation. Abu went further than Sara in demanding justice when his more devious tactics failed, and paid the price of losing his job. Sara felt herself to be in no position to protest: withdrawal was the only weapon she had.

Abu's second experience of domestic service ended with another incident which illustrates the way in which he saw domestic work, much more clearly than Sara, as a degrading experience. 'That Indian I went to work for, though I only stayed a week ... it was exactly like this: "Don't use my lavatory [he said]. If you want to go, ask me for permission and go outside". I asked him, go where? And he said to go to that free one – yes the municipal one ... I told him, "fine, I'm going to work for you? Yes. Well, if I have to go outside when I need to relieve myself, don't think I am going to clean your lavatory. There's no way I'm going to clean your lavatory for you to use, and I am prevented from using it!" He was furious, we really quarrelled. "Do you want the job?" "I want it!" "Then just because you can't use it, doesn't mean you shouldn't clean it". [I told him] "Aren't I a human being like you" ... in the end I told him I didn't want his food either, for wasn't I a man like him? We were just the same'. Abu left the job after a week.

Against this stirring account of Abu's moral outrage, his recognition of, and refusal to submit to subordination, and his relinquishment of the job on a matter of principle, I set his story of the 'good employer', Walji, for whom he worked loyally and unstintingly for years, despite a work load that (to me) seemed excessive. Walji's family consisted of fifteen people, and Abu was the only servant. Washing all their clothes and pots took several hours a day. 'Banyanis never leave their clothes to pile up – they wash every day, unlike other people ... So many pots. They are not like us who just have one dish – they prepare so many! But I was used to it'.

His 'willingness' in this case was not as nakedly instrumental as Sara's, but presented as due return for the decent treatment he received. Abu was insistent that employers 'are not all alike', though in comparing the terms of his work for Walji with the lot of other servants he seemed to be making the point that in general domestic work is exploitative: 'I have seen how other servants are made to work until they are tired out ...' 'Some employers expect you to start work at 6.30am – but for me it was 8 o'clock ... as if I were going to the office'. 'They were not hard on me like some other employers are. I have seen how it is for other workers'.

I was struck by the domestic metaphors which he used in describing the 'goodness' of this family. For example, he said: 'for me, it was as if I were at home'. And: 'they treated me as if I were their child [*waliniona kama mimi ni mtoto wao*]'. 'They helped me [to get married] as if I were a member of the family [*mtoto wa nyumbani*]'. These comments jarred on me, because they did not seem to describe the familial arrangements either of his employers' home and family, or his own.

First it was evident that whilst Walji's family developed a close bond with Abu, trusted and appreciated him, the employment mode is not a familial one, and he was not in any real sense incorporated into the family. Abu says: 'they treated me as if I were their child' – but their own children did no housework. He ate his midday meal with the children, but not with the adults: 'Once I had got used to them I ate at the table together with their children ... they told me to sit and eat with the children ... and when we had finished I took the pots and washed them'. It is clear that in his own home Abu is a decision-maker, indeed the key decision-maker. In this family he was not 'at home' in this sense at all: he was subject to the decisions of others, and had no say in their family affairs. At best, one might say that he was assimilated into a status which had echoes of perpetual childhood, and that most of his time was spent with the women of the house, some of whom worked almost as hard as he did (though at more interesting and less back-breaking jobs – cooking rather than washing clothes) and were probably marginalised from family decision making too.

What he appreciated about this household was that it gave him a sense of autonomy in carrying out his work: 'no-one told me what to do ... I knew what to do ... Those people were totally different [from other employers] – there were no "words"'. They were also generous in their way, giving him money and presents when he married (though they did not raise his wages), cast-off clothing, food, loans (which had to be repaid). More than this, they did not demand services which would have been demeaning to him: that he should wash female underwear, for example. There was a degree of 'respect' – and Abu felt very strongly that 'as human beings we must show respect to each other'. And given that he was telling me this story in retrospect, its 'happy ending' may also have coloured his view: 'my hope was that I could stay with them for ever, if I was to stay in town at all ... I told them that given the way we got on so well, if they left for Europe I could not see myself working for anyone else ... So they thought long and hard and then they suggested that it would be better for me to start learning shoemaking and repair ... if I could get the hang of it then that would be a step up for me. It would be like my ticket ... I thanked God for granting me this progress'.

Abu was remarkably uncomplaining about the fact that Walji did not, at first, pay him even the government minimum wage. 'They began with a lower wage because that is what we agreed upon, and then, because we got on well and I stayed for a long time they were ready to pay me more'. Earlier he had given me a fuller account of how this shift was achieved. Indians, he told me, were well aware that the government insisted on the minimum wage being paid, and did not want to be caught. So they made it a condition of employment that if officials from JUWATA (the government-sponsored union) came to enquire, the worker would say they received the correct amount. Abu agreed to this condition. One day JUWATA people encountered him sweeping outside, asked him if he worked there, and then enquired about his wage. Obediently he named the minimum wage of the time (Sh160 – in fact he received only Sh120). They asked to see the lady of the house, and she told the same story. Then they asked to see his contract of employment. The woman was flustered and claimed that, 'he has only been working here for a few days, we haven't got it yet' (he had in fact been employed for some time). They returned to see her husband, and told him that Abu must have a contract. So the employer got a contract, and 'gradually increased my wage until it came up to the "government wage"'. He did not go beyond this wage, even though he worked with them for so long.

Abu seemed to be content with this, the value he placed on the job and his 'good' treatment outweighing the poverty of the wages. At any rate he did not perceive – as I expected he would – that JUWATA might be an ally for him in negotiating a better deal from his employers. He never joined JUWATA, and when I asked him why, he said: 'Well, if you get on well with your employers, if there is mutual satisfaction [mapatano], then you have no need of JUWATA'. He did not want to offend his employers by joining – 'people who joined JUWATA were seen as troublemakers. They might find it difficult to get another job if they fell out with their employers'. And whilst he appreciated the minimum wage legislation, and recognised that not to pay it was to break the law, he added that: 'the government is up there, far away – it does not reach down into every corner, or the affairs of people like me. We have to take things as we find them, and we wouldn't get jobs if we insisted on our rights'. Like Sara, then, he viewed the worker as a lonely individual, facing a powerful employer. If you want work you have to endure their terms; if you cannot, then you leave. Occasionally you strike lucky.

And yet, Abu did have his limits, and there were, as I have described, points in his life when he was prepared to insist on his rights – 'as a human being [binadamu]'. He was also conscious of being a gendered human being, 'a man' (mwanamume). I was interested in the way he squared this with being a domestic servant for so many years, and in the curious contradiction between his view of himself as a 'child of the house' in his employer's establishment, and his sense of himself as a 'man' in his own house.

I tried to explore this in relation to his first experience as a servant in Korogwe: did he see the job in gendered terms, and how did he know how to do it? His reply illustrates the ambivalence of men's relationship to such work: 'If it's necessary, you just have to do it'. He knew how to wash clothes because he had always washed his own. 'Ironing I knew how to do because I ironed my own clothes at home'. But sweeping – 'well, it's true men don't do that at home, but I had been watching women sweep all my life, so I knew how it was done. Now I had to do it, so I did it. Washing pots? Yes, at home, it is your mother or your sisters who do that for you, but still I managed somehow'.

On the one hand he was proud of his ability to do domestic work: 'I could do any kind of housework ... I knew how to do all the work ... I knew how to cook ... I knew what to do'. On the other hand he devalues and disparages his own achievement in this: 'It's not highly-skilled work, you can learn as you go along'. To be a 'house helper' did not have the same status as being a cobbler. A cobbler was someone who has skills and is expert in their performance (*fundi*). Was this because the *fundi* is typically male?

Whereas Abu could live with the indignity of doing jobs like sweeping and washing up, because as wage labour, these were jobs that other men were prepared to do, there were aspects of domestic service which he perceived as directly threatening to his masculinity. The major one of these was the fear of being asked to wash intimate or soiled clothing, especially that belonging to women (though I discovered that most women servants also drew the line at being asked to do this). Abu called it 'secrets', and when I looked puzzled he explained. 'Yes, intimate things. I am a man ... in some houses they put them in with the other clothes, and you are working with the women, they put them together for you to wash ... we human beings, we must have respect ... clothes like that you must wash yourself. You wash them yourself ... You know I am a man, and it's not good, it's bad practice, against our customs ... They can't insist I do it, it's respectful [not to ask] ...'. Abu's usual composure was lost in this passage – this demeaning possibility was clearly very threatening to him, and particularly as a man.

Within his own family, Abu sees himself as the central figure. He never brought his wife to live in town, though she visited him occasionally, and he returned home as often as he could. Although he presented himself as the main economic support of the family, saying of his wife: 'she is relying on me', it was clear that his wife fed the whole family in his absence from her cultivation, occasionally selling any surplus.

To be a servant is not only to be poorly paid, exploited and subject to indignity, it is also to be doing work which men do not do at home. I probed this particular issue further with Abu, by asking questions which were evidently, in his terms, 'outrageous' in their questioning of his sense of manhood, and which generated a degree of hysteria in response. He was telling me about his wife's work on the land and in the house, and I had 'innocently' asked if he helped out with housework at home. 'When I'm there? No! when I'm at home, mama, I have so many things to attend to. I am really busy. And the business that we men are involved in …' This led on to the following telling exchange:

> JB: Men's work is different at home?
> Abu: It's different. We men do the heavy work – that's what we do. But housework – I don't know why, cooking – no, we don't take part in that.
> JB: Let's say your wife were sick?
> Abu: The wife is sick. No then, what we would do would be to call on a neighbour. If my wife is ill and she needs help, my neighbour there, the wife of my brother, my in-law – she will come and help. Or my mother might come and help out. I am not allowed to step into her shoes – it's a matter of respect, for us. I can't enter the kitchen at home. My mother is nearby, and my in-law, or my younger brother – one of them will come and help. That's the way we do it at home.
> JB: If your wife realised that you were doing work like this for other people …? What would she think?
> Abu: For other people. Well, to be honest I can't deceive you into imagining that [my wife] understands completely what kind of work I do. She just knows that I am a household help [slight hysteria, speaks excitedly and fast]. Akakaka! Even if she knew, it's not easy for her to ask questions: this housework – why don't you do it here? She must be respectful – I mean between she and I – can she tell me what to do? She can't. She can't. I really don't think she could – but I have never seen such a thing, nor do I expect to hear [the argument] that because you do housework there you should come home and wash the pots – no, no, it couldn't happen. Not at our place.

The struggle which Abu was having in dealing with this question is transparently clear, and it would appear that for him, it is not even a legitimate question. In effect he deals with the contradiction by keeping the two worlds as far apart as possible. This distance is both material – the hundred miles or so that separate his village from the town – but it is also a gendered social distance maintained by his insistence on his wife's 'respect' towards him.

Abu's life story is concerned primarily with his struggle to improve himself, first through education, and later through wage work. Working as a servant was the first rung on the ladder, and through his success in finding a kindly employer he was able to marry, and then to better himself through acquiring what he perceived as 'skills' in shoemaking and repair. Even this was not an end in itself – he describes it as a 'ticket' – either to better wage employment, but better still as the basis for self-employment. At the time when he did the tape he was looking back, but also planning to go forward. To become a trader, and to combine this with farming, was what he was aiming for. His striving was linked to his masculinity: 'The reason ... that a man works [is] in order to be independent. To support yourself and your family'. But realistically he added: 'You don't have much choice in what you do for a living ... Work is work'.

CONCLUSION

In a study of life histories it has been argued that 'women's narratives ... stress the centrality of gender to human life and thought' (Personal Narratives Group 1989:263). Certainly this is evident from Sara's account, where being a woman is referred to as a particular burden. Unlike Abu she made no grand statements of universal principle relating to human rights and perhaps did not recognise herself as having such rights.

My thesis here, however, is that men's narratives may also emphasise gender, though their mode of gendering is different (a point which is also made by Caplan 1997:229). The way in which Abu saw his life as the unfolding of a plan, his pride in remembering how he had asserted himself ('am I not a man like you?'), his unquestioning view of himself as breadwinner,[3] and his work as a means to independence, was very different to Sara's 'getting by' and her view of work as a means to avoid men's oppression. It may be that it is precisely because Abu had to work in a job which challenged normative views of masculinity that he found it necessary to stress his manhood.

Abu's narrative indicates the extent to which gender relations remain the same in rural Tanzania. His wife was a piece which fitted exactly into the jigsaw of his existence, allowing him the space to consider and plan self-improvement, which for Sara was almost impossible. Her story shows that women who break 'free' from male dominance in marriage struggle to survive, but that survival is possible. As servants, women work a 'double day', returning home at night to 'further unpaid domestic duties' (Johnson 1992:137) whilst men rely on wives for their own domestic service.

Although their relations with employers were clearly of a class nature, and despite a political culture which initially at least emphasised new identities such as that of 'worker', neither Sara nor Abu displayed a politicised class consciousness. They evidently see themselves as part of a network of significant others (mainly the urban diaspora of kin, plus neighbours) who are crucial to securing work or a place to live, maybe even sanctuary in times of real trouble. They also identify with 'other workers' in knowing their 'place' in society – 'we people who don't get much', 'people at the bottom', 'people like me [down here]', and they are quick to distinguish themselves from 'the big ones' or those on the make amongst their fellow Africans. Whilst their felt experience of exploitation is sharp and bitter – the augmentation of worktime or of workloads for the same pay – neither is consciously a member of any organised group based on common class or work interests.

Abu, like Sara, viewed the worker as an isolated individual facing a powerful employer. If you wanted work you had to be compliant rather than challenging and to devise individualistic strategies to make work tolerable. Sara had more to lose here – nothing to sell but her labour power, no land, and no spouse to keep the home fires burning and her children fed while she insisted upon her rights. Her survival stratagems were the more devious then, though several lengthy periods of work with the same employers testified to her belief that they worked. Abu could afford to stand on principle occasionally, though in the end he was dependent, like Sara, on the luck of the draw in finding 'good employers' and his gender was little protection against degradation. It was Sara more than Abu who subscribed to a view of 'miracles'– that some employer (usually European or Asian) would be (as in one oft-recounted story of her mother's brother) 'so grateful ... that they built him a fine house of eight rooms'. The genre of 'success story' is a potent one.[4]

Neither were able to conceive of more collective action to improve their lot, and were cynical about 'socialist' institutions which promised to do precisely that. The state onslaught on class power and attitudes – admirable in itself, had adverse consequences for those to whom they meant work and a livelihood, and for whom real alternatives were not available.

3

A TOUCH OF CLASS – AND GENDER

The stories of Sara and Abu lead us to reflect not only on the differing experience of men and women in domestic service, but also the changing circumstances in which their subjective knowledge of class relations has been formed. If the central focus of this book is on domestic service as a class phenomenon, the point is that in postcolonial Tanzania class relations and alignments have been shifting and reforming. 'Class' is conceptualised here as the formation of relations of solidarity, exploitation and accumulation in the field of production, but it is also understood to be a vital and creative cultural process of performance and display. Whilst domestic service plays a significant role in the reproduction of class relations through its material and symbolic functions, some have seen it as a very ambiguous or anomalous kind of class relationship.

For many writers it is gender rather than class which is emphasised in accounts of domestic wage labour. Because the common assumption in the literature is that housework is gendered female, domestic service is uncritically taken to reflect the gendered power relations of family life. In Tanzania, where the actors in this drama are gendered in an unusual way, universalistic (and many local) conceptions and stereotypes are thrown into disarray. A case study in which domestic workers are male is not merely an idiosyncratic example of limited interest, but demands that we reconsider the usual assumptions.

In pointing up the way in which class formation is lived out through domestic struggles which are gendered (and often also racialised/ethnicised) we hear echoes of some very old questions, here given a new resonance. The domestic labour debate of the 1970s demonstrated that housework, in its various guises, touched on the great debates of social and political theory – Marxism, feminism and the emancipatory project. A spate of subsequent studies of housework as paid labour confirms that it has lost none of its power to raise challenging and difficult questions. Recent work has seen it as personal narrative, as neo-liberal project and as an instance of globalisation.

REINVENTING DOMESTIC SERVICE

Domestic service is an institution which appears, disappears and reappears in many different times and places. Its frequent reinvention in a range of guises may be a response to very different class pressures and circumstances. The reemergence of the domestic in the industrialised world in the late twentieth century put paid to any notion that this was a 'premodern' institution, destined to become 'obsolescent' with the consolidation of industrial society (as was argued by Coser 1973 or Laslett 1965).[1] Rather, it seemed to play different roles at different points in the emergence and unfolding of capitalism, its most telling feature its linkage to emergent class divisions.

Initially developing out of mutuality between households and encompassing both domestic and farm work (Laslett 1977; Johnson 1984), it later took on the form of apprenticeship as occupations began to be specialised and social divisions widened (Laslett 1977; Lasser 1987). Whilst the unit of production was still the household, servants were employed in direct production of goods as well as services and hence became aides to accumulation; but domestic service did not disappear as production was externalised to factories and workshops. Some argued that as the productive role of domestic service diminished, it was superseded by its contribution to status maintenance. Veblen is the most significant exponent of this position, arguing for the emergence of a 'leisure class' in industrial societies which conspicuously withdrew from direct engagement in productive activity and engaged in displaying its 'non-productive consumption of time' (1899:46). Domestic servants contributed to this manifestation of status, especially if they were numerous and their uniform distinctive (56). A similar class significance has been discerned in twentieth-century America, in 1930s Bolivia and in postcolonial industrialising Malaysia (Rollins 1985; Gill 1994; Chin 1998), suggesting that this was not a specifically European phenomenon but linked to modernity. The argument is persuasive and elegant, but we should not lose sight of the fact that classes are not formed and consolidated through polishing the capacity for display and that domestic service can facilitate more foundational class projects.

Developed capitalism may itself create pressures to which the reemergence of domestic service becomes a 'solution'. A new set of arguments refer to its function in absorbing labour or reconfiguring the labour market. In the advanced capitalist societies of Western Europe, the reemergence of domestic service has been associated with recession and male unemployment (e.g. in Britain in the 1920s: Taylor 1979) as well as with the growth of households with two partners in full-time employment (e.g. in Britain in the 1980s: Gregson and Lowe 1994). The persistence of 'old' institutions in new settings suggests that they may respond to new and contradictory demands – the struggle of female employers to cover their own domestic 'responsibilities' in order to hold onto paid work, the dramatic fluctuations in supply and shifts in the gendered conceptualisations of labour as well as to the enduring forms of privatised family existence in a class-divided capitalist society.

Domestic service also reappears as labour immigration from less developed areas of the world (Enloe 1989; Colen 1990; Chin 1998), reflecting the uneven reach of capitalism, the opening up of a global market for cheap household labour, the needs of immigrants for a foothold in a new country and of their governments for foreign currency in the form of remittances. Both Chin and Enloe claim that state and international agencies have engineered and facilitated this situation. In rapidly industrialising Malaysia the state developed an explicit policy of legalising the import of foreign domestics from the Philippines and Indonesia when the local supply of willing labour dried up, absorbed into more lucrative work in export-oriented multinational factories. Chin describes these policies as contributing to Malaysia's 'modernity' project: 'Middle-class consumption of foreign female domestic workers' labour (provided by the transnational capitalist labour market in domestic servants) is part of the Malaysian state elite's promotion of enhanced middle-class consumption of goods and services as symbolic of personal and national progress' (15). For Enloe it is the promotion of neo-liberalism through international agencies such as the IMF which creates both the demand for domestic servants (as public services are cut back) and the supply, through the extension of market relations.

If domestic service can be associated in one place with industrial growth and an expressive consumptionism, in other places it can be held to be more reflective of the failure of growth or of the contradictions of uneven development (Sanjek and Colen 1990:177). Servants may be employed precisely because industry cannot yet supply labour-saving household appliances, and imported goods are too expensive for most. This is the case in many developing countries (Shindler 1980). A more contradictory situation is described for South Africa, where capitalist industry did develop the capacity to produce household devices, but its market was undermined by the very cheapness of labour which the state also fostered through its policies towards black Africans. As Van Onselen noted for the early part of this century: 'despite the great hope placed in the cook-oven in particular, the Witwatersrand could not be recast in the mould of American capital so easily. In a society where domestic labour was cheap, household appliances were considered expensive, and thus South Africa continued to assume its own distinctive capitalist profile' (1982:21).

In other places domestic service may facilitate the consolidation of classes struggling to accumulate in very uncertain environments. As class divisions emerge in the South, domestic work often involves young people working in an apprentice capacity (Sanjek offers an example from Ghana: 1990). The supply of servants may reflect the existence of a grinding and desperate poverty in some areas whilst in others intermittent spurts of growth are accompanied by opportunistic accumulation for a few. A recent report disclosed the practice in West Africa of traders 'buying' children for as little as £10 in Benin and Togo and selling them on as domestic workers to wealthy families in Nigeria for around £200. The headline spoke of the 'scandal of child slaves' (*The Voice*, 29 Sept. 1997). In contrast to Malaysia where the import of domestic labour is highly regulated within the terms of overall state policy linked to national development, these transactions occured outside the remit of state control.

CLASS PROJECTS

If domestic service is reinvented in a variety of economic and political settings and as a response to distinctive localised pressures, there is one common feature to its form as wage labour: domestic service is a class phenomenon. Whilst appearing as a purely private and domestic solution to shortages of labour within the household, the employment of servants simultaneously speaks to a diversity of class projects within the overall ensemble of class relations – to accumulate through exploitation, to demonstrate material and social success, to survive through labour, to secure and improve conditions of employment. The state, especially in contemporary settings, often plays a vital role in regulating the flows of labour or the conditions of employment and in facilitating or impeding accumulation processes which frame the employment of servants.

As a class phenomenon, domestic wage labour throws up some challenging anomalies. Many writers have seen domestic service as an institution in which precapitalist or preindustrial forms of class relation are enshrined, despite its contemporary (and now predominantly capitalist) context. The relationship between servants and their employers is seen to have overtones of feudalism or slavery in the degree of control which employers expect to exert over servants' lives. '[D]omestic service is ... predicated on the premise that it is the person of the servant, not primarily her skills, that is hired' (Tellis-Nayak, 1983, 68). Domestic service is therefore characterised by Tellis-Nayak as a relationship of 'patron-clientage' rather than wage labour; by Chin as an 'essentially premodern institution' (1998:4) and by Callinicos as 'quasi-feudal' (1975:61). Writing of South Africa, Bozzoli summarises the position, adding colonialism as another servile context for labour relations:

> Domestic work is normally cast as the ultimate experience of the colonised. Women who perform what is perceived by most as degrading work of a personalised nature, in the intimacy and feudal-like confines of the white household are, quite rightly, viewed by modern-day interpreters as victims of a system capable of inflicting particularly humiliating forms of subordination. (1991:104)

These appearances are clearly linked to the privatised location of domestic work. In contrast to industrial forms of production, domestic work is conducted in the home as workplace. The opportunities this affords to employers for treating servants as less than human, and for isolating these workers from others has often been noted. The assumption that this inhibits organised forms of proletarian class consciousness and breeds a passive subjectivity is also well-entrenched in the literature. The recruitment conditions of domestic workers are optimal for setting them in competition with each other, and indeed it is argued by most writers that domestic servants are 'almost unable to organise collectively' (Wrigley 1991:327, citing evidence largely from Latin America, but also Gordon 1985 on South Africa; Gregson and Lowe 1994:236 on contemporary Britain.)

Rather than seeing domestic service as embodying 'slavery' or 'clientage' or 'feudalism' in settings where these are not the general prevailing social relations, some analysts place servants firmly within the class of wage labourers, either on technical or political grounds. For Cock (1980), writing on apartheid South Africa, this is done in classical Marxist terms of the domestic servant's relationship to the means of production:

> the paid domestic worker is firstly a wage labourer and thus subject to the discipline of the wage, with the corollary that the worker receives less than what she produces, the surplus being appropriated by her employer. Secondly she plays a critical part in the reproduction of both labour power and the relations of production. She is thus an important element in the indirect production of surplus value for capital. (1980:14)

This formulation owes something to the debate around the domestic labour of the housewife in capitalist societies (see below). Like servants, though without the benefit of the wage, housewives were engaged in reproducing labour power in a material and ideological sense, that is to say, renewing the capacity of others to work (who are more directly exploited). Despite this parallel role, Cock assumes no alliance of political interest between the two parties. Domestic service is class exploitation, not a version of family relations or of gender solidarity.

Bozzoli (1991) offers a more complex and contradictory account of domestic service as wage labour, but also as class project. Based on the personal narratives of women of Phokeng (South Africa), it underlines the way in which theoretical accounts of the servile nature of domestic work may be contradicted by the actors' own subjective evaluations. Women often saw domestic work as having allowed them to achieve autonomy from family pressures and build a long term future in the urban areas as members of an aspirant 'respectable' working class.

Within Tanzania, domestic servants have not only been viewed as an 'exploited' element of the working class (Mascarenhas and Mbilinyi, 1983:18), they have even been celebrated as proletarian heroes (Shivji 1983; compare Gill 1994:143). Contrary to the view that servants are unable to organise, the evidence for Tanzania shows that in the colonial period they were amongst the first to be unionised and in 1956 they played one of the foremost parts in a wave of strikes which swept the country. These particular events and their explanation are explored in Chapter 9: they were not unique to colonial Tanganyika but were paralleled in other parts of Africa. I will also consider the apparent passivity of domestic workers in Tanzania today. The historical evidence of militancy amongst domestic workers seems to confound Shivji's orthodox Marxist position on class activism: 'The common economic situation of workers being at one place and being the sellers of the same commodity – labour power – unites workers in combinations ...' (Shivji 1983:13). Of course domestic servants are not as workers concentrated together, but isolated, each one facing individual oppression. Despite this, in colonial Tanganyika and elsewhere in Africa they were occasionally able to combine and to voice their rejection of employment conditions – and this demands explanation.

The evidence of proletarianisation is not to be found in organised political activism, nor is its foundation to be discerned in the exploitative character of the employment relationship (as Cock argues), but, as Seccombe puts it: 'The proletarian condition is produced and reproduced by means of the worker's separation from the means of production' (1980:39) and being set adrift with nothing to sell but their labour power. What has often been missing from accounts of domestic service is any analysis of the extent to which men and women are deprived of alternative means to a livelihood other than to sell their capacity to labour. In many parts of Africa we cannot yet speak of a proletariat in this full sense of the word since wage workers continue to some degree dependent on the pre-capitalist sector (petty commodity or subsistence production of agricultural and craft goods) for family survival. This feature adds to the ambiguous class character of the domestic worker, who is not only operating in the privatised domain of familial production of use values, but like most other workers is semi-proletarianised. But as Stichter has pointed out for early labour history in Africa: 'even a migrant and semi-proletarianised work-force is capable of individual and collective labour action' (1975:30).

Marxist class analysis is essentially relational, so that a determination of the class character of domestic service must require a scrutiny of the nature of the employing class as well as the employed. Shivji indicated the ambiguous character of the ruling class in Tanzania by way of the title 'bureaucratic/state bourgeoisie' (1976). The question as to whether this class, with its varied fractions, is an accumulative class, and if so, by what means it attempts to acquire and expand its capital base, is relevant to the issue of domestic service, for we may hypothesise that an acquisitive class would be less disposed to employ servants simply as a mark of status to underwrite their ease and comfort. Rather, in their concern to augment capital, they might engage servants for more instrumental purposes, freeing household labour for more productive enterprise or for creating such enterprise on a household basis. A comparison can be made with industrialising Malaysia where Chin argues for an employing class whose overriding objective is consumption and the assertion of a distinctive life style – though this may be an effect of the theoretical lens through which the phenomenon is understood (1998:184). The projects of the employing class are not always realised – as for example when the pool of labour they have relied upon for servants dries up – workers preferring less servile or more rewarding employment and conditions to be had elsewhere, or where accumulation is impeded by state or economic crisis and once-dominant classes are no longer able to live in the style to which they were accustomed. If class formation has powerful structural and material determinations it is also a field where agency has a forceful influence on outomes.

Domestic service as gender subordination

Whilst the institution of domestic service is inconceivable except in class-divided or dividing societies, it is its gendered character that is often to the fore, with the assumption that servants are everywhere female. Along with this go other assumptions – that the work and its relations reflect the usual patriarchal order of domestic settings and that no further explanation is required of worker passivity. Here is one example, drawn from an account of domestic work in contemporary Britain:

> waged domestic labour can only be understood and accounted for in relation to its unwaged form, and the ideology and identities which underpin it ... [Domestic work] is permeated ... with highly traditional ideas about the gendering and form of specific types of domestic labour and with a strong sense of working for love as opposed to money. (Gregson and Lowe 1994:5–6)

What is striking about this formulation is the specificity of the phenomenal features of domestic wage labour described. Set this against the situation in Tanzania, where 'traditional ideas' about domestic labour derived either from rural African households or were imported by colonialists and where the colonial gendering of domestic service as men's work confounded all of them. These were men who joined an emergent, unstable urban proletariat working for survival money, unencumbered by notions of housework as 'labouring for love'. Clearly gender is at issue here in quite a different way.

Because domestic service has been seen as an archetypically feminine occupation, and because housework (domestic labour) was for a time seen as the vital clue to the subordination of women, particularly in capitalist societies, it was feminists who stimulated a renewed interest in domestic wage labour. Given present pluralised and apolitical conceptions of gender it is useful to remember the passionate and polarised politics out of which the domestic labour debate arose. With its beginnings in the late 1960s, in the protests of individual women against men who took domestic skills and their product (comfort, cleanliness, meals etc) for granted, it later developed into a theoretical challenge to Marxism by feminists who argued that Marx maintained a 'guilty silence' on the important question of how labour power is reproduced – or, to put it more simply, how the capacity of workers to create profits for their employers is maintained day by day and renewed over the generations. Domestic labour was seen as the most important element in this process (Seccombe 1974).

By the end of the 1970s this debate had run its course, and domestic labour was no longer seen as the only key to understanding women's oppression (Molyneux 1979). Not all domestic labourers were women (single men also had to reproduce their labour power), and not all women were domestic labourers (some could afford to pay others to take over this task for them). And whilst initially it had seemed a powerful argument against capital to see how it appropriated the products of an invisible army of housewives, the 'functionalism' of this position (that domestic labour existed only to serve capital) deadened its impact (Bozzoli 1983:159–60).

The domestic labour debate nevertheless raised central questions about the ways in which labour power is reproduced in capitalist societies, and by implication how labour power is created and maintained in all societies. For capitalist societies it also focused attention on the character of domestic labour as privatised labour with an indirect and usually hidden relation to capital, thus raising questions about the apparent failure of capitalism to capitalise these socially necessary tasks, and thereby about the uneven development of capitalist relations of production even in advanced capitalist societies. Furthermore, it generated questions about worker solidarity in this sphere, for whereas the common objective position of housewives was taken to be a sufficient basis for collective action by those who organised the Wages for Housework campaign, others identified the barriers in the way of such mobilisation to be the atomisation and privatisation of household work (e.g. Seccombe 1974:23).

Crucially, the domestic labour debate did not establish a necessary link between domestic labour and women's subordination, although it was this aspect which was borrowed when the terms of the debate were transferred to the study of paid domestic labour in historical or Third World settings. In the mid-1970s, feminists began to write about domestic service in Latin America (e.g. Smith 1975) and in nineteenth- and twentieth-century Europe (e.g. Davidoff 1976; Taylor 1979). In all these cases the 'servant class' was overwhelmingly female and this was taken to be its definitive and most significant feature. Moreover the predominance of women in domestic work was assumed to be a logical extension of women's domestic role. It was seen as a simple case of women transferring skills learnt at home to the marketplace, or, to present it from another perspective, carrying out their traditional servicing roles in a more exploitative setting.

There is an irony in this, of course, for in considering paid domestic work it is no longer 'women' as a unitary category which is at issue. Some women take on domestic labour as a paid job in order that other women may withdraw from it. And domestic service is a context in which power relations between women come to the fore: an aspect which later studies came to reflect on (especially Rollins 1985, writing from the receiving end as a domestic worker; and Palmer 1989, who speaks of her 'personal dilemmas' as a feminist with a commitment to gender and racial equality who yet had always benefited from domestic help).

The present study throws another complication into this view of domestic service as the subordination of women: in many parts of Africa the majority of domestic servants have always been male. This is also the case in parts of Asia (Sharma 1986), whilst in eighteenth-century Europe and earlier, male as well as female servants were common (Laslett tells us that 'males slightly exceeded females', 1977:43; see also Burnett 1974:143). Evidently the question of the sexual division of labour in the domestic sphere was not to be explained unproblematically either as an outcome of women's 'natural' capabilities for homemaking and child care or as an obvious and automatic transfer of talents from the home to the labour market (a debate to be considered further in Chapter 5).

Although debates within feminism highlighted some of the characteristic ambiguities of domestic labour, whether performed as private service or as wage labour, they misled us in equating its contradictions with those faced only and always by women.

The gendering of domestic service as a class phenomenon raises other contentious issues, for it seems likely that at some points men and women may have distinctive interests to pursue or battles to fight. We need to reflect on why Bozzoli's women of Phokeng clearly had plans of their own; on the way in which men come to inhabit the 'female' tasks of housework; and on how women servants resist collusive assumptions about their 'love' of housework. Could it also be that the reason for militancy amongst servants in colonial East Africa was because they were predominantly male?

SUBJECTIVITY AND POLITICS

A parallel can be drawn between gender and the question of 'race', where again it is all too easy to project particular circumstances into a general rule. Gaitskell et al.'s insistence that 'domestic service, especially in colonial societies, has a racial character. Almost everywhere in the world it is performed by "socially inferior" groups: immigrants, blacks and ethnic minorities' (1984:88) indicates a confusion of phenomenal forms with the essence of the relationship. By definition, those who perform menial wage labour are thereby rendered socially inferior, but that there are sometimes 'racial' differences between employer and employee is not the determining factor here, but class. In many cases there is no 'racial' difference between mistress and servant – in nineteenth-century Europe for example. The social fact of class difference can itself of course be provided with an ideological rationale drawing on racial or biological mythology (the IQ debate would be a telling instance of this). In the South African setting, every social fact is charged with racial significance, but the danger in seeing 'race' as integral to the employment relationship here (Cock does the same, when she speaks of the 'triple oppression' of class, race and sex endured by female domestics) is that it clouds our understanding of relations between employers and servants of the same 'race'.

There is an almost apologetic tone to Gaitskell et al.'s admission that black people in South Africa may also employ servants:

> Although some black women do employ domestic servants them-
> selves, and although the relationship may [sic] manifest a servile or
> class character, it does not resonate with the overall structures of
> racial domination in South African society. Rather it may contribute
> to an awareness of class differentiation within the black population.
> (1984:89)

Johnson also asserts of her experience in Southern Africa that 'the relationship I saw between black employers and their servants was different to that I saw in white households' – the former often friendly and coop-erative; the latter formal and markedly unequal (1992:146). Such mutuality is unlikely to be more than a short-term phenomenon, at least at higher class levels. Hansen reports a very different view from Zambia. 'Zambian [employers] forget, servants say, that you are a fellow black – or rather that they are black themselves ... Zambian employers resort to hierarchical practices of interaction with their servants. In their view, although they are of the same race, servants are still other' (1989:249). It is important not to discount the possibility that the oppressed can become oppressors, and that women together are not bound in sisterhood if divided by class.

This is underlined in another way by considering women's liberation movements in the South. Johnson points out that the domestic labour debate did not have much resonance in southern Africa because 'many of the women in key positions in these [women's] organisations don't have to do their own domestic chores' (1992:146). Wrigley is even more hard-hitting:

> The women's movements [in Latin America] typically are led by
> middle-class educated women who themselves employ domestic

workers. This helps reinforce the image of the feminist movement as
class-bound, serving the interests of the privileged ... domestic workers
remain on their own – all too often disdained by the labor movements
of their countries and equally slighted by middle-class feminists.
(1991:326)

Many voices: domestic service re-presented

In employing class and gender as framing concepts in this analysis I aim to
problematise their use; this is not intended as a 'sinking back into reductive
essentialisms' (Baden and Goetz 1997:20). It is worth considering the
extent to which postmodernism, with its exploration of personal narratives
and its fracturing of the concepts of gender and class, challenges the
arguments so far formulated in relation to domestic service.

To press the claims of subjectivity, meaning and actor orientation in both
theory and method has a long and honourable history. In studies of
domestic service we find Tellis-Nayak (1983) as well as Sanjek and Colen
(1990:178) bidding for an 'actor-centred approach'. An intense interest in
actor perspectives as purveyed through personal narratives is also of long
standing. Anthropology and some forms of sociology had a tradition of
collecting such accounts, building on participant observation. Marxist-
inspired cultural studies also impelled labour and feminist historians to seek
out first-hand accounts of those whose voices had never been heard. A spate
of studies based on diaries or life-history work was produced, some more
innocent of, others more inspired by, postmodern critiques of conventional
biographical endeavour. Where this work offers an inner view of the
experience of domestic service we should grasp it eagerly.

The work of Liz Stanley on Hannah Culwick, an English domestic
servant who had a long-term, complex and troubled relationship with her
male employer in the latter part of the nineteenth century, casts an acute
and self-questioning eye on the evidence this throws up of 'power' relations
within a transgressive relationship (1984; 1992). Using this exceptional case
to highlight the ordinary, Stanley also focuses on the relational aspects of
power as a never-ending outcome of struggles rather than as a property of
socially given categories. Working from Hannah's diaries she aims not to
disclose the 'true' Hannah but a recognition of the complexity of the woman
and her own [Stanley's] shifting responses to that complexity.

Reflecting on labour and women's history through the medium of personal narratives has raised challenging questions about the experience of
colonial and postcolonial lives. From Tanzania there are biographical
accounts of women slaves, of political activists, of 'modern Tanzanians' (all
men!), of churchwomen and of 'unsung heroines'.[2] Amongst these there are
one or two men and women who speak of domestic work and its conditions
in ways that offer insider views of the experience – often bitter ones. One of

the problems of personal narratives is that the individual case is all too easily taken as representative of the whole. The value of the exercise lies in our placing the narrative in some kind of setting and asking searching questions about its narrator as well as critically subjecting the researcher's objectives to scrutiny: are they presenting the speaker as an exemplar (of oppression, of resiliance, of strength)? Why and how have they selected and interpreted the case? If Stanley is right to cast doubt on the notion of a 'privileged' or 'final' account (1992:176) what happens to the quest for explanation or under-standing?

Gordon's collection of life histories of South African servants (1985) is also useful in its telling of more complicated stories from within the service relationship. Although the handful of servants described here are almost certainly exceptional in their ability to articulate their experience and in their eagerness to improve themselves (they were mainly older women with a 'career' of domestic service behind them, and Gordon does not discuss their typicality) they are not as cynical, as passive or as victimised as the servants Cock had earlier described. Several were active unionists, others had stood out against domineering mistresses. Conversely many of them talked of warm relationships with employers. Gordon's work suggests that the personal loyalty demanded and occasionally achieved by employers may erode the class solidarity of workers. Clearly the experience of domestic service is not all of a kind, even where class oppression feeds on gender and race subordination.

If the concept of class can break up before our eyes through the device of personal narratives (though this is largely an effect of focusing on individual subjectivities rather than on aggregated social data), the concept of gender is equally fragmented by the postmodernist gaze. A particularly relevant example here is the pluralisation of 'masculinities'. Radical feminism's monolithic version of masculinity was punctured through pre-postmodern accounts such as those of Cockburn (1983) and Willis (1979) on working class men. They pointed up the contradictory nature of being male as well as being a worker: the way that male workers assert a masculinity of skill, pride, strength, competence and control in work despite their subjection to capital; the fragility of masculine power faced with the arrival of female competition smuggled in through new technology; the way that older men harden up younger men through their initiation into work; the way that a male worker's reputation is based on his ability to bring home the money 'won in a masculine mode in confrontation with the "real" world which is [seen as] too tough for the woman' (Willis 1979:197). Certainly it was the contradictions which struck me when men become domestic servants.

Postmodernism has fractured our simplified view of gender as a bipolar system: it re-presents it as negotiated, playful, pluralistic, dynamic, shifting etc. (Cornwall and Lindisfarne 1994; Mac an Ghaill 1996). Feminism has had problems with this as have those whose roots in Marxism have not yet withered: inequality, exploitation and oppression disappear from view or become merely discursive forms of resistance. Most recently the worm seems to have turned again, particularly in the study of masculinities: the notion of 'hegemonic masculinit/ies' resurrects power relations (Connell 1987), there is a questioning of the view that 'all practices are effects of discourse' (McMahon quoted in Collinson and Hearn 1996:213; Ramazanoglu 1993) and the emancipatory project is redrawn:

> feminist interpretations of postmodernism seem to offer a productive way forward. They focus on the fluidity of processes of gendering and, when they are linked to the new feminist politics of location, they offer new ways of using comparative insights to combat inequality ... if we locate and describe the multiplicity of competing masculine identities in any given setting we automatically begin to dislodge the hegemonic versions of masculinity which privilege some people over others. (Cornwall and Lindisfarne 1994:4)

And yet 'locating' and 'describing' remain intellectual activities – not unimportant, but hardly the stuff of active 'dislocation' of entrenched patterns of power. This new genre of thinking about masculinity may help us to formulate questions to address the fact of male workers, largely under female orders, located in the home as workplace. Could they turn this into a powerfully embodied 'masculine' experience? In aiming to do so, were they not at risk of being labelled insubordinate *vis à vis* female employers? How did the title 'domestic help' reverberate in their own homes or with other men in jobs deemed more manly?

What this kind of analysis does not do is to investigate (or offer modes of investigating) the ways that men in this position might act together, or with other workers, male and female, to demand better terms and conditions for their labour; or how domestic employment as a servant is different from the domestic labour of wives, or from 'homeworking' where employers devolve responsibility for the production process to workers in their own homes. With its focus on the construction of identities (albeit understood as a social process) it often loses sight of the relational aspect of production.

Postmodernism rejected class as a structuralist metanarrative *and* as an emancipatory project; it thereby also rendered the concept of 'class culture' meaningless. The institution of domestic service refocuses our attention on the cultural construction of 'class', for it may contribute to this process not only by symbolising status and facilitating its maintenance, but also by its role in reproducing the next generation. At higher class levels servants may play a bigger part in the care of children than parents do. The contradictions inherent in having one class of persons actively socialise children who will claim another class heritage has often been noted.[3]

Putting this in other terms, we can say that domestic service plays a part in the class drama of display and rehearsal. Evidently the scale of the drama rests on the accumulative success of the employing class, but these features act as markers of its extent. It is important to investigate the cultural construction of class in countries where emergent class formation may proceed silently or flamboyantly, either against the grain of other interests built on state ideology, locality, ethnicity and family, or incorporating these elements in more powerful coalitions of social identity. One aspect of such an investigation is clearly domestic service, both in its capacity as regenerator of present labour power and as reproducer of future labour power.

Postmodernism first rejects the notion of class as part of a totalitarian metanarrative based on essentialism; it then begins to build it back in as a form of personal identity. A similar process occurs with gender. Although much of this, with its emphasis on diversity and difference, is at odds with the politics of coming together,[4] it does head off unrealistic views of how solidarities might be achieved. It also focuses attention on the possibility that difference might be woven into and enrich, as well as hinder, creative coalitions. It leaves us with the problem of explaining solidarity where it occurs, against the odds: 'every man must remember that what befalls another will react on him. These are the laws of our association of Boys'.[5]

4

COLONIAL DISCOURSES

'A bit of nonsense this one' (Colonial official's comment on the file of the African Cooks, Washermen and Houseservants' Association, c. 1951)

In borrowing a Foucauldian concept of 'discourse' to reflect on those fragments of the colonial record which touch on domestic service in Tanganyika, I affirm that the term is a useful one with which to denote the voices of the past which confront, engage with or silence one another, evidencing 'modes of representation' of Self and Other more than faithful accounts of 'what really happened' in colonial society. The focus here is not on whether (or how) the texts reviewed are historical evidence of real events or processes, but on their ideological or discursive features. Foucault suggests that we consider conventions regarding what is 'sayable' at a particular period, how this 'discourse' is 'deployed' in a 'practical field' and how it relates to other discourses and is potentially transformatory.[1]

Whilst employing the now all-pervasive term 'discourse' and setting up the task as one of 'discourse analysis', I draw as much on a Marxist culturalist approach, or on an Althusserian notion of 'reading', as on Foucault, for I engage also with issues that Foucault specifically rejects as concerns: with who speaks, and with what is not said, the 'silences'.[2] Whilst Foucault argues that reflection on the 'conditions of existence' of particular discourses are part of the project, it is important to recognise that these go beyond the discursive field to enclose socio-economic and political contexts, which cannot be dealt with in the same way.[3]

To write of colonial discourses is to emphasise that these are largely productions of hegemonic positions within a politico-economic order that is now past. My approach here is to seek out themes, perspectives, forms of argumentation, inconsistencies and taken-for-granted assumptions in the archive, as well as exploring how policy issues are selected for action and discussion, and how debate is sometimes foreclosed, whilst, on other occasions, extended and transformed. Some of these records offer a glimpse of dialogue and of oppositional discourses; they by no means represent an undifferentiated or unchallenged 'official view'. Putting this in another way, we can say that these are discourses around power, some of which had more impact than others.

The Tanganyikan colonial archive is far from full on the topic of domestic service,[4] even whilst the attention paid to it speaks of its key relevance to colonial concerns. Why is it worth further consideration? I want to argue here that colonial discourses continue to reverberate through contemporary understandings of the institution. Some of these discursive elements can be stated as assumptions: that the best domestic workers are men; or that ethnicity marks both the nature of demand and the conditions of supply. But in addition there are the expectations which most employers continue to have of servants (and vice versa) and which are clearly presaged in colonial discourses. What seems to have been lost (and this is of interest in itself) is the assumption that domestic service is a matter of 'official concern'. Deliberately excluded from postcolonial official statistics, it is no longer formally linked with matters such as working conditions, gender or subject-status. If the topic itself now escapes the official gaze, there is also minimal 'oppositional discourse' around domestic service.

In this chapter I look at four sources of colonial discourse(s). One derives from the national archive of colonial records and consists of official files and reports – a source which is normally cited in a factually 'evidential' way, without attention being paid to its conditions of production or its internal dialogues, its sifting of external input or its project of achieving an 'offical position'. A second source is in instructional manuals produced for 'new-comers' (from Europe). As they would be setting up house in Tanganyika it was imperative to socialise them into local convention in the matter of domestic help. The third source is contemporary newspapers where repor-tage and debate of official policy in this field surfaced from time to time, as well as formulation of outraged responses to domestic servant militancy. I will also look briefly at a colonial novel which devotes more space to this subject than was usual.

Each of these sources is addressed to a different audience and hence subject to different conditions of existence. The degree of mutual recognition is worth noting however: what discourse analysts call 'intertextuality' (Kristeva 1986). Official files contain press cuttings and drafts of letters to the press to put the official view; instructional manuals are written in the consciousness of colonial laws and official constraints upon employers; whilst the press is constantly commenting upon the actions of officialdom. Having introduced each source I will explore the themes which they discourse upon with domestic service as the object of concern, and in particular class and gender relations. In no sense are these themes explicitly voiced: indeed the concepts employed here are alien to the social thinking of colonialdom. They are expressed in implicit ways and this is a reflection of their imbrication in social life and the politics of colonial rule. Discordant voices – and how they are silenced – are also addressed here.

SOURCES OF COLONIAL DISCOURSE AND THEIR AUDIENCES
Official records

The records of colonial officialdom represent one example of colonial discourse where a certain kind of self-interest is writ large. I refer to the archives surviving in Tanzania – 'preservation' being a very random matter. Despite the material being essentially fragmentary, it speaks loudly of another world. Its impact is heightened by the conventions of the medium. These were officials writing essentially to each other: memos, notes, annotations and informal records of meetings are enclosed in the files as well as formal reports and copies of official letters. These people did not expect to be 'overheard'; many of the documents are not intended for public consumption. Given that there is much that is 'off the record', officials felt free to express views of colonial 'subjects' that were at best patronising, at worst disparaging. Such views were mirrored by an unquestioning faith in the superiority of Europeans and the justice of their civilising mission in Africa. Though considerable effort went into the production of bland public documents where such views were self-censored, it is clear that officials did not expect to have to answer to the local African population (until independence was in sight).

Colonial officialdom was also self-evidently aware of itself as accountable to higher authorities: to the Colonial Office in Britain, and, since Tanganyika was a territory held in trust by Britain on a mandate of the League of Nations (later the United Nations), to even more august bodies still. The devising of self-serving or masking accounts of local actions was never far from the minds of the authors of the letters and reports which crowd these files.

Then there were the sometimes uncomfortable relations with those Europeans, also resident in colonial Tanganyika, but whose concern was not with 'the advancement of the African' but more nakedly with profit, and with the freedom to establish relations of employment unfettered by offical regulation. The interests of employers (not themselves always in harmony) had to be fielded or accommodated within the official ideology of developing the territory for the benefit of its people ('development' and 'people' being ambiguously interpreted at various times).

The voices which speak out of the files are those of Europeans talking to other Europeans; they are also those of men speaking to other men in a world unquestionably dominated by men. When questions relating to gender occasionally arise, the authors feel free to be lofty and dismissive, or to adopt a tone of amused tolerance, even when the claimants are their own womenfolk (as they would see it).

The non-official parties to the dialogues and negotiations with which officials dealt day by day sometimes present their own cases within the dusty paperwork of the files: letters, petitions and reports of meetings are often carefully noted and preserved. But in the files at least, it is the officials who have the final say.

Far from official discussion around the institution of domestic service being marginal, or a footnote to weightier concerns, it is evident that it was highly pertinent to the central social relationships with which colonial officials were concerned and to their presentation of these in self-serving forms. Issues such as labour relations and conditions, the growing militancy of Africans as workers and subjects, the preservation of ethnic distinctions, the proper place of women and the contestable power of colonial officials in mandated territories are all illustrated in commentary and policy relating to domestic service.

Instructional manuals for 'newcomers'

Various government pamphlets and Handbooks were produced to inform newly arriving officials about conditions in the territory – and more important, to initiate them into what was expected of Europeans in this setting (e.g. Government of Tanganyika 1930; East African Office 1948). Most of these publications contained advice regarding the employment of servants – and especially about how much they should be paid. Ignorant newcomers were held to threaten existing understandings about wages and to spoil the market.

Another source of instruction was the Women's Service League of Tanganyika (WSLT), founded in 1927 by European ladies 'to promote the interests and well-being of the women and children of Tanganyika'. The official *Handbook of Tanganyika Territory* noted one rather narrower aspect of its 'useful work': to run 'a registry office for native servants for the benefit of [European] residents both in Dar es Salaam and up-country' (Government of Tanganika 1930:489). The WSLT produced its own advice (published by the Government Printer) to those new to the territory and justified their 'notes' as follows: 'they will give the newcomer just the information he or she requires' (WSLT 1947).[5] The care taken to engender new arrivals was evidently responsive to the domestic nature of the information to be imparted. They explained their objectives in producing *Notes on African Domestic Labour in Dar es Salaam*:

> Many questions come to the minds of employers at the present time – especially to the minds of newcomers to the Territory – as to what should constitute fair emoluments, hours of work, duties and the like for their domestic staff. (WSLT 1948:1)

Borrowing from dramatic protocol as much as from Foucault we might say that new actors needed to be taught the lines regarding 'what could be said'. Such pamphlets were written in a lofty European tone, quick to point out the inferiority of African servants – they spoilt clothes by their violent methods of washing, they broke or ignored 'new-fangled gadgets' (1947:3,10), garden boys were 'not satisfactory' ('All Africans need careful supervision and it is difficult to supervise during the heat of the day' 1948:4) and so on. Conversely there is the patronising view that, 'The African appreciates any interest ...' allied with the blatantly instrumental: 'better service will be forthcoming' (1948:6).

The position of European women in this colonial setting was a highly ambiguous one, whether they were wives or, more rarely, independent, single women. Occasionally the wives of officials, planters, missionaries or entrepreneurs were employed (often as nurses or secretaries), whilst some single women occupied official roles in their own right.[6] These were women caught between colonial privilege and male patronage. Donaldson conceptualises their situation as: 'contradictory ... both colonised patriarchal objects and colonising race-privileged subjects' (1993:6).

Contemporary newspapers

My focus here is on newspapers in colonial Tanganyika which addressed themselves to a largely European audience, though they were evidently also read by some sections of the Asian population and increasingly by Africans.[7] English-language newspapers disclose a broader view of European society outside of, and not always in sympathy with, the aspirations and routines of officialdom. For a brief period after the First World War, for example, the *Tanga Post and East Coast Advertiser* spoke up for 'Planter and Commercial' interests which were often opposed to those of the colonial state; whilst in the period leading up to independence in 1961 the *Sunday News* found itself objecting to government policies on a number of occasions (facilities for European education, taxation, the 'value for money' of colonial officialdom and so on), whilst at the same time lending support to the 'multiracial' United Tanganyika Party (UTP), which the Governor of Tanganyika hoped would steal support from TANU, the Tanganyika African National Union.

Despite distancing themselves from the 'official' view on matters of crucial concern to the European population of the territory, those who wrote for English language newspapers shared with administrators an unquestioning assumption of European superiority and preeminence. At times it is as if the world they inhabit is a solely white world, caught up in its own closed social circle. The social whirl of parties, game hunting, amateur theatricals, and the latest arrivals from Home serve to distract them from preoccupation with the cost of living and the difficulties of life for Europeans in the tropics.

The mango and the palm

The Mango and the Palm (1962) is one colonial officer's autobiographical novel recounting the time he spent as a District Officer in Tanganyika (and other colonial postings) in the 1950s. What is noteworthy about this book is that it seizes with wry humour on the issue of dealing with servants, and tells several anecdotes of interest on the matter. This is remarkable because, as Strobel points out, the reminiscences of colonial men rarely mention the difficulties and joys of 'homemaking' in new and trying circumstances (1991:21). This is a women's genre.

It is this unusual streak to Darrell Bate's book that makes it difficult to categorise – as well as to visualise the audience that he intended to reach (or did reach – a largely female audience?). Compared to other sources of colonial discourse, this book alone confronts the issue of gender head-on, even whilst it has no name for it. It exposes the contradictions of a situation in which it was taken for granted that 'real men' did 'women's work' and illustrates how people from diverse backgrounds were affronted when this unspoken rule was transgressed.

DISCURSIVE THEMES IN COLONIAL DISCOURSES

Focussing only on domestic service as an object of discourse, the whole superstructure of colonial society is revealed. This can be immediately illustrated by the term 'boy/boi', which was not only shorthand for 'servant' (taken for granted as male) but also had a much wider compass, congruent with the category 'native' or 'the African'.[8] All these terms were employed as categorical forms through which Africans were homogenised, denigrated and belittled. Inherent in the term 'boy', when applied to an adult male, was an infantilisation which summed up the view of many colonials that Africans were immature, not yet 'ready' for self-government, that they were under perpetual tutelage. In the domestic servant role, the 'boy' was often assimilated to the status of children in the family home. When Africans began to organise and protest against colonial rule there was talk of the 'growing pains' of development.[9]

By the 1950s the broader public usage of the term 'boy' had been abandoned and it became acceptable only as a job description.[10] And whilst the term 'native' went on being used up to the late 1940s in official documents it was increasingly being superseded by the usage 'African'. By 1951 official doubt was even being cast on the title of a key legal Statute, the Masters and Native Servants Ordinance: should the term 'native' be removed from a pamphlet describing its remit? But it was decided that no change be made.[11] However the very title of the statute indicates the way that employment relations were founded on the feudal/patriarchal domestic model. Whilst the term 'native' was beginning to sound questionable in the 1950s, using the term 'Servant' to cover all (African) wage employees (and 'Masters' to mean all employers) did not yet seem inappropriate.

When class relations hide behind ethnic labels

In these colonial sources there is no vocabulary of 'class' as such. It is 'races' which are seen as the major actors on the stage of colonial political and economic life, and the identification of people in these terms is nearly always preeminent. It is not that ethnic/racial labels are code for 'class' or a way of disguising class attitudes. Ethnic labels are shorthand for quite different and (by the 1940s and '50s) unspoken causal assumptions: that social distinction is the product of genetic difference or of unbridgeable cultural gaps.[12] We are not witnessing here simply a process of 'Othering' (with 'The African/Native' and 'The Asiatic' as the key Others). As Foucault reminds us, discourse is deployed in a practical field and in this case the substance of discussion is the management and maintenance of political and economic power. Conversely, ethnic pride and privilege (as Europeans), and the determination to preserve it, were expressive not simply of ethnic distinction but of positions within a colonial polity within which class interests shadowed political imperatives.

In practice ethnic labels acted as broad ideological brackets, within which more practical distinctions were made. In some senses these 'descriptive labels' themselves carried an ethnic marker. Thus 'undesirable sojourners', 'coolies', 'lower grades', 'tax defaultors', 'agitators', 'semi-literate', 'mission-trained' and even 'workers' or 'labourers' would be understood by all as signifying Africans and no other ethnic group. The same applies to the single example of 'class' terminology found in official files, where a mention of the 'wage earning classes' is immediately followed by pointed references to examples of misbehaviour amongst African government employees (Tanga District Officer's Reports 967.822:1936).

These general points are amply exemplified in references to domestic service in colonial discourses. Two kinds of compelling interest (not always complementary) can be discerned in these discourses. One is that of state power, whilst the other speaks of the demands of employers. Employers of domestic servants were deeply concerned with their efficiency and loyalty but also with keeping wages low and having the unfettered freedom to employ the cheapest kind of labour (including children). The discourse of state functionaries revolved around how to deflect or suppress political unrest, how to mould the economy in such a way that the colony could be made to pay and how, through skilful representation, to avoid criticism of their actions by the 'public' or by higher authorities.

The issue of domestic workers enters into this in regard to state intervention in the economy: when minimum wage legislation is discussed – or skills training or the exclusion of juveniles from the labour market. It also arises when servants are the instigators of political unrest. And we should not forget that state functionaries were usually employers of servants themselves – or at least lived in households where domestic labour was paid for, with wives in charge of its management.

State power and domestic service: 'official lines' and the fielding of interest groups

The centrality of domestic service to colonial concerns is illustrated in a lengthy file (V14/32744, 1944–9) on the wisdom of legislating for a minimum wage to be applied to domestic servants – an issue raised for consideration in Tanganyika by a British Parliamentary report. In the course of exploring this possibility and turning it down, other policy imperatives emerge and are shown to be related. In particular, it is held to be axiomatic that if the wages of servants were raised, an immediate consequence would be 'an influx of natives' into the urban areas where most domestic employment was located. This was to be resisted at all costs (ibid. 1944). Although it was occasionally conceded that servants' wages were 'sub-economic', officials found all sorts of rationalisations for this – there were other perks of the job, it was because 'Asiatics' paid such low wages, it was due to a large number of juveniles in employment, and anyway: were servants really value for money? A decision not to pursue minimum wage legislation for domestic servants was taken out of motives which were far from disinterested, but expressed in a language of rationality and efficiency in the utilisation of labour.

We may begin at the end of this story, when the official 'line' had already been carefully formulated, with a letter from the Governor of Tanganyika to the Secretary of State for the Colonies. The Governor advises against minimum wage legislation for servants on various grounds, the main one being the need for 'influx control'. The argument, however, is framed in racial terms which present 'Africans' as contented, 'Europeans' as generous, and 'Asiatics' as employers with lower standards (and the Governor as presiding over a well-run colony). 'There are many indications that this occupation is popular with Africans ... Asiatics usually give their servants full board while Europeans are accustomed to let their servants take all the water, fuel and soap they require ...' In noting the lower wages paid by Asian employers, he explains carefully that: 'The majority of Indians live simpler lives than Europeans. Their houses are smaller, they keep different hours and their standards of service are less exacting' (V14/32744: 29 November 1944).

This letter underlines the accountability of colonial officials to higher authorities even on such 'trivial' matters as pay for domestic workers, but it also illustrates the acceptability of a racialised vocabulary not only in Tanganyika but also in Britain at the time.

The issue of wages for servants (and its ideological frame of racialised assumptions) had arisen initially in regard to the employment of juveniles in domestic work. In 1943 the employment of children under twelve had been prohibited by ordinance. There was one exclusion – juveniles employed as domestic servants. The prohibition had apparently come about due to the pressure of missionaries in Tanga Province, where many children were employed on sisal estates. Concern for children's well-being struggled with self-interest: a letter on file from missionaries complains that 'our schools are half empty' (1937). Following the prohibition, estate managers were told to lay off juveniles. It was clear that they found this a restraint on profits, and unfair: 'Mr Karimjee [owner of a large sisal plantation in Tanga and a member of an official Labour Board] considered that the same prohibition that applied to the employment of children on estates should apply to those in domestic service'.[13] Local Labour Department officials also defended juvenile labour in agriculture as 'healthy outdoor employment', the wages from which benefited families and thereby the children themselves; it was not agricultural labour but domestic service which was unsuitable for children.[14]

The advisability of extending the ban on juveniles to domestic employment was then discussed at the highest level. Officials were asked for statistics on the numbers involved, and these were reported in a public document (Minutes of the Labour Board, 2 July 1945). Reference to an International Labour Office conference on the matter held in the same year reminds officials of external surveillance. Although the statistics had been collected separating out employers under racial headings (they are in the file in this form), the public document aggregates all races together simply as 'employers'![15] A decision was finally formulated in 1946: to extend the ordinance, making it imperative for juvenile servants to return to their parents each night. This very limited constraint seems to have been aimed at reducing immigration into urban areas, rather than protecting children. Given the pressure of conflicting interests the colonial administration found itself holding the ring, and claiming a more far-reaching rationale for intervention in the market: namely to 'control the entry of undesirable natives into townships'.[16]

Behind the scenes, but preserved in notes and memos in the files, are hints of other power struggles that went into achieving public pronouncements on such matters, and the extent to which these were imbued with racialised expressions of class interest. Despite the fact that sixty-seven European employers were found employing juvenile servants (8 per cent of the total in large towns outside of Dar es Salaam where no breakdown was attempted) the opportunity is taken to castigate 'Asiatic' employers: 'some of the children employed in households, particularly Indian, are the veriest 'totos' [babies]' engaged for 'domestic drudgery'; whilst employers of such labour in Dar es Salaam were 'mainly Indians' employing 'under-nourished' children. There is a barely disguised glee in the speculation that 'if these cheap household servants and nurse boys were not available to Indians they would have to employ older servants at better wages or look after their children and do their household work themselves' (V14/30136, quotations from 1943, 1939). In Tanga the Labour Officer presses home his point about different kinds of work for children by referring to domestic service as 'the worst [form of occupation] ... especially as it is practised in the urban districts ... by Asiatics and Indians under conditions of employment which can frequently be described as abhorrent in the extreme' (4/652/28, 1942: letter to Labour Commissioner).

The implicit contrast in all these statements about Asians is with Europeans: as 'reputable' employers, providing their servants with decent wages and conditions, demanding high standards, certainly not exploiting youngsters as cheap labour. Conversely Africans appreciate employment, even low wage employment, and their children do not need protection from exploitation in the same way as the European child would. When the rules were being discussed in Tanga this contrast is made explicitly by the Labour Officer: 'at that age [12] he [the African child] is much more developed than our own children. It is better for them to be employed than to indulge in mere pleasure or idleness, with all its accompanying evils' (4/652/28, 1942).

Officials were also personally affected by minimum wage legislation which undermined the freedom of employers to pay low wages. One official noted that 'unqualified and incompetent servants [were] demanding wages far in excess of their capabilities' (V14/32744, 1948, Memo from Labour Commissioner). If the government were to intervene in setting wages, then should they not also concern themselves with ensuring the efficiency of servants through training schemes? (This suggestion brought other interests into play as we shall see below.)

Officialdom saw its role as one of protecting the interests of Africans who could not protect themselves, but also of mediating other interests in a way which would allow for the more efficient running of the economy: a discourse of benevolent paternalism tempered by rationality. It is also evident that external surveillance (real or imagined) required hypervigilance on the part of local officials whose authority was constrained in a mandated territory.

Domestic workers: the moral agenda mediated through the press

The European press might use racialised vocabulary that was little different to that of officialdom but its project and the pressures upon it were different. To prosper it had to cater to the views of its audience as well as aiming to mould them. The major source of my sample survey of this press was a newspaper (*The Sunday News: SN*) which clearly had Europeans as its predominant clientele, but Europeans who, in the 1950s, were increasingly aware of the 'writing on the wall' in regard to African aspirations. Whilst opposed to African nationalism they nevertheless saw themselves as 'fair-minded' and not illiberal. Despite this, 'European' self-interest frequently surfaces as the driving force of opinion – Europeans as employers, as taxpayers, as parents of children needing 'European education', even (once!) as 'non-natives'. This last, residual, category is inclusive of Asians with whom they occasionally noted some commonality in position – both seemed to have to pay too much for their children's education, both had a higher tax burden than the African, neither were welcome as members of 'Mr Nyerere's party' (TANU), and the women of both communities were said to be subject to 'insults in the streets' from Africans (*SN* 30 Dec. 1956, 27 Jan. 1957).

Being 'European' did not necessarily translate into support for the government where it conflicted with private interests, especially on taxation. An editorial of 30 December 1956 rails against 'the bilkers and the dodgers' (disclosed in the next sentence as 'African males') who were not paying up, whilst 'European taxes' were increased. Europeans would be 'only too willing', as employers of African labour, 'to make the necessary deductions at source ...' The sting in the tail is that 'we would [also] be asking: are we getting full value for money from the Civil Service? The answer would ... be a flat "No". The Administration is too top-heavy ...'

If the language of both press and official sources is framed in terms of 'race' rather than class, there is a contrast between them in emphasis when it comes to the issue of domestic service. What comes over in the European press is a concern for the 'moral order', whereas official records speak more in the language of 'management'. The image of servants which the press upholds is almost one of semi-feudal 'retainers': loyal, reliable, trustworthy. It is newsworthy when real servants live up to this image: 'The house of the magistrate was broken into when the ayah and two children were asleep. The ayah awoke, gathered up a child under each arm and stood by the open window and shouted for help ...' (*SN* 2 June 1956:1). Or when a gang broke into the house of a 'white hunter' and terrorised his wife and children: 'Meanwhile, her African cook, who had been shot in the leg, had gone ... to raise the alarm' (*SN* 22 July 1956:1). It was taken for granted that the labour of servants could be deployed to cement relations between equals: 'People are very kind in Tanganyika [reported a visitor to the country]. My new friend had got his boy out of bed [at dawn], had my suit ironed ...' (*SN* 14 October 1956:10).

It is also newsworthy when servants do not live up to the image. A magistrate was reported to have said of a man who posed as a servant in order to rob a house that 'the type of crime he had committed could destroy trust in servants and mean loss of employment for hundreds of Africans' (*SN* 20 May 1956:2). Even worse if African servants were seen to pose a 'moral danger' to children. The case of a nine year old girl having suffered sexual 'interference' from a 'shamba boy' (gardener) is commented on in explicitly racial terms as: 'the current scare of the moral harm to young

European children left in the unsupervised care of Africans' (*SN* 15 April 1956:1,14).[17]

Wage levels are also a moral question rather than one of economics. Europeans were used to a buyers' market in domestic labour where they could dictate terms and Africans would be 'grateful' for the favour. When this is put at threat by a 'houseboys' strike' for higher wages, the tone changes. The *Sunday News* (21 Oct. 1956:4) put the employers' position histrionically: 'If wages are increased to the level most African workers would like them to reach, employers will either consider using fewer but more efficient – non-African – workers – or else welcome everything that automation – despite the high capital cost of new machines – can give them'. Quite which 'non-Africans' would be prepared to work efficiently for less wages than Africans were acccepting is not made clear, and the possibility of substituting machinery for labour was limited in a setting where the available domestic equipment (according to a WSLT pamphlet) was 'deplorably primitive'.[18] But *in extremis*, the editors and feature writers were even prepared to consider doing the work themselves, rather than be at the mercy of 'agitators' in their kitchens. This discursive response will be considered below.

Domestic service: the discourse of gender

Whilst gender distinction and gender inequality pervaded all areas of colonial life, 'gender' was a category not yet formulated in social thought. However, its reverberations were highly audible in discursive terms, wherever reference could be made to 'women', whether in official, semi-official (WSLT productions sponsored by government) or unofficial (media) forums. What is striking is the way in which the issue of domestic service brings gender relations to the fore in quite unexpected ways.

As the overwhelming majority of servants were men, one might have expected this to occasion some commentary. Instead this inversion of gender relations was completely taken for granted,[19] even in the genre of 'advice to newcomers' such as that put out by the WSLT. What is drawn to the readers' attention is rather an exception to this rule: 'Boys have usually proved more satisfactory as nurses to children than have women, *but* it is more fitting to have women as nurses for female children' (my emphasis, 1948:4).

This cultural blindness is exhibited on another occasion in the mid-1940s, through fascinating cross reference to policies on domestic workers in postwar Britain. Enclosed within the file on Domestic Servants (V14/32744, 1944–9) are brochures from a commercial institution in the UK – the National Institute of Houseworkers Ltd (NIH) – describing courses in domestic skills as well as appropriate citizenship and social skills.[20] Here it was deemed appropriate to aquaint the worker with 'her place in her circle of friends and neighbours, her relations with her employer and fellow workers against a background of the ... development of industrial relations'. The female gender is used throughout these brochures.

What could be 'said' in colonial Tanganyika was by now 'unsayable' in Britain – and vice versa. The NIH is very careful never to use the nomenclature 'servant' (inappropriate in Britain under a postwar Labour government?) and presents itself as offering opportunities for *self-improvement* through the skills of 'Homecraft'. The Minister of Labour (Ernest Bevin) even offered an introductory note, describing 'domestic work [as] a skilled trade which has a great contribution to make to the wellbeing of the nation'. There were subsequent attempts to set up training schemes for domestic servants in Tanganyika (which apparently came to nothing) but there is no reference to the wisdom of the NIH. The language must have seemed dangerously radical in the context of colonial Africa, perhaps particularly where servants were men.

Although in Tanganyika it was generally unthinkable to have female domestic workers (ayahs excepted), it was thought proper for African women to be domesticated. This theme crops up both in the press and in official records. Education for Africans should entail agricultural schools for boys, but for girls, 'training in domestic affairs, cooking, needlework and mothercraft ...' (Archives: 4/652/28:1942). And a report in the *Sunday News* headed 'Wonderful work by African women' described an exhibition of clothes, food, furniture and pottery, all 'made from local products and ... within the scope of any African housewife to produce'. The high-profile exhibition was put on by Domestic Science Teacher Trainees and attended by the Director of Women's and Girls' Education in Tanganyika as well as a visitor from the Colonial Office. The prevalence of this theme of 'domesticity' in education for African women has sometimes been employed as an explanation for the gendering of domestic labour (see Chapter 5). It makes no sense here.

Feminists have often noted the way that 'men' are discursively and generically treated as the norm, whilst women are presented as special cases or even deviations. In official files 'The African' is always gendered male. References to African women are not only rare but nearly always an adjunct to others who take centre stage. For example, the file on Employment of Women and Young Persons (Archives 4/652/28: Tanga Labour Dept:1937–48) barely mentions women's labour, and this is true throughout official records of the time. Juvenile labour is centred here; elsewhere women are mentioned only as helpmates to male workers. The 'African wife' is normally an asset to her husband, rather than a cost (she was even estimated to eat less: 'wife's food may be taken as 75 per cent of his own').[21] There were always exceptions: a wife in town was only useful if she 'has not been spoilt by "This Freedom" and civilisation, and is prepared to help keep the home together' (District Officer, Dar es Salaam to Provincial Commissioner, 10 Jan. 1928).

Domestic service was also linked to attempts by women – though more particularly European women, to liberate themselves from domesticity[22] and take on more public roles. The arguments they deployed to transform their position, and the discourse of male power which was used to silence them is very telling. One theme was that of female suffrage. When the colonial government instituted an elective system of local government in 1955 (Coulson 1982:113) male householders were eligible to vote, together with a few (mainly European) women who were independent property owners. The demand for European married women to have the vote was supported by the European press, and the claimed 'official reply' was deplored: 'if housewives were allowed the vote, then houseboys who live on the premises would have to have it too' (SN 8 Jan. 1956:4). The equation between women and domestic servants was a galling one. To give the paper credit, it argued that 'houseboys' should have the vote too.[23]

The press even allowed space for European women to argue a limited case for liberation – at the expense of African servants of course. The issue was 'working wives'. A woman contributor put the case – that families needed the extra money to make ends meet, and that it was not neglectful to leave children with servants: 'Do they want us to dispense with African ayahs? ... that surely would cause great hardship to the Africans as well as inconvenience to us ... and are not the children in just as much moral amd physical danger if their mothers have gone out on good social works as if they had gone out to earn some money?' (SN 22 April 1956:12).

During the strike arguments were rehearsed for dispensing with servants and sharing domestic work within the family. In an article headed: 'No houseboy? You'll get by ...' the contributor waxes eloquent about doing without:

> Englishmen ... I do not think I know of one who will not help his wife if she is single handed ... Provided she does not demand perfection she may be pleasantly surprised to see how eager hubby is to make himself useful ... Children are usually quick to enter into the spirit of things ... you will ... enjoy the freedom from rigid routine, so essential when there's African staff. (SN 16 Dec 1956:3).

More 'normally' though, European women expected to have servants and to enjoy the freedom from domestic chores that this allowed.

European women might become involved in public life through transferring the management skills they had aquired in running their own households into the public setting. The key organisation in which they were able to do this was the Women's Service League of Tanganyika, which was active in welfare work. The WSLT also ran several informal employment registries to place servants of good repute. In 1948 they approached the colonial administration with a proposal for government funding to allow them to set up an employment bureau for domestic servants in Dar es Salaam. Their proposal came at a time when officials were formulating a position on the extension of the minimum wage to servants and is included in the relevant file (V14/32744: Domestic Servants 1944–9). Their letter notes that 'the domestic servant element' exploits newcomers who know nothing of local practice, and that this is to be avoided 'at the present time when the African is going through a transitional period and an understanding with the European should be maintained'. A Bureau could help in holding the line, and it should only register those servants prepared to improve 'their standards of work and their attitudes towards their work' (ibid. 26 August 1948).

Given that these women here echoed the sentiments of men of their own class and race in terms of relations with Africans, the response to this proposal is telling. At first it was viewed favourably, and Mrs Haylett of the WSLT was called in to discuss the matter with an official. He noted that, 'There would have to be a whole-time manager – almost certainly a woman as it really takes a woman to deal with female employers' (ibid. 2 Oct. 1948). Implicitly it is assumed that the Registry will serve only European employers – 'the ladies of Dar es Salaam'. Estimates are put together as to how much it will cost to set up and run the Registry, and other details of its operation discussed. By the following year it is understood that the WSLT will run the Registry and devise training schemes for domestic servants. But then suddenly the tone changes: it is asserted that in Dar es Salaam servants were becoming difficult and that female management would not work: 'European male supervision is essential' – and the cost of this to be £50 a year, compared to the £30 previously reckoned to be adequate to recompense a woman! Even more damning, officialdom remembers that it is supposed to be acting in the interests of the country, not only of Europeans. One official asks cautiously: 'is it intended that government subsidise a scheme for Europeans only?' (ibid. Dec. 1948). And eventually a higher official dismisses the whole project as a self-serving attempt to keep servants' wages down in the interest of employers: 'one of the main reasons behind the pressure for the establishment of a registry was the fear that African servants' wages were rising steeply ... and that the establishment of a Registry would help to ... minimise this tendency' (ibid. memo, Provincial Secretary, July 1949).

Class interest has turned a discussion purportedly about a minimum living wage for servants into pressure towards maximum wage legislation! Officials also found themselves fielding concern expressed by the Dar es Salaam Chamber of Commerce (a report published in the *Tanganyika Standard* of 2 March 1948 is enclosed) that the 'wages of African servants are virtually double today what they were two years ago and the work they do is about half as good as it was then'. As European employers, officials concur in such views; but as public servants in a Mandated Territory they were obliged to explain the 'low' wages of African workers to external assessors. Spurning an initiative of European women allowed them a local escape route from the dilemma without loss of face.

Another facet of this discussion is the way other ethnic groups are marshalled to devalue the case of the WSLT. There is a singular reference to the views of an 'Asian clerk' in the Secretariat: a registry is unnecessary since 'employers sent out their servants to look for new boys' (1 Sept. 1948). And the Labour Commissioner suggests that the 'houseboys' union' also carries out this function, eliciting thereby the view of the WSLT that the 'present African-run registry appears to work rather as a Trades Union' (13 Oct. 1948). On other occasions officials would have put this precise view themselves, but it seems evident that when women articulated colonial discourse it did not have the same weight as when men did so.

Turning Girls into Boys: engendering domestic service

Darrell Bate's book *The Mango and the Palm* indicates that some colonials saw a contradiction between the taken-for-granted feminine nature of domesticity and the male labour force which upheld it in the homes of the better-off in Tanganyika. Bates was a District Officer, who in the late 1940s was posted to Tanga and later to Pare District. He expends a whole chapter on his hiring in Tanga of Asumani, an old Muslim man, as a cook, and the later addition of Katie, a 'Cape Coloured woman ... girls of mixed blood often made excellent nannies' (1962:19–20). Asumani, who 'looked to me ... like a bachelor's cook' (i.e. one who did not appreciate 'Memsahib' interfering in his kitchen) is described affectionately and with a touch of pride: 'In the morning he came with his belongings. He didn't carry them himself of course. He was now after all a man of status. He was the Bwana Shauri's cook' (17). When they left for Pare, Asumani went with them as 'part of the family' (77) – the familial motif is one I shall discuss further (Chapter 8).

In Pare men were 'too clever by half' and 'too proud to fetch and carry' – they would not make good servants. 'So we decided, as an experiment, to see if we couldn't turn the girls into boys' (78–9). Bates then expands on the term 'boy':

> In East Africa servants in the house are called Boys, both in English and in Swahili. This disparaging and misleading title is a survival from the days when people, on both sides, didn't know any better, but it had stuck like a piece of legal Latin, until everyone, again on both sides, had come to take it for granted and forgotten how it started, or why or what it meant.

Having made this wryly liberal statement, Bates proceeds in the next paragraph to refer to a widow of thirty as a 'girl', and without embarrassment to admit to hiring a juvenile of thirteen as the other 'girl'.

He describes in great detail the process of teaching them the domestic requirements of Europeans ('the oddities of a European house': 82) and then recounts 'amusingly' how the younger girl was pinched in the bottom by one of his European guests at a party. He also reports on how much the male cook disapproved: '"The place for women" [Asumani] would say, "is *not* in the house"' (82). Whilst European visitors were said to be 'often impressed with the success of our experiment' the people who were most startled were 'our visitors' own Boys when they were travelling with their masters. One would hear them shout, "My goodness the Boys here are girls", or words to that effect ... it provided them with good after-dinner talk to astonished audiences in the more civilised towns where Boys were really Boys' (82).

By the late 1950s there is some rethinking about this taken-for-granted sexual division of labour, occasioned both by rationalist notions of 'labour efficiency' and by the predicates of the 'moral order'. The former is put into words by M. J. B. Molohan, Senior Provincial Commissioner, in a small booklet published in 1957 on *Detribalisation*; the latter by Lady Twining (whose husband had previously been the Governor of Kenya). A comparison between the two modes of argument is instructive.

Molohan's view is that urban women – by implication African:

> have time on their hands and so become a liability. I have always felt that more encouragement should be given and more facilities made available for women to obtain paid employment. The opportunities in industry are not as yet very great but it is ludicrous that domestic service in Tanganyika should be the perquisite of the male. The territory cannot afford for much longer the luxury of locking up so many able-bodied men in this unproductive sphere of employment for which women are far better suited and equipped. (1957:40)

Lady Twining advocated:

> the replacement of houseboys by women as an important step towards the further advancement of the African ... Women in the home as housekeepers and cooks would absorb the ways of civilisation more rapidly than men and ... they would not tend to slip back into native ways as men did once they returned to the reserves. (quoted – without comment – in *SN* 14 Feb. 1957)

The contrast between these two arguments (which arrive at the same conclusion) is notable. For Molohan both domestic service and women are negatively marked – both are 'unproductive'. For Lady Twining women are seen in a glowing light as carriers of 'civilisation' and the home as a cradle where such virtue was nourished through cleaning and cooking. Both look to the future – for Lady Twining 'the future advancement of the African' which entails discarding 'native ways'; for Molohan an industrialised economy in which both men and women were fully employed in wage labour. This vision was not realised; the proper place for women is still not as domestics and Boys are still men.

DISCORDANT VOICES/COUNTER DISCOURSES?

'Discourse transmits and produces power; it reinforces it, but also undermines and exposes it, renders it fragile and makes it possible to thwart it' (Foucault 1984:100).

Colonial discourses are transparently about the maintenance of hegemonic power initially exerted by superior force rather than ideological embrace. By the late 1940s in Tanganyika, however, discordant voices were demanding to be heard, and officials had to work harder at upholding an official line. This was by no means merely discursive resistance: it was anchored in competing structures new and old which threatened the colonial edifice. One set of overriding structural relations have been mentioned at several junctures – those of international bodies, such as the United Nations under whose mandate Britain ruled, as well as its offshoots such as the International Labour Organisation. But we may also include here the Colonial Office in Britain, which in the postwar period was envisioning the impossible – a gradual withdrawal from Empire. Each of these bodies demanded new ways of thinking and behaving with regard to colonial subjects: that overt and gross exploitation be eliminated, that the labour of women and children be counted and their rights protected, that workers be allowed to organise. And colonial officials knew themselves to be under surveillance.

This is illustrated in a lengthy file concerning the activities of a domestic workers union, registered in 1945 as the African Cooks, Washermen and Houseservants' Association (hereafter African Cooks), but whose registration was cancelled in 1950. The name of the file: 'UN Visiting Commission 1951: Petition: African Cooks ... (etc)' (V22/37681) indicates its seriousness for colonial officialdom, underlining the point that they could no longer 'speak for' or 'represent' African views, since Africans themselves now had direct access to higher authorities.[24]

During 1951–3 this association bombarded colonial officials with petitions and demands – and it did not stop there: letters were also sent to the Colonial Secretary in Britain, the Queen and the United Nations Secretary General, and a meeting between them and visiting UN officials was scheduled for mid-1951. These actions exposed colonial officials to possible censure and forced them into humiliating if haughty explanations of the essentially contemptible nature of the Association and its concerns, as well as official translations (from Swahili) of views it did not think worthy of putting on paper. The iron fist in this velvet glove was the use of the Special Branch to investigate the association's leader, Saleh bin Fundi, and the continuing refusal to register it as a legitimate trade union.

Indeed their letters are abusive, intemperate and injudicious. During the course of the one-sided correspondence (replies, if any, are not preserved in the file) the African Cooks adopted a new name, 'Tanganyika Government Union No. 3', believing, according to the police, that 'recognition by UNO put them on a par with government' (letter from Special Branch to Political Liaison Officer, Dar es Salaam, 21 Oct. 1953). At a time when in neighbouring Kenya the Mau Mau rebellion had led to the killing of several Europeans and African chiefs and the imposition of a State of Emergency, it was asking for trouble to write to the Queen as follows (with copies to the Governor, and African worthies as well as to the Governor of New York):

> We ask that this Governor should be suspended or sent back to England. He is not fit to stay here in Tanganyika ... African [chiefs] are likely to be killed by their people because he [the Governor] deceives them ... [and they] are very fond of bribes ... the Kaiser did not deceive us, he only treated us justly and we loved him ... I do not want to hit people with machetes as is done in Kenya .... (10 Sept. 1953).

It is not surprising that the letter was regarded as inflammatory[25] as well as embarrassing to the administration.

In the host of letters which preceded and followed this one, it is notable that the vocabulary of 'race' was adopted by the oppressed as well as those in power. Using the language of 'race', these men[26] subvert it by denying the colonial hierarchies of 'race'. The letter to 'Her Majesty the Queen Elizabeth', ends:

> Now let the Europeans of Tanganyika work without pay and rent their houses and pay their servants with their own money and use their purses for all purposes as we do: this will make it necessary for them to go away for they will have no profit. We ask [for the removal of] European, Indian and Arab ... we are tired of your people. (ibid.)

The leaders of this association do not simply turn the imagery of race 'on its head'; they openly speak the language of material interest. Europeans take land, they make profit, they pay exploitative wages. This recognition of material differences is also extended to the African population. The writers accuse Europeans ('you people') of listening only to

> the well to do Africans who do not care about the poor other Africans; those are the people who are fighting for their own interests, not for

the others. The common town people are those who know the needs of the people because they can starve for two or three days, but you ... hold your meetings with the rich people so you cannot find out the difficulties of Tanganyika Territory. (Two letters to the Colonial Secretary both dated 14 April 1951, one from Saleh bin Fundi alone and the other signed by him and five other men)

They return continually to the material conditions of domestic service. Employers paid so little that their servants went hungry, they were given no time to rest, no clothes or other perks and were dismissed without reason (ibid. petition to UN 1 Sept. 1951).

Is this a 'counter discourse' (in Foucault's terms)? Certainly there is no way that it constitutes power at this point. This is language that can only be regarded as subversive. The letters are opened by the Special Branch, returned from the Colonial Office and the UN with queries, and responded to by the Governor of Tanganyika without consultation with the senders. It is also contrived that the Union leaders fail to meet the visiting UN Mission (1951). Nevertheless there is here a discourse of resistance which undermines and exposes those in power: the UK Government found itself having to explain matters to the UN when the Association's officials failed to turn up (in letters presumably drafted by colonial officials on behalf of the Governor). It does so in the predictable ways of power dealing with insubordination: the Association was derided as 'unrepresentative', it was not properly managed, its leaders were 'self-seeking' men of 'doubtful integrity' especially in relation to members' subscriptions. 'The Labour Commissioner and his staff were nevertheless most patient', but eventually were compelled to cancel the registration of the Union. 'There was evidence' (not produced) that up-country members were 'relieved' at this outcome, but the Dar es Salaam leaders were aggrieved at losing their income, and this explained their subsequent spate of letters. As far as domestic servants in general were concerned, their conditions of employment (by 'reputable employers') were very pleasant and their wages had risen considerably in recent times (ibid. undated, but c. Sept. 1951).

The Association sent further petitions to the UN in October and November 1952, asking first for jobs for their members in America. Again the Governor found himself having to explain to the Colonial Secretary, so that he could report to the UN, that these men were actually unemployed domestic servants who refused all offers of other work and had been 'advised to return to their home districts' (ibid. Nov. 1952). They did not, penning off instead another letter to the District Commissioner in Dar es Salaam, described by Special Branch as 'offensive' as it claimed that 'Africans ... were the true owners of the land' (ibid. Dec. 1952). After the final insult of the letter to the Queen, sent in the following year (1953), the Governor is again busy explaining to the Colonial Secretary that Saleh bin

Fundi was 'intensely anti-Government and anti-European' and that the Association's claims had no substance. Of course, poll tax (an exclusively African tax) had been increased, but this was to 'finance new and expanding social services'. The abusive and offensive communications had led government eventually to refuse either to respond or to meet the persons involved – and he recommended the Colonial Secretary to do the same. If he must reply then he could say that 'registration of such a union will again become possible only if and when an association is formed showing itself capable of understanding the principles of trade unionism' (ibid. 4 Nov. 1953).

Although officialdom is forced to cover its back, it has the power not only to define but also to deal with the situation: extra-discursive power. This power – to define *and* dismiss – is summed up in one official comment heading the file: 'A bit of nonsense this one'. And ultimately it persuaded the UN of the same, ensuing in a description of the African Cooks petitions as 'manifestly inconsequential' (ibid. 1 July 1953).

Saleh bin Fundi thereafter fades from the historical record. But Africans, as workers and as colonial subjects, went on to challenge the colonial order, and domestic servants were once again in the thick of events. This emerges in the press as commentary on events of the mid-1950s, when domestic servants and hotel workers (now united in a Union of Domestic and Hotel Workers) initiated a general strike in Tanganyika. Denoting this 'the houseboys' strike', the European press is full of stories of heroic Europeans pitching in, both in hotels and at home, to the claimed discomfiture of the strikers: 'Some ... have found to their amazement that the Bwana and Memsahib have managed very much more than adequately without them, and have decided to economise on servants ...' (*SN* Editorial, 9 Dec. 1956:4). This trivialisation of the issue is belied, however, by the hysterical insistence that the strikers must have been led astray by 'a gang of rabble rousers ... men rich by African standards ... hooligans ... unemployables' (ibid.). The undifferentiated concept of 'The African', or 'The native' begins to seem less serviceable.

There is no doubt that the domestic workers' strike shook up the old order. When 'faithful' servants go on strike, the overwhelming response of their employers is one of betrayal. Wage claims were described as 'unreasonable', the union's actions as 'sinister' and 'ridiculous', whilst firm action from the government 'will win nothing but approval from the *loyal* servant' (my emphasis, *SN*, Editorial 2 Dec. 1956:4). There is a determined presentation of willing strikers as a minority: 'response from hotel workers and houseboys was far from one hundred per cent. Many reported for duty as usual but widespread intimidation by agitators was used to increase the numbers of men idle' (*SN* 9 Dec. 1956:1). Many 'reluctant union followers' were said to have returned with pathetic excuses as to why they had been absent (ibid. Editorial:4), whilst employers were portrayed as revelling in their own retort: 'Yes you can come back, but you do not get that rise I promised'. And: 'In the huts, market places and bars of the native quarters this weekend, Africans are beginning to ask themselves where they went wrong'.

In this return to the generic 'Africans' there is a recognition that the significance of the strike went far beyond issues of wrongful dismissal (its purported cause), wage levels and poor conditions of service – though these claims were noted and rejected. The strike was seen as 'a trial of strength' (ibid. 2 Dec. 1956) as the Union threatened and delivered sympathy strikes across the economy. It was understood to be against 'employers' (here code for European employers and by extension Europeans in general) and the 'government' (an attempt to undermine the whole colonial order).

Female employers felt the betrayal and loss of labour more deeply than men. But it is also women who express some of the most forthright comments. A letter to the *Sunday News* penned by 'Housewife' as the strike proceeded, put forward a novel point about racial stereotypes – novel at least in the colonial context: 'The fact that all the houseboys are Africans does not give anyone the right to say that the strike was called against Europeans or Asians. It was called purely as a protest against low wages and the dismissal of workers ...' (16 Dec. 1956:3). Housewife's letter provoked a strong reply from 'Portia': 'Union leaders themselves come out with statements such as "Share your wealth – or get out of our country". Such sentiments could hardly be described as normal labour dispute language. We have no desire to start racial arguments – we can only hope the majority of Africans will share this view' (*SN* 30 Dec 1956:3).

The language used by 'Housewife' is a remarkable break from convention, a fracturing of colonial discourse from within. Even 'Portia's' letter conveys a different tone: 'we can only hope' she says (hope being considerably thinner than the certainty underwritten by coercion); whilst the concession to democratic forms is also notable: 'the majority of Africans'. Ultimately the point is that a strike merely of 'houseboys' is seen to presage the collapse of the colonial order.

CONCLUSION

What may be concluded from this review of colonial discourses will not be fully appreciated until we have explored the institution of domestic service in more contemporary times. In highlighting the issue of domestic service in this archive, however, a view of the whole colonial architecture of thought has been disclosed. Straddling, as it does, the world of 'unproductive' domesticity and that of waged work, as well as the relations of men and women, and the mediating/coercive role of the state in all of this, domestic service is a symbolic metaphor for the whole.

The colonial state relied on force to establish its authority. It did not need to create ideological hegemony or to strive for cultural unity within the country as a whole. This was left to missionaries. Colonial discourse should thus be read as a private language of the ruling class, rather than as public utterance. It was declaimed to restricted audiences who were 'in the know'. At the same time it was not itself fully consensual – we are occasioned a glimpse of plural and contradictory discourses here relating to colonial relations and to the colonial mission, some of which were more effective than others. And it operated in a context where external surveillance from above was a fact of political life, the terms of which changed over time. 'Public discourse' (an achievement of official striving embodied in communiqués and formal pronouncements) was addressed to a non-official audience (largely European) but with an eye always on the powers above (Colonial Office, UN etc.).

It seems clear that the discourse, whether expressed in official files, documents or newspapers, begins to be censured as it becomes apparent that 'others' are listening in. Even then, the ways of thinking and expression voiced by oppositional elements are shocking to the ears of those who rule: they literally say the unsayable. In evaluating the inflammatory writings of Saleh bin Fundi or the 'sinister' demands of the Domestic and Hotel Workers' Union, Gramsci's term 'counter hegemony' seems appropriate (Gramsci 1957). Domestic servants became part of an emergent historic bloc of diverse social forces in which popular (African) feeling was unifying around an anti-colonial discourse. And returning at last to Foucault, discursive resistance is not yet sufficient to make a revolution.

MEN AT WORK IN THE TANZANIAN HOME: HOW DID THEY EVER LEARN?

'I didn't know how to wash up or clean floors – at home our sisters do that'
(Male house servant)
'It's just natural for them [men]. They know'   *(Female employer)*

Men's successful performance of domestic service in Tanzania is neither 'natural' nor a product of their usual socialisation.[1] What I explore in this chapter, is how men learnt to do the job and whether this is seen as a transgression of 'masculine' behaviour. I shall show that workers hold inconsistent or situational ideologies regarding gender and work (housework being unmanly at home, but manly if it generates a wage packet). Employers too hold contradictory views, their view of men as the best and most suitable domestic workers conflicting with their own domestic arrangements in which women take the major responsibility.

The historical predominance of men in domestic service in this example offers a mirror image to more familiar patterns of domestic work as a female ghetto, often explained as the transfer from the home to the work place of domestic skills, the lowly status which devalues those skills and the demeanour of subordinates. It is recognised to be rare for men to move into occupations which society has categorised as women's work (McElhinny 1994:170). Where men rather than women have always been the dominant labour force in domestic service, it is clear that an apprenticeship in gender subordination is not essential to acquiring domestic skills for wage work: class subordination is sufficient in itself to produce this effect, whilst class differences render the ideological link between gender and domesticity a contradictory one. This case also throws into question the thesis that gendered forms of occupational segregation in developing countries are simply imposed from outside.

Recent analytical studies have focused on the gendering of work as a question of identity and cultural construction whereas earlier work saw it as a matter of socialisation processes or structural constraints. Debates about the relative weight of patriarchy or capitalism have given way to discussion around the diversity of 'masculinities'. And whereas these debates have largely drawn on evidence from the developed capitalist world they have also featured in accounts of developing societies.

The account offered here encompasses 'living memory', with the earliest reminiscences of servants and employers[2] relating to the 1920s. Within this period much has changed, but domestic skills, when performed as wage labour, are still seen as 'male skills'. Men are employed to clean and cook, to wash and iron, to garden and to guard houses, occasionally even to mind babies.[3] As I shall show, most of these tasks were sex-stereotyped amongst Africans themselves as 'women's work', and commonsense might have led us to expect a predominantly female workforce in this occupation, certainly a preference for those assumed 'naturally' to have these skills – i.e. women. This is only now beginning to happen, and, in this particular case, men have ended up doing 'women's work' better than women.

SOCIALISATION AND SKILLS: THE DEBATE

The older debate about the gendering of work focused on the way in which appropriate skills were defined, acquired and evaluated. The skills mobilised in domestic wage work are of two kinds, the first 'performance skills' (technical aptitude in the performance of tasks), the second 'presentational skills' (the successful adoption of appropriate demeanour – in this case humility, willingness, deference etc). It used to be argued that what made domestic service a 'woman's job' was the transfer of technical skills and appropriately deferential attitudes from the family or school to the work-place. Later studies put more weight on what happens in the workplace rather than on processes prior to employment.

The original thesis was formulated in feminist writings on the developed capitalist world: 'women's work' and the lowly status accorded to it, was argued to be an extension of women's domestic role. The socialisation of women was defined as an apprenticeship in acquiring the relevant skills, and the relative cheapness of women's labour explained as the appropriation by employers of women's domestic skills, ideologically and materially devalued (Oakley 1976; Taylor 1979; Phillips and Taylor 1980). It was then reworked to explain gender segregation in wage work in Third World countries, most notably in the case of factory work by Elson and Pearson (1981a; 1981b) but also in the case of domestic service (Cock 1980).

The assumption that socialisation generates appropriate and ready-made skills for wage labour is not however proven. In trying to apply it to the case of domestic servants one would have to question the presumption that domestic skills are common to all households and hence readily transferable from one to the other. Such skills can in fact be shown to vary by class, and hence what is learnt at home in one class is not always the most useful knowledge for the work place. This is compounded when ethnic/cultural differences are added to those of class.

The other variant of the socialisation thesis focuses on the ideological preparation of labour. Writing on South Africa, where today the vast majority of domestic workers are women, Jacklyn Cock argued that black women had been 'educated for domesticity'. Both missionary and public bodies saw this as the goal of the education which they offered to African women (other examples could be multiplied: e.g. Gaitskell 1986; Hansen 1989:127, fn.151, 181–2; Musisi 1992). The thesis has come in for considerable criticism (Gaitskell et al. 1984; Hansen 1989:136–7), partly because it cannot explain the predominance of men in domestic service in South Africa before 1911, but also because few of the thousands of female domestic servants were educated, and few of the mission-trained went into lifetime domestic service (indeed Van Onselen tells us that 'the "mission kaffir" [was seen as] ... the worst possible type of servant': 1982:40). Although the manifest aim of formal education for African girls may have been to fit them for domestic service, this in itself does not explain a predominance of women in this occupation.

Where men are performing domestic tasks for wages their socialisation cannot usually be adduced as the explanation, and hence arguments which focus on the workplace itself are more useful than those which reduce skills to a 'reflection' of processes elsewhere (Beechey 1987; Walby 1988). This perspective borrowed from the the work of Braverman on the way skill had been transformed by the emergence of industrial capitalism (1974). It argued that notions of skill are socially and ideologically constructed, not as a simple reflection of the gender hierarchy, but as an outcome of political struggle, especially over the length and form of training. Gaskell argued that male workers often had the political muscle to force employers to subsidise lengthy periods of apprenticeship, thereby controlling and restricting the numbers in a particular field. This was 'a process of managing the image of skill as much as it is learning to do a job' (1986:379).

A study by McElhinny (1994) on the way in which women become police officers is pertinent here. She explored the gendering of police work following the integration of women officers in the United States. What she reveals is that women officers adopt men's styles of work, but that they then define their skills simply as 'professional': 'they do not interpret their behaviour as masculine' (1994:167). McElhinny also adapts Bourdieu's concept of habitus to explain how women 'become men' without the predisposing characteristics of upbringing. Experience within the job is what moulds them; experience is then translated into norms rationalised by 'nature' or 'commonsense' which come to structure later interactional engagements (165). This is also the way that, once in the job, men in Tanzania made domestic service their own. They became 'workers', not 'women' – albeit not workers with much capacity to exert political leverage over employers.

MALE SERVANTS/FEMALE SERVANTS IN TANZANIA

That men performed successfully as domestic servants in colonial Tanganyika is confirmed by those who employed them. 'The men were more efficient with normal housework – and more in tune with the ways of Europeans'. S was 'very loyal ... a good cook and able to improvise ... [on safari] he often cooked bread in a hole in the ground covered with tin and firewood ... He could also organise packing ... He was a good "shopper" and could negotiate for eggs, meat, veg etc with the best' (personal communications from European colonial employers).

That men perform this job successfully today is attested to by the continuing practice in Tanzania of employing them in preference to women, even where there is a choice, and even amongst the more recent employing class. Glowing testimonials to their aptitude, skill and utility are frequently offered, as in the following: 'Boys[4] are more useful because they will work both inside and outside ... Girls can't do heavy work. They are slower than boys and they like to chatter. Boys are industrious and speedy.' (African employer). And if colonial employers thought men fitted to child care (WSLT 1948:4), so too do contemporary employers. An African employer sang the praises of her previous 'houseboy': 'he was exceptionally good ... he helped to look after my daughter from being a baby. He was quick to learn. I had no worries'. Only two employers out of the sixty I interviewed claimed that women (as one of them put it) were 'more attuned to the idea of housework' than men (African employer). This is to be contrasted with the opposing view that men here do not even have to learn how to cook, wash and iron: 'It's just natural for them. They know' (Goan).

If we listen to what male servants, who are predominantly migrant labourers from rural areas, have to say about domestic skills we would hear a different point of view: 'At first I found all this [washing, helping to cook, cleaning the house] very difficult. At home all that is done by our mothers'; 'I wasn't used to doing those kind of jobs. Mama does that work at home – our job is to herd the cattle and goats'. Men also deny that they help their wives in such tasks at home. A cook tells you that at home his wife cooks all the food, and most men are offended at the suggestion that they might assist with housework: 'I never sweep at home'. Not even to help your wife? 'Maybe, but I would have to know what the problem was first' or as another put it: 'I might, if she were ill'.

So far, so familiar. Conversely, many men in Tanzania expect to wash their own personal clothes, especially best clothes, and if the clothes are to be ironed they will do this too. Women are far less likely to know how to iron than men.[5] Ironing might then be seen as a 'male skill' which could be transferred to the work place, though the irons with which such men would be familiar would be heavy charcoal irons, whereas those in use in the homes of employers are now almost universally electric.

African women also have expectations regarding the aptitudes and domestic behaviour of men: 'A man can't rear a child'; 'A husband expects his meals to be ready for him, at his convenience'; 'At home, girls are taught housework and to cultivate – their value as future wives depends on it'. Observing the sexual division of labour in the homes of ordinary Tanzanians one sees that it is women's responsibility to prepare food, to clean and to care for small children, and that husbands are either absent from the domestic scene, or, if present, they do little more than dandle babies, sleep, eat, or sit around with friends. A Zanzibari employer said: 'Our men do nothing – never clear anything away, leave their pots on the table, never wash their clothes'.

Young children's play is clearly gender-differentiated: small boys make ingenious lorries and cars out of tins, sticks and bits of rubber, whilst girls are to be seen 'cooking' sand and mud in coconut shells. Confirmation of this domestic division of labour can be found in other accounts which touch on gender and household work in Tanzania (Koda et al 1987:30, 50, 66; Mbilinyi 1987:116).

In Tanzania then, men do not enter employment as servants with ready-made domestic skills: rather the opposite, they have to overcome an aversion to performing what is seen as 'women's work'. Conversely what a girl learns at home may be neither appropriate nor marketable knowledge for securing domestic work at a higher class level. The home conditions of poor peasants do not prepare them for the kinds of work they are expected to perform in the houses of the well-off. Peasant houses are built of mud and wattle, with thatch roofs and beaten mud floors. Furniture is minimal – beds and stools, occasionally a table. The source of fuel for cooking is firewood, the kitchen in the main room of the house or a separate hut. The homes of employers are not only much bigger ('a separate room for everything' as one ex-servant put it), they are typically built of stone, brick or concrete, with glass windows, expensive and varied items of furniture, kitchens with piped water, electric stoves and generally refrigerators, occasionally even washing machines. The work demanded by the employer, and the standards set, bear little relation to what a girl might learn at home.

Thus one African employer who had two teenage girls from the countryside working for her explained that when there was washing to do she called in the young man who is her cowherd. She explained that the girls were still learning – their mothers had taught them cooking, but washing bedsheets (by hand) was heavy work and they couldn't do it well. (By implication one kind of housework was regarded as requiring masculine strength!). Another complained that her female servant, 'still forgets to dust and to clean the cooker – they don't have those kinds of things in their own houses' (African employer). A woman domestic worker, Lia, explained to me in detail:

> We don't know how ... Our ways of doing things are not the same as those of Europeans or Indians. For example, in my house I have no bottle brush – if we want to clean a bottle, we put sand in it and shake until it is scoured clean. So if I come to work and see a bottle brush, will I know how to use it? Or the lavatory – at home, we have a hole over a pit which we swill down with water occasionally; or in the countryside, people are used to just digging a hole, doing what they have to do, and then covering it up. Eh Mama! if you come and see a shining lavatory, a flushing one, would you know how to clean it? And cooking – we don't grind spices for example. Every tribe has its own way of cooking which you have to learn.

Even when Africans go to work for each other they must acquire these skills: as one Sambaa woman explained, her Chagga employers had to show her how to cook 'Chagga food' (bananas and meat).

The agenda for child care amongst the well-off is also at odds with what a peasant girl would already know – so that the Goan woman who employed Lia saw no contradiction in saying that 'neither of us knew how to look after a baby when P was born', even though Lia had already had three children, one of whom was now grown up. One could indeed argue then, that women, far from having an advantage over men in the pre-knowledge of appropriate domestic skills, would in fact have to 'unlearn' familiar domestic habits, whereas men have no such conflicting socialisation to break with.

There is a further instance where domestic service does not build automatically on pre-existing gender-related socialisation. In Tanzania, as in most of Africa, it is women who do the bulk of the agricultural work for subsistence needs (Mascarenhas and Mbilinyi 1983:94–5). When it comes to hiring a 'garden boy' however, no employer thinks of taking on a woman – this job, like that of watchman, is unquestioningly male-gendered in Tanzania. Not only is there a lack of coincidence between the home and the work place as far as skills are concerned, there are also some significant gender cross-overs of skill taking place.

Clearly skills transfer is not an adequate explanation of sex-stereotyping in this occupation. If men do not enter domestic employment with skills learnt at their mothers' knees, then this cannot be used as an explanation of their predominance in that occupation, or their status as a preferred workforce. Men must aquire the appropriate skills in some other way, generally on the job. And if men can learn such skills in the course of their job, then so too can women.

EMPLOYERS' VIEW OF DOMESTIC SKILLS

Employers expect to have to train servants to their own requirements, assuming no prior skills in either women or men. 'Individual employers liked their individual ways', was how one ex-colonial put it, whereas an

Asian family in Tanga today described how their servant had 'worked for Indians before, but we still had to train him, especially in how to wash clothes. He insisted on rubbing them with his hands, but we do it differently – we lay the clothes on the floor and scrub them with a brush'. An African employer explained how she had to train the young woman who worked for her: 'She didn't know how to iron or cook or dust. I had to show her how to wash my khangas [wrappers], how to hang them to dry in the shade, and not to iron them but to fold them in a special way'.

Men were and are seen to be quicker to learn domestic skills than women, although employers give varying accounts of how long this takes: from two to three days up to several months. No matter what sex the servant, the period of training was recognised to be a testing one for both sides, entailing assertions of power on the part of the employer and bids for autonomy on the side of the servant. Employers did not always win the battle; servants were able to exert some independence in defining standards of work. From the colonial period: 'Cook No. 1 cooked quite well ... but his kitchen was very dirty and untidy. He had previously worked for a single man who had never entered the kitchen. My incursions were regarded with disfavour ... in his opinion "everyone has their own job"'. And from more recent times: 'She refuses to learn to iron, she says it "burns her blood"' (Asian employer). 'We are still not satisfied – he is dirty ... always forgetting to sweep the cobwebs away. We have to stand over him all the time' (Asian). A European employer said of her male servant: 'My boy was already trained. At first I tried to insist on him doing things my way, but it became boring, every day reminding him. [For example] dusting – he does it merely as a favour, not because he thinks it is important – they think it is a European thing – they don't do it at home. You have to live with patterns of work they have learnt from other employers'.

The interest of employers in the performance skills of their servants would seem to be a twofold and contradictory one. On the one hand, servants can be paid low wages precisely because they are defined as 'unskilled'. We have seen that in the late 1940s, when there was pressure from Britain on the Tanganyikan colonial administration to set a minimum level to servants' wages, this was resented on the grounds that servants were neither well-qualified nor competent enough to claim such wages. Various attempts were made to set up training schemes, all of which foundered. Alternatively wages could be kept down by employing those who could claim no prior training: 'If a housewife is capable of training a cook, a young boy would be worth teaching, and could be employed for a considerably lower wage than one with experience' (WSLT 1948:5). A modern twist to this same employer self-interest is evidenced in the comment of an African woman on the practice of bringing young girls from the rural areas to be servants in the town: 'they are so ignorant they are grateful for anything ... they have not yet learnt to be greedy'.

Conversely, a trained servant contributes much to their comfort and well-being. 'Servants trained by German residents knew how to do housework well' said one ex-colonial; '[I] usually found trained servants', said another, 'though not always to our own standards. [The] English tended to employ those employed originally by English, Germans by Germans, Asians by Asians etc. Greeks – well they did not bother much' (personal communications). It was generally necessary to pay higher wages for more specialised servants.

Present day employers also recognise the benefits they can derive from skilled servants: 'I expected to have to train her, but she already knew the work' explained an African employer: 'She told me she had previously worked for an Asian family. Her standards were higher than mine! When you got up in the morning she'd already have swept and washed the floors'. An African employer compared her male servant with the young woman she also had working for her: 'I taught both of them, but the girl didn't learn properly – she can't wash the nappies or clean and she is a poor cook. But the boy learnt fast and now he is incredibly good – cooks beautifully, cleans and polishes assiduously, is always eager to help and never seems to be tired ...'.

As this last quotation suggests, employers were concerned about more than performance skills. Less tangible features of the relationship such as willingness to work, loyalty, honesty and reliability were characteristics they appreciated almost more than technical skills in servants. In the old days this could take a decidedly feudal form, as described by one elderly European woman: 'When I ran a temperature or did not feel well, O slept before my bedroom door (without my knowing it). When I found out, he excused himself that he could not sleep at home thinking that I might need him ... the old boys addressed me as *Bibi Mkubwa* (Grand madam).' One old servant's testimonial summed it all up: 'He is a very faithful boy. He has never missed a day's work and is completely honest'.

Things have not changed so very much in Tanzania today. The kind of servant who is appreciated is one who 'does what he is told to do, doesn't answer back and is polite'. An Asian woman praised her two servants (a man and a woman): 'They work willingly, without making faces – that is most important'. Dishonesty in servants is a frequent cause of complaint, and both male and female servants are blamed for this. But it is female servants who are more often felt to lack the respect necessary for the servant role – they are frequently said to be too familiar and too inquisitive about their employer's affairs. They are also said to be unreliable: 'girls are always sneaking off to neighbours' houses or to town, and leaving the house unprotected' (African employer).

TRAINING IN DOMESTICITY: THE SERVANTS' PERSPECTIVE

From the point of view of domestic servants, the acquisition of skills has a different significance. If employers can be persuaded to recognise particular skills, then this may be utilised as a lever in bargaining for higher wages, especially if specialisation restricts the supply of labour in these fields, thus leading to a better price for labour. It is only when workers are organised that these mechanisms can work effectively; otherwise they may have an adverse effect, leading individual workers to invest in the acquisition of specialisms which are neither adequately rewarded nor appreciated.

During the colonial period it was common for European and rich Asian employers to have a complement of five or six servants, each one a specialist: a cook, a cook's assistant, a headboy, a houseboy, a washerman, a nurseboy or nursemaid, a garden boy etc. In 1948 a cook could earn over Sh100 a month, although the average was nearer Sh65 or Sh70. 'Houseboys' earned around Sh60 a month, female ayahs (nursemaids) around Sh50, whilst 'garden boys' only earned Sh35 (see WSLT 1948:2 ; Archives V14/32824). However, the WSLT was insisting that the 'present cost of living' made the specialised servant prohibitive: 'It should be the policy, whenever possible, to try and reduce the number of servants by encouraging them to undertake more than one kind of work ...' (6). Nowadays few employers have more than one or two servants, and general ability is more in demand than specialised skills.

The Union of African Cooks and Houseservants was never strong enough to restrict the numbers entering domestic work in the colonial period, and despite organised domestic and hotel workers calling the 1956 strike they were unable to force employers into paying better wages (see Chapter 9). But in earlier colonial days, the supply of houseservants in Tanganyika did not match demand and wages were relatively high compared to other types of work. Even in the early 1950s the average male wage was only around Sh40 per month (Shivji 1986:65), whereas, as we have seen above, domestic servants were mostly paid Sh50 and above, and some specialised servants were able to earn double this amount.

Since Independence, the pool of migrant labour in urban areas has expanded, without much corresponding expansion of industry. In this situation which threatens the existing workforce of domestic servants, it is impossible for workers (men or women) collectively to impose controls over the entry of new recruits, or put pressure on employers to recognise much in the way of skill/wage differentials. Individualistic competition is intensified, but this does not mean that workers no longer have an interest in acquiring skills. Servants themselves recognise that an aptitude for domestic work, or the capacity to learn quickly, is still a matter of economic survival.

Servants who have spent a lifetime in this occupation are conscious of the fact that both technical abilities and a studied deference are crucial factors in securing their jobs. One old man, in telling me of his experiences in the immediate pre-war period, imitated the high-flown and patronising tones of his European employers – 'Bring tea boy!' 'Boy! Fetch water for bath!', but he also remembered his responses: 'Yes Memsa'ab, ready Memsa'ab'. A woman in her fifties, who had learnt cleaning in a school run by Catholic Sisters was eager to tell me how the Sisters had taught her to wash floors and polish window panes, but also that 'if you found anything left by the children you went and put it in the office': the *show* of honesty was vital. Many old servants were proud of the fact that they could be trusted with money to go to the market, be left in charge at home and so on.

Today, displays of humility are less required by employers, or at least were resisted by workers in the context of socialist Tanzania. 'They used to call us "Boy", but now they say "worker"'. Still this man affirmed that his employers 'call me by my (first) name', although he, like most other servants, does not reciprocate, but uses a term of respect. They are conscious that they should not be too familiar with employers: 'I don't know what my employer's work is. A servant can't ask too many questions'. And the proper demeanour of 'willingness' was seen as necessary to getting and keeping work. One woman said that her daughter would have no chance of getting a servant job: 'You have to have a cheerful face, not let your face fall or look sulky if you are asked to do something. She couldn't keep that up!' Conversely, a servant had to put up with bad-tempered employers without answering back. Servants might be asked to do degrading or demeaning tasks and they should not demur – like washing underwear for example. A young man described another instance: 'They have a dog. And for a Muslim, if the dog sniffs at you, you are polluted. I have to ... feed it and bath it with tick medicine. I can't refuse or they will say: "If you don't want the job, be on your way". So I keep quiet'. The capacity to endure insults, to put on an appearance of docility and eagerness to work, to feign respect even where you did not feel it – all this was recognised to be necessary if one were to keep one's place. The modes of servility had to be learnt on the job by hard experience.

Technical aptitudes seem to have been acquired more willingly. I discovered that there were three major ways in which either men or women learned how to become adept in cooking and cleaning. The first and most obvious was that they were taught by employers, usually the woman of the house. Men in particular boasted of their ability to learn quickly. One who had worked for Indians said his first employer had shown him what to do – 'but me, I only have to be shown once and then I understand. I learn fast'. They saw the work place as one in which a set of conventions at variance with those of their upbringing applied, conventions to which they were prepared to adapt in order to survive: 'At home all that is done by our mothers. But I didn't feel bad doing it – I wanted to learn so that I could earn some money'. They described how they were taught to wash floors, to cook, to adjust the dial on an electric iron. And how some employers were kind and helpful whilst others were never satisfied, constantly found fault, and docked their pay if they broke or lost things. 'She used to rub her finger along the top of the cupboard and say: "You not dust here!"'.

Some men denigrated the domestic skills they had learnt, such as the man who said he worked as a servant because: 'If you haven't any skills (*ujuzi*) you have no choice. It doesn't take much learning'. But his comparative reference was telling: 'I am ashamed when I see people with whom I went to school and they have big jobs like doctors and managers'. Other men however, spoke with pride of their ability to 'polish the floors until they shone', or of particular skills which they had struggled to acquire: 'The hardest thing to learn was ironing – it really needs skill – you can easily burn the clothes'.

Women learnt in precisely the same way. A woman of twenty who went to work for a European described her experience. 'I didn't know how to do the work, but the woman said she would teach me. She showed me how to wash windows, clean the floors and sweep, also to do all their washing. She taught me not to use so much soap' Why? 'Our clothes are very dirty so we use a lot of soap but Europeans' clothes are cleaner'. Other women told of how they were introduced to 'red floor polish', and told how to clean the floor not by 'sloshing water all over it and spattering the walls'. One woman explained how her Asian employer had taught her how to make chapatis, and to prepare many different kinds of vegetables with a variety of spices: 'they don't just throw spinach in with some coconut milk like we do'. Women recognised that the skills of the workplace were different to those of the homes from which they had come, and that this was partly to do with ethnic differences, but also to do with material class distinctions: 'their house had painted walls and electric light everywhere, lots of furniture, clothes and radios ... there was so much washing to do because they were always changing their clothes'.

There were two other ways of learning marketable domestic skills. Men in particular talked of learning from fellow workers: 'The other servants showed me what to do'. In the colonial days this was more feasible because each household had several servants. A boy might come in as a 'cook's *toto*' (assistant) or as a houseboy under a headboy and work his way up in the job. One old man described how he started work in the 1920s as a nurseboy, living in with his European employers. Gradually he was taught by other servants how to do housework, and more importantly, what Europeans expected of servants. In later life therefore, he knew what was expected of him, he 'didn't have to be told anything'. One of the ex-colonials provided an interesting twist to this: 'we once found that our headboy was charging the cook's *toto* a small monthly amount for being trained in housework!' – but whether or not this was a common practice I cannot say.

Nowadays learning from other servants is not so easy as few households employ more than one. But I still found several instances of it. A young man told me how other servants had explained to him how to clean and wash floors, though he too insisted that 'it doesn't take much learning'. Another said that the nursemaid in the first house he had worked showed him what to do: 'what the mistress expected of you and what she didn't like'. For employers this is a cost-free method of training (indeed the existing staff are expected to see it as evidence of the trust in which they are held). Several employers described older servants being left to train the younger ones.

A final mode in which skills are transmitted is outside work altogether. Although neither men nor women learn these marketable domestic skills in the normal course of socialisation, the skills once learnt were sometimes passed on within families. This was especially true of Indian culinary arts. An African woman described to me how she hoped that her ability to cook would get her a servant job – 'I can cook egg chapatis and pilau and many different dishes like that'. How did she learn? 'My father worked as a cook for Asians, and he taught my mother, and she taught me. And now I have taught my son: when he cooks you would be astonished – he cooks like a woman'. One man told me that before he got a job as a houseboy his father's brother, who had also worked as a servant for many years, explained the work to him. Another man learnt by moving in with his brother who was a live-in servant. By watching and helping him he became adept in the job. Men also described how fathers or brothers had taught them to iron their school clothes, so that later all they had to learn was to use an electric iron. Occasionally it was male friends who passed on the skills. In all these ways, then, we can see men learning domestic aptitudes, not as part of the usual pattern of male socialisation, but as a specific apprenticeship for wage labour. Their mentors are as likely to have been men (whether family, friends, or other servants) as women.

Wage rates for domestic service are in theory governed by minimum wage legislation, although this is widely ignored by employers. In 1986 the minimum monthly wage was Sh810, but the average wage uncovered in my survey of employers in Tanga was just below Sh800. The highest wage was a very exceptional Sh1800, the lowest Sh400. The calculations which determine wage levels are quite complex, but we can say that skills, whether of performance or demeanour, are only recognised reluctantly by employers. The only domestic workers who can claim a skill increment are cooks, but very few specialised cooks are hired today (I found three amongst ninety-seven domestic workers). Long and loyal service may be acknowledged by occasional wage rises, though usually only after a period of grumbling on the part of the servant. The longest serving employee I discovered in my survey was still paid only Sh1000 a month, after forty years service in the same household. Moreover, if employers move away and servants are forced to seek new work, they do not carry with them those increments accrued from lengthy and skilled service.

There are two kinds of skill which can more readily be translated into market advantage. One of these is laundering and the other is cooking. It was nearly always men who saw an opportunity in this. Thus one old man told me how, whilst working for Europeans, he had observed the washerman very carefully. 'I wanted to know how to wash and iron so that I could use this knowledge for myself'. Later he set up as an independent laundryman, a job he was still doing thirty years later. Self-employed laundrymen are a common sight in Tanga, and many acquired their skills through private employment. I have never seen a woman doing this job, either in a private house or as an independent artisan, even though women do washing at home.

However, a woman told me how she had learnt to make *sambusa* (a savoury snack) in the course of her work as a servant, and how she later established a business with her children and a neighbour, cooking and selling *sambusa*. Knowledge of the arts of cooking are more especially prized by male servants, however, and they feel aggrieved if employers will not pass on these skills to them. Although few cooks are now employed in private houses they are better paid, but more importantly, these skills can be transferred to a considerably more lucrative occupation – that of hotel work, where good cooks are regularly poached by competing entrepreneurs. Both in private houses and in hotels, cooks are almost always male. Given this situation, male servants may be prepared to endure low wages if they are learning skills which can be advantageous to them later.

CONCLUSION

Accounting for the lack of men amongst the workers in 'world market factories' in South East Asia, Elson and Pearson reach the following conclusion: 'If men are to compete successfully, they ... need to acquire the "nimble fingers" and "docile dispositions" for which women workers are prized. But for this they would require to undergo the same social experience as women ... to experience gender subordination.' (1981b:155). As this case study shows, men, like women, can learn nimble fingers and servile dispositions on the job; they need bear no relation to processes of gender subordination; class domination is sufficient in itself.

I am not arguing here that women's – or men's – pre-market skills (and the ideologies of gender inequality by which they are evaluated) are irrelevant to gender segregation in the work force, only that these skills and ideologies are not a sufficient explanation (and in some cases no explanation at all) for this phenomenon. Pre-market skills and ideologies are not transferred unproblematically to the wage sector, though fortuitously they may sometimes be appropriate. In the case of domestic service, what women do at work is not simply an extension of their domestic role, because domestic labour is transformed by the terms on which it is carried out. The skills and attitudes appropriate to the wage sector are a product of the structure of relationships (power, hierarchy, solidarity) in the workplace itself, rather than an outcome of processes of gender socialisation, especially when the material base of such socialisation is marked by class (and often ethnic) distinctions.

In an attempt to explain the limited patterns of incorporation of women into the Ghanaian wage economy Scott eventually concludes that: 'This situation is the outcome of exclusionary mechanisms introduced by a foreign state and based on alien ideology' (1986:179). Such an explanation would not work here, because not all the employers of servants – even in the colonial period – were foreigners. Even if they had been, it would be difficult to see the employment of male servants as a manifestation of an 'alien ideology', for if Europeans brought any assumptions with them about an appropriate work force for domestic service it would have been that it be composed of women.

Hansen (1986a; 1989) offered another explanation for the phenomenon of male domestics in Zambia: it was a consequence of female employers' fears of the sexuality of female servants. Perceiving young women to be 'sexually loose and tempting to male employers' (1986a:22) they prefered to employ men even when women were available for domestic employment. African husbands and fathers concurred in this view of the matter, and looked with disfavour on their womenfolk becoming servants.

In my view the 'sexuality argument' pays too much attention to the demand side of the equation, which is at best only half an explanation.[6] It assumes that the gender composition of the servant labour force is determined by female employers, more than by the kind of people who present themselves for such work. In choosing not to employ females, women employers seem to be acting as much out of fear of the sexuality of their own menfolk as of the sexuality of female servants. In considering the converse instance (in South Africa) of female employers' fears of the sexual advances of male servants, which led to the moral panics denoted 'black perils' (see Van Onselen 1982:45–54), Hansen links it unconvincingly with the contrasting histories of each employing class. Did female employers trust their men more in South Africa than Zambia? Did women servants behave less provocatively? It seems unlikely.

I would prefer to argue that the home as workplace is a profoundly contradictory context, in which the intimacy between family members is brought into uncomfortable liaison with the distance required between class unequals. In all cases these contradictions have to find a workable solution, rules have to be established about degrees of 'familiarity' and physical proximity, and sex and marriage have to be separated from the employment relationship. But in the day to day close encounters of domestic life there is always the potential for sexual interest to overstep the social boundaries of class, and then to spin off gendered or generational conflicts within the family (see Gill on Bolivia 1994:74–6). What is at issue here is not just sex of course, but power, usually that of male employers over female servants, but also that of males (even servants) over females. I discuss these matters further in the context of the micropolitics of the home as workplace (Chapter 8).

If we are to find a more convincing explanation for the continuing predominance of men in this occupation we need to look not just at the demands of employers, but also at the terms on which they are satisfied. This is essentially a question about the supply of labour and about the reproduction of labour power, and it is one which I will explore in the following chapter. The point here is that in colonial Tanganyika the stereotype of 'domestic servant' was moulded in male form as an outcome of processes of male labour migration. In the early colonial period male domestic servants were also able to demand wages comparable or superior to those of workers in other occupations. Once this act of ideological rethinking had been forced on employers and workers alike, its persistence was remarkable and we can see confirmation of the habitus thesis proposed by McElhinny. As Scott remarks: 'once gender segregation has crystallised in an occupation ... it exerts a strong normative pressure on the market: there is resistance to substitution even when supply and price conditions change' (1986:160).

In Tanzania such conditions are now changing. Growing pressure on rural households has led to a rise in the number of women migrating to towns. Women have begun to compete with men for jobs at the bottom of the occupational hierarchy and are now actively seeking jobs as maids of all work in private households. If they are to compete with men already established in this field, they must offer their labour cheap. The average wage for women servants in Tanga in 1986 was only Sh670, compared with Sh956 for men (employer survey).

Women who offer themselves for work, however, come up against resistance from employers who have been accustomed to think of men as having more to offer in the domestic setting. Although women are now more available as domestic workers, and more in demand in some quarters for their cheapness, men have continued to hold their own overall because they are still regarded as the 'best men for the job' and are motivated to sustain this view amongst employers. Like the police officers whom McElhinny studied they do not see the skills they use on the job in gendered terms of masculinity or effeminacy. These are skills learnt in order to get work and to earn wages, and it is their wage-earning ability that defines their masculinity and asserts their identity with other men. The comments of three men underline this conclusion: one emphasised his eagerness to learn these skills 'so that I could earn money'. Another denied that paid domestic labour was women's work, adding: 'don't other blokes do it in hotels?' the third insisted that 'a lot of other men are doing it, otherwise I would not do it. No-one thinks anything of it, though it's true that work is done by women at home'.

Discussing threats to masculinity in quite a different setting Collinson and Hearn have argued that some men 'make a highly conscious effort to retain a clear psychological and symbolic separation between the spheres of paid work and home' (1996:67). For these men, as labour migrants from faraway rural areas, the physical separation of work and home provided added protection against unwelcome comparisons – as we saw in Abu's case (cited in Chapter 2). But more significant is that masculinity is seen to be less threatened by domestic work when it is performed for a wage. Masculinity becomes contingent on the situation and location in which it is enacted (Sweetman 1998); at work confirmed by the capacity to acquire skills and to provision families irrespective of the nature of the work (a perspective which they share with women workers), whilst at home defined by a marked symbolic distance from domestic labour (which women facilitate).

6

GREEN WAVES: THE SUPPLY OF DOMESTIC LABOUR

Since Independence the occupation of domestic worker has begun to be feminised, at least in relation to 'inside' work. Whilst the extent to which this is happening cannot be definitively confirmed, much is suggestive of how and why. Feminisation is not an outcome of changing employer preferences but the unintended outcome of dramatic and far-reaching dislocations of gendered modes of rural livelihood in the colonial period and beyond.[1] The growing feminisation of domestic service has coincided with an increase in the rate of female migration from rural areas. In this chapter I consider the determinants of labour supply, using evidence culled from life histories and from accounts of the area from which migrants predominantly come. As the lives of these men and women encompassed other wage work and forms of livelihood besides domestic work, the picture which is revealed is of a migrant working class in formation, one which is the outcome of strategies differentiated not only by gender but also by generation.

Labour migration marks the beginnings of a process of proletarianisation by which relations to the land as a means to a livelihood are eroded, and men and women seek to sell their labour power in the market place. In practice the unfolding of events is rather more complex and proletarianisation often incomplete. It is rare in this case for peasants and subsistence farmers to be completely dispossessed of access to land, or for complete families to join the expanding army of wage labourers. It is rather that the capacity of small holdings to sustain whole families has been progressively undermined in most parts of Tanzania. Survival demands that some must leave whilst others stay.

If there were no sex or age differentiation in peasant production, or in rights to property and the product of labour, then this experience of semi-proletarianisation would be the same for all. In this case, as in many others (e.g. South Africa: Bozzoli 1983, 1991; Van Onselen 1982; Senegal: Mackintosh 1989), it is clear that men and women, and to a lesser degree young people as compared to the more mature, join the army of wage labourers on unequal terms and out of different material circumstances. Exploring this difference I ask why the migratory flow of women and young people from the countryside seems to be increasing, so that there is an expanding supply of such labour entering the market for domestic work. I concur with Bozzoli

(1983:144; 1991) that this needs to be explained in terms of domestic struggles within peasant households in the context of increasing pressures on peasant agriculture – adding that these gendered struggles continue within the urban setting. For women in Tanga, as for the women from Phokeng, domestic service often offers a first foothold in the urban economy (Bozzoli 1991).

There is a curious contrast between my life histories of men and women who constituted the pool from which servant labour is drawn: two very different stories were being told which shed light on the discourse and practice of these gendered struggles. For men, wage labour in town was clearly part of a patriarchal and familial strategy for survival. They retained their land in rural areas but left wives to cultivate it or planned to marry at home in order to do this. Nearly half of the women migrants who told me their life stories were married too, but they were not cultivating at home; they had established themselves in town, sidestepping patriarchal strategies. How had they achieved this? And how could the behaviour of unmarried women here be understood, in a context where marriage is not only the norm but also an insurance against female destitution in the rural areas from which they had come?

FEMALE MIGRATION AS RESISTANCE?

In Tanzania various hypotheses have been put forward as to why rates of female migration have been increasing. These range from the frankly sexist (a rising tide of 'immorality', evidenced by prostitution, illegitimacy and the insubordination of wives) to culturalist arguments about how the education system raises the aspirations of all youngsters in ways that cannot be satisfied by rural life (the arguments were reviewed in Mascarenhas and Mbilinyi 1983:36, 121–37).

Another hypothesis was offered by Mascarenhas and Mbilinyi when they asked whether : 'the increasing rate of female migration ... is not a form of protest against the patriarchal family relations?' (1983:122). Men expect women to produce the family food, they expect to command the labour power of their wives and daughters and generally to control its product; some women may resist these impositions. The state also had an interest in women's labour. Since independence women's labour in agricultural production had intensified in consequence of the extension of peasant cash crop production. Government initiatives in various guises (settlement schemes, 'socialist' villages, coerced villagisation) meant that women were expected to add cash crop production to their already heavy burden of household labour and the cultivation of family food. In Mbilinyi's terms: 'the ruling class used the state apparatuses to extract surplus in an absolute sense, by intensifying the labour of all producers, but especially women, and increasing that portion of the labour product which was marketed' (1985:123).

Women's willingness was not infinite and some rebelled by leaving the rural areas. This suggests a theory of female labour migration which sees women as actors in their own right, rather than simply the creatures of men. Each leaves as an individual; but in aggregate the departure of women has its social roots in gendered inequality.

Sender and Smith (1990) discuss the same process in terms of men's response: 'married men [attempt] to resist the proletarianisation of their wives, in order to maintain their own control over the household economy' (65) – a control maintained through violence and the 'brutal appropriation' of women's labour (66,67).[2] A gendered struggle appeared to be raging, with Sender and Smith arguing that men are the winners: the only women who become wage labourers are those whose 'freedom' comes out of potential destitution: the divorced, the unmarried, widows left with insufficient land or without sons, none of whom have a secure claim to be provided for by men (59). There is some truth in this, but it is not the only story – evidence to be cited points to single and married women achieving the same release from rural toil through resourceful manoeuvres.

Sender and Smith studied one part of the Usambara area from which the majority of servants in Tanga originate. Their focus is on wage labour as agricultural workers in adjacent large farms and estates. Entry into such work does not in fact provide the 'escape route' for women that Sender and Smith suggest.[3] Even on their own estimates such women can barely subsist and (like men) would evade such labour if they could. The real escape route, as many see it, is in making for town.

Rising rates of female migration to urban areas can thus be interpreted both as a tactic of survival and as a form of resistance, whether against the men who benefit from the existing organisation of production, or against the state which builds on this arrangement for its own purposes.[4] This thesis is at odds with some Marxist and neo-Marxist theories of labour migration which were predicated on the now discredited assumption of a universal and necessary transition to capitalism in the South (critically reviewed in Cohen 1987). Capital demanded cheap labour drawn from precapitalist enclaves whose conservation thus found its rationale. The questioning of this functionalist teleology would seem to be particularly relevant in a case such as that of Tanzania, where capitalist forms of expansion were resisted until the 1980s and state intervention has been striking. The rise in female migration has occurred, moreover, in a period when capitalist production stagnated rather than expanded. The 'migration as resistance' thesis requires us to understand the migration of both men and women in the context of diverse pressures on peasant agriculture, of which capitalist expansion may only be one.

The changing pattern of female migration into urban areas does not tell us everything about the supply of domestic labour and why women are now more available for domestic work. Men continue to apply; and there are other ways of earning a living in town. Why do women, and indeed men, choose this work, rather than any other?

SOURCES OF DATA

Data from the mid-1980s (culled from my employer survey) allow us to discern the features of the then currently employed cohort of servants. The continuing predominance of male labour in domestic work is notable (nearly three quarters of the total). The men employed were older – 45 per cent of them over thirty-five; whilst two thirds of the women were under twenty-five. More than half (of both sexes) were Sambaa people (the majority of whom were also Muslim).

For a longer and more detailed view of those who form the pool for domestic labour, I draw on the life histories of servants and ex-servants (78 cases: 44 woman and 34 men). The vast majority (90 per cent) of these servants and ex-servants were migrants into the city (all of the men and 82 per cent of the women). Some were young people who had only recently arrived; others were elderly – many planning to return to the rural areas from which they had originated, whilst a few were now settled in Tanga. Not all were first generation migrants: many had fathers who had themselves commuted from rural areas to work in towns, some now retired home, others still working. Ethnically they were quite diverse, though again the Sambaa were the most prominent (54 per cent of the women and 82 per cent of the men). The men and women were fairly evenly matched in terms of age, though the average age is higher than the cohort of servants from the employers' survey.

The two oldest men in my life history set had come to Tanga in the 1920s, one a Digo from a village not far away, whilst the other, an Ngoni, had come as a twelve year old from the far south of Tanganyika to work on the sisal plantations. The earliest arrival amongst the Sambaa men was one who had first come in 1939, and there were three others who had arrived in the 1940s.[5] The rest of the men had arrived later, with the largest proportion having first come in the 1970s.

None of the women in my life history set claimed to have come before the Second World War, though there were several women here as old as the oldest men. Amongst those who had been in Tanga the longest were two (a Sukuma woman and a Mnungwa) whose parents had been sisal cutters on a nearby plantation. The earliest arrival amongst the Sambaa was a woman who had come in the 1950s, though we know there were Sambaa women in Tanga in the 1930s.[6]

From these life history sets it is possible to extract accounts of the experience of migration into domestic service which reflect its social composition in the mid-1980s. Later visits to Tanga and to the Usambara area (Lushoto district) from which most servants originate added to the analysis and enabled me to assess changing currents in the flow of labour.

CLASS PRESSURES; GENDER DIFFERENTIATION

Men and women often provided comparable accounts of their reasons for leaving the rural areas. Both spoke of deteriorating conditions for rural survival – land shortage, drought and poor harvests – as a background to their exodus. Both emphasised their need for cash in addition to the fruits of their own labour on the land. Both young men and young women saw themselves as having been a burden on parents struggling to make ends meet. At first sight the pressures which led them to migrate appeared class specific rather than gender specific – i.e. as the conditions for their existence as independent peasant or subsistence farmers were undermined. A telling example is what happened to the Sambaa people (also called Shambaa/ Shambala) in the Usambara mountains, around a hundred miles inland from Tanga town. It is worth expanding on this case since Sambaa people have become the major contributors to the supply of domestic servants in Tanga.

More than fifty per cent of the Sambaa interviewed were from Mlalo, a part of the Usambaras particularly hard hit by erosion and high population density. Women described these circumstances even more graphically than men. 'We left because the land was exhausted', said one; 'There is land, but it has been eroded. It's become like a desert' said another. Land shortage was also mentioned: 'There are so many people in Mlalo that the farms are too small – an acre or less'.

The increasing marginalisation of poor peasants is not a simple outcome of population pressure and ecological degradation, although peasants themselves may perceive these crises as the root cause of their hardships. Both capitalist and 'socialist' developments have had an impact on reducing the capacity of poor peasants to survive. This is evidenced in the alienation of land for capitalist agriculture, or the emergence and expansion of a kulak category (peasants who hire labour); as well as by state intervention. The history of the fertile highlands of Usambara illustrates these pressures.

From the early colonial period European settler farmers were encouraged to alienate land in this area. Sambaa people did not work willingly on settler farms and plantations; from the German period onwards they had to be coerced: by interspersing alienated land with areas reserved for Africans, by forced labour levies and by taxation (Iliffe 1969:135–8, 160). Over time, land alienation and population pressure led to the encroachment of Sambaa agriculture on increasingly marginal areas; with the clearing of forest land and steep slopes, soil erosion began to be a serious problem. Colonial interventions on this matter were sometimes bitterly resisted (e.g. the Mlalo Rehabilitation Scheme in the 1950s: Cliffe et al 1969; Feierman 1990). It was a Sambaa woman who told me about these attempts at land reclamation – herself finding the Sambaa at fault for abandoning practices like terracing after independence. The land of her own family had had to be relinquished: 'The soil washed away, down the mountainside'.

The problems of land shortage and soil erosion did not disappear with political independence. Although the government nationalised the land in 1964, landowners were not dispossessed and people were still able to buy land and to sell their inherited rights to it, allowing social differentiation amongst the peasantry to intensify. Whilst the capacity of Usambara agriculture to sustain the poorest members of the local population has continued to decline, this period has also seen the expansion of enterprise by richer peasants and privately owned estates producing for profit (food and export crops such as tea and coffee) in the least eroded and most fertile land – especially on the lower slopes and in valley bottoms (Attems 1969; Cliffe et al. 1969; Glaeser 1980; Sender and Smith 1990).

Such production relations survived the phase from 1967 onwards in which 'socialist agriculture' was heavily promoted by the state. In the Usambara area more forest land was cleared to create 'socialist' villages, thus heightening long-term ecological vulnerability, whilst the already better-off were able to hi-jack the opportunities for expansion so created (Cliffe et al 1969; Sender and Smith 1990). Such experiments had rather less impact here than in some other parts of Tanzania, since the land was already intensively cultivated, and there was little room for communal farms. Only one woman mentioned an obligation to work on the village farm. The creation of state marketing boards was another feature of this period and between 1980–5 official prices for agricultural products fell in real terms (Maliyamkono and Bagachwa 1990:149). Men noted that legal trading opportunities were consequently inhibited, though parallel markets began to flourish (ibid.:75). One man spoke of having set up a small shop in Mlalo when these developments occurred: 'And then Nyerere said that everything had to be shared – we should share the businesses too [village shops were to be run by the new "socialist" villages]. But I didn't want to share so I abandoned my shop and came to Tanga'. Neither men nor women saw themselves as resisting pressure to increase production – their energy was already fully applied to this task.

Out-migration from this area for those most heavily pressed has been noted for more than fifty years. Not all of this migration entailed the search for wage work in urban areas. Sambaa people moved gradually to colonise new areas of lower plain land in Muheza and Korogwe districts where population density was much lower, though families often maintained a foothold in both upland and plains areas. Out-migration from Lushoto has generally been a preferred alternative to working as agricultural wage labourers within it. Local capitalist and kulak enterprises have consistently experienced shortages of labour (Sender and Smith 1990). Wage work on tea plantations such as those in the Amani area, half way to Tanga, was regarded as not much better than casual agricultural labour locally, though some worked there.[7] Most migrants sought wage work in towns such as Tanga, but some went further afield, to Dar es Salaam or even to Kenya.

A report by Cliffe et al. on the Usambara area in the late sixties notes that:

> Of 121 heads of households surveyed, all but 12 had spent some time away in paid employment ... The type of work done by heads of households mostly comprised unskilled labouring and domestic service. The younger generation tend towards more skilled occupations – drivers, clerks, salesmen and teachers – although domestic service is still common. (1969:20)

The patterns delineated here were not those of emigration: the household heads interviewed had returned to the rural areas, after a period of paid work away, in response to 'needs for supplementary income' and as a 'temporary relief' in a situation of local land and population pressure (21). This pattern of migratory oscillation between peasant production and paid employment is still the predominant pattern in Tanzania, despite some stabilisation of the urban work force (noted as early as 1979 by Sabot: 200).

Despite the constraints on peasant agriculture there were few migrants who did not continue to cling on to their land, poor and inadequate though it might be in most cases.[8] None of the men I interviewed from this area were landless, though some only had a claim on family land yet undivided.[9] None saw themselves as abandoning farming to become permanent wage workers: 'You don't give up your land' said one man, 'but if the sun scorches the crops and the harvest is bad you need money'. This man had first come to Tanga from the Lushoto area in 1948, and had spent most of his life since working as a servant, but with periods (in one case seven years) back at home, cultivating. Now he is old and, having supported his six children through to adulthood, the land is a refuge to which he is planning to return.

Nor did the women here come from families destitute of land. If they had abandoned eroded land or lost rights to it, they had often acquired other plots on the outskirts of Tanga – a process which I will describe below. Land was almost more important to women than it was to men, since access to it determined their capacity to feed their families: a task all agreed was the responsibility of women.

Only men were perceived as 'heads of household' in Cliffe et al's study in the 1960s, and it is therefore only male migration which is commented upon. Evidence of the extent of migration from this area is often illustrated by reference to the unbalanced sex ratios found in the Usambara area. Sender and Smith for example, note that: 'the ratio of males to females in Lushoto district has remained at around 87 since 1957, significantly below the levels for the region and the whole country' (1990:5). By the end of the 1980s it had fallen again to 84 (Census, 1988). The point being made is that out-migration from the Usambara area is high relative to the national average. The argument requires an assumption, never explicitly stated, that out-migration from the area was, and is, overwhelmingly male migration. (If the same number of men and women left the area, then there would be no imbalance, even though migration might be higher.) Whilst it is primarily men who leave to seek wage work, women have always been part of the migratory flow: and not just from the Usambara area but from other areas in Tanzania. The velocity of this flow is now increasing and it is beginning to take on a different character with more independent migration by women.[10]

If migration is largely a response to pressure on land, one aspect of this is that peasants may feed themselves but have little surplus to sell. The rising need for a cash income to cover children's school expenses, pay taxes, and to purchase items like clothes, sugar, salt, kerosene or tea, is experienced by women as well as men. Clothing is a key item here, mentioned over and over again as a reason for leaving home to seek work (see also Bozzoli 1991:86 on South Africa). People born in the 1920s and '30s mentioned it as often as those born in the '50s. Tanzania's infant textile industry has never been able to provide cheap clothes for mass consumption, nor indeed a ready supply even of expensive clothes. The poorest were at their wits end to afford clothing – indeed in the early 1980s it was reported that 'people in many parts of the country had very little to wear' (letter to *Daily News*, March 1986). Eventually the government allowed the import of secondhand clothing, and it is this which people from the countryside hope to be able to purchase with their wages.

An additional pressure on women to find cash came in 1984 when the government imposed a Development Levy on all adults over eighteen, women as well as men (Sh220 per annum). During a debate in the National Assembly in July 1986, when members questioned the imposition of this tax on women, the First Vice President stated that 'since the Party and the Government had insisted upon the equality of women and men ... and in recognition of the fact that women lead in creating wealth in the villages ... they will continue to pay tax' (*Uhuru*, 1 July 1986, translated from the Swahili). He noted that in the previous financial year women had contributed the greatest share to revenue from this source.

Whilst the intention of this tax was probably to increase the marketed production of crops, the role which male taxation played in impelling men to migrate in search of wage work in the colonial period suggests that this new tax exerted a similar pressure on women (Bujra 1990). As one woman said of it: 'a wife cannot be without money now'. Increasing female migration could be seen as an unintended consequence of government policy, whilst the proclaimed formal equality of women disguises considerable inequality in terms of their access to both land and cash incomes.

GENDERED LAND RIGHTS AND MIGRATION

Most men still control land in their own right in Tanzania, whilst women's rights are conditional, generally on marriage. This has not fundamentally changed despite new formal relations of ownership and allocation of land imposed by the state following the nationalisation of land and the Village Act of 1975 (Mascarenhas and Mbilinyi 1983:28).

The Sambaa case is not atypical. The Sambaa kinship system is strongly patrilineal, and marriage patrilocal (Feierman 1974:33–4; Mitzlaff 1988:24–5). Men inherit land from their fathers, allocating fields to their wife or wives on marriage on which family food can be grown. It is the responsibility of a wife to produce a subsistence for her husband and children. Men may cultivate some fields themselves, especially for the production of cash crops, though the wife's labour is often called upon here too. Sons inherit land from the portion allocated to their mothers. Daughters do not inherit land unless there is no son; they are expected to marry and to be provided for by husbands. The bulk of agricultural work is carried out by women, as well as all the work of the household and the care of children (Mitzlaff 1988:28–32). It seems probable that over generations of forced and then voluntary conscription into the army of wage labour, male labour input has become increasingly marginal to the requirements of subsistence production, and women's responsibilities have grown.

For the Sambaa and for many other peoples in Tanzania patterns of male labour migration are heavily dependent on keeping intact this system of male control over productive assets and women's labour. I want to look at this situation through the eyes of both men and women migrants in Tanga, because they do not always perceive it in the same way.

MIGRANT HUSBANDS: DOMESTIC CONTROL

To sustain men's lives as migrant workers a wife at home who would work the land and feed the family in their absence was vital. Seventy per cent of the men I interviewed were currently married and nearly eighty per cent of these had left their wives in the rural area. They took this arrangement for granted: 'It's not our custom to have the wife in town', said one Sambaa. 'I can't carry her around with me like a bag all the time. She is cultivating the farm'. 'I did not allow my wife to live in town – she has her responsibilities back home, for the land and the children', said another Sambaa. Whereas their wives had spent short periods in town – perhaps before they had their first child, or between busy periods of cultivation, they were not expected to live there: 'I returned her home', said a Pare man. 'She cultivates there, I work here'.

A man without a wife at home is in an insecure position. He may have rights to land, but it will be used by other relatives in his absence. He cannot count on receiving any product from it unless he remits savings to those who work on it; it does not constitute guaranteed security against his sickness or unemployment or retirement. This is why unmarried men are eager to be married; and divorced or widowed men are few. The two widowed men here had left their land to be cultivated and their children to be brought up by their grandmothers.

That men should command women's labour is also taken for granted. 'What she cultivates is mine', said one Sambaa man of his wife's efforts. And whilst another man's comment indicates recognition of the worth of a wife at home, his conclusion is clear:

> [my wife] can manage, she doesn't need me. I can stay in town ten years and she doesn't sit at home waiting for orders – she makes the decisions – what to plant and when to harvest. If there are extra beans she sells them and uses the money to buy clothes for herself and the children. I know nothing of it until I go home and she tells me what she has done, and says: 'and here are the savings'. (but see below!)

In line with these expectations men were careful to return to the countryside to marry: 'It's better to go home and marry a girl who knows how to work and has respect. Town women have little respect and they don't know how to cultivate' (Sambaa).

Once married, the aspirations of male migrants reflect their control over land and labour. Men's aim was to 'raid the cash economy' (as Watson once put it: 1958) for the means to secure their independent operations as peasant farmers: to buy land, and thereby to increase their production of cash crops. Only a few were successful in this; for the majority migrant labour became a treadmill from which they could not escape and their working away for wages became merely a condition of survival for their family at home. One man, who left home to seek the wherewithal to marry, worked as a servant for several employers, but never earned enough to buy more land. Between jobs he returned to the one acre plot of land inherited from his father, there trying to survive with his wife and children. When I talked to him he had once more been driven back to town by hardship – the harvest had been spoilt, their food supplies ran out, and he was again looking for work. Another man said: 'There is not enough land for me to live there as well as my wife and children. There would be no money'.

There were many men here who sent home money to enable their wives to hire agricultural labour on a casual basis. But for most of these it was simply a matter of replacing their own labour at a lesser cost (urban wage rates being greater than those of casual rural labour), rather than expanding the scale of their operations. For the majority of these men, the rewards for wage work had been meagre. Perhaps a better house at home, built with blocks or a corrugated iron roof, or, more likely, just clothes, bedding and cash for taxes and school fees.

Only a minority have generated investment in agriculture out of wage work. Nine men claimed to have been able to purchase small amounts of land, but only two of these were growing regularly for sale. Four others had been fortunate to inherit enough good land to plant coffee or tea or vegetables for the market. The cash these men put back into the rural enterprise, for hiring labour, and for marketing, can be seen more properly as investment leading to accumulation. They could be described in class terms as 'straddling': one foot in the proletariat, the other on the ladder to kulakdom (Cowen and Kinyanjui 1977). Only three were prepared to consider giving up the security of their urban employment however, one to retire and the other two with plans to become agricultural traders, selling the surpluses of others.

Only two men had successfully exploited employment as a means to sustained accumulation, but in neither case was this out of the average domestic worker's wage. Yahya was only thirty-five, the third son in a large family whose parents were peasant farmers. He had left home as an adolescent, come to Tanga and almost immediately got work as a cook's help in a restaurant. This enabled him to learn how to cook and he was eventually employed by the wealthy owner of a Tanga club who paid him three times the minimum wage in order to retain his services. Meanwhile Yahya had inherited a little land from his father, but he now purchased more. He delayed marriage until he was nearly thirty, but now sends money to his wife to hire labour to cultivate vegetables and fruits for sale on some of his fifteen acres of land, whilst she grows the family's food on the rest. The key to this man's success was his good fortune in finding hotel work, which pays much better than private service.

The other man's achievement would be much harder to repeat today. He was in his fifties and had recently 'retired' to full time work on his farm. He had only ever worked as a servant, but this included two lengthy periods of service, the second to a very wealthy Asian employer for whom he became 'headboy'. For nearly fifteen years he received good wages and free benefits like housing, and when his employer emigrated to Canada he enjoyed a lump sum of severance pay. His family were not very poor peasants, so this man had inherited several fields on his father's death, and purchased additional land on which to grow vegetables for the market. This was the man who 'did not allow' his wife to live with him in town: she was busy augmenting his income at home. By the time he retired he had accumulated fourteen acres of land. Employers such as his hardly figure on the scene today, and few domestic servants would be able to accumulate in this way.

These exceptional cases prove a more general rule: that men's control of land and labour was undermined by the land poverty suffered by most of them. Wage labour of the kind these rural migrants were able to find does not generally allow for the accumulation of savings which can then be transferred into agricultural expansion. To achieve this on a servant's wage was possible only by way of long term service to wealthy – and generous – European or Asian employers, or by finding remunerative work in hotels rather than private employment. These cases also demonstrate that the labour of a wife is as crucial to expansion as it is to survival. If she can be kept in the rural area she will oversee the employment of wage labourers and the transport of produce to her husband for sale in the town, as well as feeding the family. Given this conclusion, why should any man consider having his wife in town?

It is impossible to draw any definite conclusions from the five cases in this set where men have their wives in Tanga, but they are suggestive. Either the man has very limited or no resources in the rural area so that his wife cannot be an asset there, or his wife's presence in town may outweigh the benefit of her being at home. There is an 'old style' and a 'new style' in these matters, though men present both as a demonstration of continuing male control. One of the oldest men in my set had his wife with him for two reasons: he had been able to acquire land near Tanga which his wife cultivated, and his better-paid job (following long-term service to a European family) had allowed him to build a house in town and rent out rooms. His views on women were patriarchal indeed – his wife had wanted to train as a teacher but he married her out of school and thought the place for wives was at home. When I asked him why women were now more often found as domestic servants he said that young women were greedy for money these days whereas in the old days 'men had control over their wives'. Another factor was that he had married a girl born in Tanga. Women born, brought up or married in town will resist being returned to a rural area.

The new style of things is represented by a younger man in his thirties who, after several years working as a servant, got a job in an Asian-owned club. He was not only very well-paid as a cook, but his wife was also paid to clean and sweep the premises, and he received free accommodation where he lived with her and their children. These favourable circumstances meant that even though he had land at home, and had built a good house there, his mother and brothers work the land rather than his wife. He said he preferred his wife and children to be with him; it was safer in town as the hospital was near by.

MIGRANT WIVES: DOMESTIC STRUGGLES

For a married woman to abandon her husband's land and to go independently seeking paid work elsewhere would generally be unthinkable.[11] The land rights of married women may be conditional, but they also have an interest in tending and securing the land even when their husbands leave the rural areas to seek work. If they are to shoulder the burden of cultivation and care for the family, however, they need cash as well as food. When the husband's remittances are intermittent or inadequate they must seek an independent source of cash, the means to which do not threaten their major security in cultivation.

The most frequent solution is to sell small surpluses of beans and maize in local markets (Mitzlaff 1988:35). I observed one such market, in Lushoto in the mid-1990s. Here the majority of sellers were women, and they sold not in order to accumulate, but to buy other everyday necessities. A second option for such women is to sell their labour to local farmers, including neighbours like themselves, on a casual basis. Several women mentioned this as a last resort, but, as already noted, the pay is low and less than men's (Mitzlaff 1988:34, Sender and Smith 1990:63–4).

If a husband's remittances cease altogether it would be grounds for divorce, an outcome which will be discussed below. Where an absent husband does not support his wife properly, or where she hears he is carrying on in town with another woman, she may take advantage of the relative autonomy of action which his absence allows. In one woman's account:

> Then she hides her savings, and when he asks what happened to the money from this year's harvest she deceives him: 'Don't you know how expensive khangas (wrappers) are these days? And the children were ill' ... or 'The harvest was poor'. If he is the type who comes wanting to borrow from her hard earned money she may give him Sh150 to help him on his way.[12]

If most wives remain to cultivate when husbands migrate, some women have different aspirations. The migrant women whom I interviewed were unrelated to the men, but half were married women living with their husbands in town and they saw this as an outcome as much of their own strategies as those of men. A few of these women had married in town (and saw this as a means to enhance their position there) but the majority arrived after being married in rural areas. Their strategy was simple: to become a resourceful help-mate to their husband in town so that he finds it an advantage to have her with him.

These women put forward a range of arguments to support their case. If they were in town then their children stood a better chance of education and access to health care was easier. They also perceived rural life to be hard: 'it ages you quickly' and sometimes reported husbands as being concerned about this – 'he said, in town we could rest a little'. However, they also accepted their responsibility to provide family food, and they conceded that it is the husband who takes the decision as to whether they come to town or not. Often, the best they can achieve is to commute backwards and forwards so that they are in the countryside to plant and harvest, visiting their husbands between whiles in town. For the Sambaa, given the relative proximity of Tanga and Lushoto, this seems to be a practice of long standing.

Complex processes of family negotiation are required to persuade a husband to allow his wife to reside continually in town, since the effect of the wife's move is the loss of labour on the land. Where that land is exhausted, this may be no loss; but where it is not, a substitute must be in place if the woman is to leave. Occasionally the man's position in town improves to the extent that he can afford to relinquish the advantage of having his wife at home. One woman described how after marriage she had been left to cultivate her husband's land in the Usambara area whilst he was away working in the docks in Mombasa. She grew beans and was able to sell a little, whilst her husband sent remittances from which she was able to save. Eventually they had enough to build a house with a corrugated iron roof, and her husband then agreed that she leave the farm to spend a year with him in Mombasa. Then, instead of returning home, where 'life is hard' she went to Tanga to join her mother and has lived there ever since, working on and off as a domestic servant. Meanwhile her husband sends money which she transmits to her brother at home. He uses the money to hire labour to cultivate their land, whilst another relative is occupying their house. Surpluses are sent to her in Tanga so that she can sell them.

A husband is more likely to agree to his wife being in town if they can find land there. Areas had been opened up on the outskirts of Tanga where people could ask for plots, and several of these married women were working land locally. In this way one peasant enterprise might be abandoned, or left to other relatives, whilst another was established.

Alternatively women ensure that whilst they are in town they are more than 'unproductive housewives'. Their husbands were mostly working in low-paid manual work, whilst a few were independent artisans or petty traders. Wives seek ways of supplementing their husband's often meagre incomes, whether through wage employment or some other means. The women reported on here had been employed as domestic servants, and had also worked or were working in small factories or as bar workers. They conceded that husbands must be asked for 'permission' if the woman wants to work, especially outside the home. The attitude of one husband is indicative. Aziza had accompanied him to Mombasa where he was a dockworker. There they shared a house with several other families, one of whom asked Aziza if she would help with housework and childcare whilst they were out at work (both were teachers). When she asked her husband he said: 'Since it's right here in the house and you haven't anything to do after making tea for me and sweeping out our room, you can do it. If it had been anywhere else I couldn't agree – you are a stranger and how would you find your way?' Aziza found nothing untoward in this – it was part of the normal constraints which she took for granted.

Even women who have come to town on their own account are subject to such conditions. One such woman who had worked independently as a servant for three years married a factory worker in town, after her father 'felt it was time for her to get married'. Her husband objected to her going 'out' to work, which she explained to me in the following terms: 'Husbands are afraid you will be seduced by another man. If you are late home they think you didn't go to work at all'. She now has a thriving business selling cassava and fried fish from home to local schoolchildren in their break-time.

It is not only that husbands may object, but also because wage labour is difficult to combine with child care, that many of these women had eventually found a way of making an income from home – often by selling cooked food, but also by weaving mats, or, most common of all, by retailing flour, beans, salt, fruit etc. which they bought in bulk. Domestic service had merely been a step on the way to this independence. With inflation as it was in the 1980s, and with the real value of wages falling, whole families could not easily be accommodated in town unless each adult contributed to the family income. One woman had set up a business making and selling savoury snacks (a skill learnt in domestic service). The labour of all her children was required – to peel potatoes and onions, knead and roll out the pastry, and to go out selling the finished product. But she then contributed more to the family income than her husband did, and has no further worries about feeding her children.

Married women in town then, are not on the whole mere dependents of their husbands, even though they may have come to town in that capacity. What men prefer, given that their own incomes are rarely enough to support a household adequately, is for women to earn money under conditions set by themselves: if not working from home then perhaps for the same employer for whom they work themselves. What they do not like is for women to organise moneymaking for themselves. Women's perspective is different. Although their income earning activity in town can be seen as part of a strategy to dissuade husbands from returning them to the back-breaking toil of cultivation, it also allows them an insurance against divorce, and a degree of autonomy within the marriage. As one woman put it: 'Never depend on a husband! When you need something you want your own money ready in your pocket'.

Needless to say, this was not a mode of expression which a husband would appreciate, so women presented themselves as loyal and hardworking help-mates. One story illustrates the way they might see themselves as the key actors in the urban survival saga. Amira's husband was laid off work, and her own attempt to earn a wage through domestic work had collapsed. Her mother's brother had land near town so she went to beg a piece of it.

> My uncle agreed so I returned to my husband and told him: 'we have land'. He said 'how can you cultivate when you are not fit and the land is far away?' 'You will take me on your bicycle'. So we cultivated. It was late in the planting season so I told my husband we should not waste time clearing the land. The grass was short so I told him, 'we'll just dig holes and put in seeds'. So we did.

This device worked, they harvested maize and her husband got another job. But cultivation was very exhausting and in addition 'a wife can't be without money' so she sought wage work again.

In all these ways married women see themselves as survivors rather than victims, and they are resourceful strategists in the domestic struggles which determine whether they remain in town or commute back and forth. They may be seen as 'bargaining with patriarchy', in Kandiyoti's striking phrase (1991:36). Women without husbands are in a different position. It is striking that over half of the women interviewed had come to Tanga as single or divorced women migrating on their own account, rather than in consequence of the migration of a husband or parents on whom they were dependent.

DIVORCED MIGRANTS

If women's access to land is conditional on marriage, then divorce generally results in women losing their rights to their husband's land. Many of the women I interviewed had returned to their natal family on divorce, to be given land by their fathers or brothers, or merely to till the same fields as their mothers. Mitzlaff notes of the Usambara area that: 'in poor families [divorced] daughters do not receive a warm welcome as competition over land has become a matter of survival' (1988:25). Of Tanzania more generally Mbilinyi says: 'For the majority [of women] upon the death of husband or divorce, the producer is dispossessed of the land and the product of her labour ... [This] helps to explain why women have moved off the land in search of cash incomes' (1985:100–1).

Divorce may be interpreted as an index of women asserting themselves in marriage, resisting male authority. Some women spoke of leaving drunkards. One woman told me how she had run off with another man, leaving her husband and children, then quarrelled with this man too. Finding herself in town with a small child and unable to return home, she had looked for work. Few women chose to be left to fend for themselves, however, especially where they had children to care for as well. In half the cases women had left children with their mothers, to whom they were struggling to send remittances; in others the children had been taken by the father. Occasionally children are brought with their mother to town if there are relatives there who can care for them. Two examples illustrate the problems and the potential for women after divorce.

Asha, a Sambaa woman from the Usambara mountains, was married for around ten years to a man who worked for Indians in Tanga first as a laundryman and then as a watch repairer. She had five children by him, and spent her time commuting between Tanga and the countryside where they had a plot of land. She fell out with her husband because he took another wife. 'He didn't care for me any more. When we slept together he kept his clothes on. And I was still young!' After divorce she had to find some way of surviving in the rural area, and at first she cultivated on land given her by her father. Then, leaving her children behind with her mother, she came to her mother's sister's house in Tanga with several containers of maize which she had harvested. She sold the maize retail whilst she looked for work. She found a domestic job and she also met a man who wanted to marry her. She had several other jobs after marriage. Eventually she was able to bring her children to Tanga and she subsequently had two more.

Zuhura's life seems to have been dogged by misfortune. She was married to a man who worked as a market trader in Dar es Salaam, but she was left at home in the Usambara area to cultivate their land. She had four children, the first of whom was mentally handicapped. After eleven years of marriage she was divorced, and although her in-laws allowed her to go on cultivating, she had lost the remittances which her husband used to send: 'the land did not bring in any income. I had to find some way of feeding and clothing my children'. She came to Tanga to join her sister, and found a job working for an Indian family as a servant, whilst her sister looked after the children. At first she nearly turned down the job because the wage offered was less than the official minimum wage. 'If it's like that', she told them, 'it's better I return home and farm. With Sh500 I shall not be able to feed my children'. They then agreed to pay her the minimum wage, and she worked happily for three years, only to lose the job when she went on leave to visit her mother. An accident in which one of her children was hurt delayed her return and she found the job taken by another. She was looking for paid work again, but selling cooked beans as a stopgap measure.

Marriages can end through divorce or death whilst women are in town, or become fraught so that women can no longer depend on their husbands. Although they may have arrived as wives they do not necessarily stay so. They then find themselves obliged to work if they are to survive. Their situation in the labour market is not necessarily worse than that of any other women – indeed the absence of a husband can mean freedom to seek a variety of ways of earning an income.

It is salutory to compare the significance of divorce for men as opposed to women. For men, the divorce of a wife generally means the loss of labour on his land, and this can be serious if he is absent and depending on his wife to feed the children. Two men in my set were divorced: one had no children and had returned to a bachelor life. The other had been forced to let his wife keep their child as he had no way of providing for her. But it is not divorce which causes men to migrate, whereas for women in the rural areas, for whom it entails the loss of their means to a livelihood, migration may follow.

THE MIGRATION OF YOUNG PEOPLE: SURPLUS LABOUR AND THE PEASANT HOUSEHOLD

So far we have considered the contrasts between the sexes in terms of migratory experience. But generational differences add a further and distinctive strand to the argument. Most young men can look forward to being allocated land on marriage; most young women can look forward only to working the land of a husband. Until their marriage young men and women must labour on their parents' land. In theory they should be allocated land by the state, which guarantees the right to land of any individual, man or woman, if they cultivate it (Village Act 1975). In practice in many areas there is little land to spare.

Young men often leave home at this point to seek work in urban areas, indeed it was rare for them to leave for the first time at any other stage in their lives. The most common scenario was for them to help parents for a year or two on the land, often after completing a few years of schooling, and then to leave in their late adolescence. Their retrospective perceptions of this were of striking out for independence and adulthood. 'I had to make my own life' said one. 'I was a man', said another, now in his mid-fifties: 'I must work. I would want a wife and I couldn't expect my father to shoulder all the costs of this – I must help'. Many men explained their departure from home in terms of the need for cash, particularly for clothes. 'I saw I had no clothes, and my friends were coming from town with clothes. They looked smart so I thought, why not me too?' 'I wanted two or three shirts, but my father was hard-pressed for money and could only buy me one. So I decided to leave and stand on my own feet'. Younger men were still enjoying their 'freedom'. For them the town represented 'the light', 'tomorrow's life'. Older men had discovered it to be an illusion.

It is tempting to take these accounts at face value, as describing purely individual initiatives, or the 'only natural' behaviour of young men striving for independence. Aggregating them, a rather different picture emerges. The land on which their families depended was too little or too poor to produce a regular surplus. Men express this by saying: 'there is no money in farming', and 'there was food, but no cash'. In particular, there was little money to share with growing sons thinking of marriage, or in need of clothing. Underlying the 'urge for town', then, was rural poverty. As Attems (1969:5) and Glaeser (1980) comment of the Usambara area, subsistence farming, particularly in the context of land shortage, is rendered viable only by the export of surplus labour – and, one might add, by the easing out of surplus consumers.

If the migration of young men is a pattern of long standing, what is striking is that young women are now beginning to follow suit. The usual pattern is for girls to beg to go and visit a relative in town, most commonly an aunt. Occasionally it is parents they go to join after having been brought up by grandparents in rural areas. Once ensconced with relatives in town, they tend to overstay their welcome at around the same time that they realise everything in town costs money. Seeing other young women working they begin to search for jobs themselves.

Rashida came into Tanga to stay with her uncle, a self-employed shoe-maker, and his family. When she had been with them for some time, 'I saw young people like me earning for themselves, so I looked for a job'. She explained that she needed money for clothes, and the example she gave was telling: 'You can't ask male relatives to buy you spare knickers for when your time of the month comes – it would be shameful'. She found work as a servant. After quarrelling with her employer she returned home to Mlalo, but within a year she had married a bus-driver and returned with him to Tanga. Many of the young women who migrate independently end up by returning home to marry, whilst others find husbands in town. But they seek husbands who do not leave them in rural areas to cultivate.

Sometimes young women are thwarted and their dreams turn sour. Bihawa came from Mlalo to her aunt in Tanga, initially to help her clear land nearby. Then she heard of a servant job and worked for several months, only to lose the job when the employer was transferred. She started training in dressmaking but became pregnant by a boyfriend who turned out to be already married. He did not marry her and has undermined her independence by forbidding her to sell cooked food at the roadside.

One of the oldest women I interviewed had run away from home to Moshi with a boyfriend in the 1940s, but he then died. She supported herself up until the 1970s through a variety of jobs in factories and twice as a domestic servant. When she was in her late forties she married a man who was a skilled urban worker and they came together to live in Tanga, where he was born. This 'freedom' was facilitated by her never bearing a child.

Not all young women make the journey to town voluntarily. Some are 'sent for' by relatives in town needing help, as Bihawa was. Only later do they seek paid work. Occasionally they are 'contracted' to work as domestic servants by their parents, sometimes for relatives. In these cases all or a part of the wage may be delivered to the parents rather than to the girl herself.

Mary had many brothers and sisters and her parents were elderly and infirm by the time she left school. 'The land we had was not enough to feed us all'. When she was seventeen, a local woman who had become a teacher in Dar es Salaam came home to look for a girl to assist her in the house. Mary was suggested, so the woman, who was unrelated to them, came to talk to her parents. 'They agreed, they saw it would help them'. Half of her wage was sent back to her parents, whilst she had the rest 'to buy clothes'.

When asked to explain why they left home single women often account for their actions in the same terms as young men, citing their wish for independence. They say: 'I was tired of staying with my parents', or 'I wanted to see new things'. Their departure is not, however, viewed in the same light as that of young men. Men in general were opposed, and expressed the view that women these days were out of (men's) control. One man said he would never agree to his daughter coming to town: 'It's not good. She will probably become a hooligan [*muhuni* – for women it carries the clear implication of sexual promiscuity]. Daughters who come to town like this are the product of bad upbringing. And when they return home it will be difficult for them to find husbands. Men would say she is *muhuni*, she won't want to cultivate, she will be "spoiled"'.

One factor which undermines paternal control over daughters is that fathers may be away working at the very time that their daughters are at home chafing to be free. To evade the perceived danger of young women's 'flight into decadence' (Bozzoli 1991:110), fathers are anxious to see their daughters married off. Young women are very aware of this, and of their fathers' reasoning. 'I might get pregnant and it would be very shameful'. 'They married me off early. They were afraid I would become promiscuous'. 'As soon as my breasts stood up I was married off'. In some cases this was pre-emptive action; in others it was a response of fathers to their daughters leaving home and asserting their independence by finding work. As soon as they returned home 'to see mama', their fathers put their foot down.

Some girls are resistant, but most are not. Indeed we may see the migration of young women as in some degree motivated by the desire for marriage, rather than a determination to be independent.[13] In some rural areas young men leave to seek wage work in urban areas just at the time when they might be courting young women, hence creating a situation in which women cannot easily find husbands. In some areas in Usambara there are more than double as many women than men in the age group 20–24 (TIRDEP 1975:34; Census 1988). Some young women believe their chances of marriage are improved by migrating themselves. If they do not find a husband in town, then, on their return, well-dressed and with cash in pocket, they will be seen as more desirable by the diminished pool of potential suitors. In this belief they counter the views of older men as to their unmarriageability.[14]

One girl whose father had insisted she marry after two years away working said: 'I succumbed to the temptation and married. It was easy to get a husband'. Other women who were listening in to this account agreed. 'Men are looking for a woman who has shown herself resourceful and hard-working'. 'They like a woman who has made good use of her time – then a man knows you will be useful to him too – you will guard and increase his wealth, tend the children, have his food ready and his clothes washed.' 'If you have good clothes men are attracted to you'. All this speaks for itself of the assumptions which such young women have about the desirability of marriage, but also of their expectations regarding their future role as wives – the theme of 'service' is overwhelming. In escaping from the restrictions of daughterhood they actively embrace another form of oppression.

Although it seems evident that young women were flouting paternal authority by finding work in town when they had only been given permission to visit relatives, it could be argued that parental resistance to such departures was more ritualised than real. Older women from these same rural areas point out that families whose land is limited find adolescent girls as much a drain on already stretched resources as boys – they eat too much, need clothes and help to marry, and their labour is marginal to production. Parents are not entirely unhappy then, when sons and even daughters want to leave home. This is reflected in young women's explanations for leaving home – not only did they want money to buy clothes, but also: 'you can't depend on your parents for ever' and 'the land was not enough to feed us all'. The departure of such women eases pressure on the peasant production unit rather than undermining it.

WHY DOMESTIC SERVICE?

The men and women described here had few marketable skills and little formal education.[15] They began seeking wage work without any particular ambition to be employed as domestic servants. Any unskilled job would do – work was work, and they did not see themselves as discriminating. As one woman said: 'if you face hardship you do anything – you would be ready to clean shit from lavatories so long as your children are clothed and fed'. Another said 'without education you have few choices'. Some did find other work – especially in unskilled and labour intensive factory work. Women might also become barworkers, cleaners or street sweepers; men might be dockers, navvies, 'turn boys' on lorries or hotel workers. People began to build up skills or aptitudes once in a job; though these capacities were not always recognised by later employers. After people had done a range of jobs – acquired by luck and often lost through no fault of their own, they might be more discriminating. Servant work is then sought by some despite its low pay and aspects of servility.

One man had worked as a servant but was now humping cement sacks into lorries. Although this was casual and exhausting work it paid well. One day, however, his old employer came looking for him to work as a servant again. He was bitterly disappointed to have missed him – the work was less arduous and 'in an emergency when you need money the boss can be expected to help you out'. The personalisation of servant work attracted others too, when compared to the impersonality of work for large organisations. A man who was working in a small factory was more than ready to agree when his boss asked him to be his houseservant instead. He stayed with the family for nine years, receiving what he felt to be 'human' consideration. A woman with a lifetime of servant work behind her made another comparison. As a servant you had an informal relationship with your employer and might receive sympathy, money and gifts, whereas an office cleaner is unseen and ignored.

Whilst domestic service is understood to be work of low status (*kazi ya chini*) and some are ashamed of doing it or prefer other work (if they can get it), many point out that it is not necessarily more oppressive than other alternatives. Barwork can be dangerous when men get drunk and pull knives; factory labour can entail working in polluted conditions or operating machines which never stop. Non-domestic employers do not always treat their employees better, nor have other types of employment expanded. By the 1990s, however, the state's hold over agricultural marketing had relaxed and older men without skills or education were increasingly looking to trade rather than employment to make a living, leaving domestic service to younger men and more particularly to women.

CONCLUSION

When men explain the movement of women into jobs such as those of domestic service by saying: 'In the old days men had control over their wives – neither fathers nor husbands would have allowed their wives or daughters to work', we hear not the voice of the past, but the reverberations of present domestic struggles. It is not that men's control over their womenfolk was ever absolute; in precolonial times there were many forces which undermined the operation of patriarchy on a domestic scale (the emergence of kingdoms such as that of the Sambaa, slavery, and uncontrollable natural disasters), and following colonial intervention domestic patriarchs were themselves subordinated to coercive demands for labour via the extension of capitalist agriculture. With the squeeze on subsistence producers men's exodus as migrant labourers ironically strengthened their hold over wives who increasingly had to bear the burden of feeding families in the absence of husbands. If anything this burden has become heavier since Tanzania became independent.

The 'socialist' experiment in agriculture did not eliminate plantation agriculture (though some sisal estates were taken over by the state) or stem the emergence of local kulak farming. In the Usambara area in particular the extended pressure on land speeded processes of ecological degradation. More recently the freeing up of commercial relations has allowed some men (and even some women) to profit from trade and move out of wage work. But peasant families in general are squeezed, and within those families women are the most marginalised as their duties are great and their rights conditional. The ultimate irony is for the state then to proclaim that their equality with men demands that they too pay tax.

It is in this context that small domestic skirmishes begin to take place, minor disputes turn into extended battles, and those who expect to control find their expectations unfulfilled. Wives pressure husbands for permission to join them in town, daughters demand to go and 'greet aunty', sons leave home. Men find themselves having to let their children go as the wherewithal to support them diminishes, and they are aware that wives who receive meagre remittances become difficult. Both married and single women are conscious that marriage is still their major route to security, though they do not trust men to deliver. The contradictions press in ever more heavily but they affect men and women in different ways, with women responding to the deepening hardships of rural life by forms of resistance to male control.

Resistance which leads to migration has no clear outcome, but it may well entail women being oppressed and subordinated in other contexts – as wage workers or as petty commodity producers. Like men they become exploitable outside the context of family relations. And once forced to seek work, men and women may find themselves gendered in the labour market and the production process in ways that differentiate their bargaining power as workers: as in this case, where women were less welcome as domestic workers than men and often paid considerably less. Gender distinctions here can not be theoretically determined – they are a matter of empirical investigation. Labour market conditions do not always favour men over women,[16] nor do they necessarily differ for men and women.[17]

Local men (especially the Sambaa) began to move into wage labour in Tanga in the inter-war years, and once there constituted a pool of 'green' labour competing for the poorest paid jobs and undercutting men from other areas who had previously established themselves in the town. Amongst the jobs they moved into were domestic work. In the 1970s another wave of green labour began to enter the local job market – that of women, and especially young women, who by the mid-'80s were making inroads into the least desirable jobs, but also those demanding the least prior training. Again domestic service was a major example. Now they began to undercut men, or more particularly older men, for their labour was offered cheap. It is this feature, the cheapness of green labour, which leads to the feminisation of domestic service at this point, whereas in the colonial period it had led to competition between men.

SERVING THE DOMINANT CLASS: CONSPICUOUS CONSUMPTION AND PETTY ACCUMULATION

'I can afford it: that is why I employ three servants'   *(Asian employer)*
'My house is the visiting card of myself and my husband: we expect it to be kept up properly'   *(European employer)*
'Maybe when my cows calve I will be able to employ extra domestic help'
(African employer)

There is a tension built into the emergence of a new 'ruling' class in Tanzania and other developing countries – a tension between the disciplined sacrifice and frugality of the drive to accumulate, and the tendency towards an expressive consumptionism which marks out a privileged section of society. In this chapter I explore the extent to which domestic service is caught up in these tendencies, which are both contradictory and complementary. I shall argue that, in Tanzania at least, the employment of servants is only partially an instance of class display. Whilst there are elements amongst the dominant class for whom servant keeping has a predominant function of demonstrating wealth and position and allowing for unproductive 'idleness', there are others for whom it is also a prerequisite for accumulation, albeit on a petty scale.[1]

At a time when the language of 'class' has been discredited in social science, swept out by the postmodernist ejection of metanarratives, it is worth exploring its use here, especially in the context of societies without a lengthy history of capitalist development. Class is defined here not in terms of gradations of wealth or income, but as a dynamic marker of social place in relation to changing economic systems. It is politically as well as economically contextualised, with emergent classes having a creative relation to politico-economic processes and structures, rather than being simply their creature.[2]

Domestic service is first and foremost an indicator of a class-divided society in which some social groupings with control over resources require others to labour for them. As we have seen, it is not only a class phenomenon; it also traverses gendered relationships and cultural reproduction. There are two aspects to any analysis of domestic service as a class phenomenon. First is the exploration of *class relations*: the organisation of labour and its utilisation in varied tasks; hierarchy as manifested in control and surveillance of the labour process; forms of exploitation and lateral relations of solidarity. In workplaces which are also homes, this is manifested in a micro-politics of class relations cross-cut by gender and ethnic power which I shall touch on here and explore further in the following chapter. The other aspect of class which a focus on domestic service allows us to consider is the unfolding development of *class cultures*. Here the concern is with processes of display and forms of reproduction of the class as a social group as well as with its political modes of defensive and offensive action. Looking at these processes from the angle of domestic service allows for exploration of both the public roles and the private lives of the dominant class in Tanzanian society. This latter feature is one which has been touched on only infrequently in accounts of African ruling classes (though see Stichter 1988; Oppong 1974; and studies of domestic service in Africa previously cited).

DOMESTIC SERVICE AND CLASS ANALYSIS

In his classic study of the 'leisure class' (1899) Veblen argues that the keeping of domestic servants, and particularly those who are manifestly engaged in non-utilitarian activities, is a key mechanism by which the dominant class demonstrates its position: 'the chief use of servants is the evidence they afford of the master's ability to pay ... the need of vicarious leisure, or conspicuous consumption of service is a dominant incentive to the keeping of servants' (62). In his commentary on Victorian England, Burnett makes a similar point, noting the existence of a vast army of domestic servants: 'By their number, dress and function they proclaimed in an outward and visible way the degree of success that their employer had attained and, by implication, conferred upon him membership of the class' (1974:176).

If the institution of domestic service acts as a demonstration effect of class privilege, this is not to be adduced as the driving force of class formation. Both Veblen and Burnett are writing of societies with well-established class divisions based on fairly mature capitalist economies. Africa is another continent – though many have supposed it to be following in the same direction. Lubeck's collection of three case studies in *The African Bourgeoise* (1987) focused on three African countries (Kenya, Nigeria and Ivory Coast) described as 'in transition to capitalism' with emergent 'indigenous accumulating classes'. What was at issue was the nature of such classes. Kitching, in the same work, commented that, whilst capitalist development would seem to call for the adoption of a 'bourgeois ideology' of thrift and industry, 'there seems to be a persistent orientation toward ... conspicuous consumption' (1987:51–2). This suggests that display may precede or inhibit accumulation, and raises the possibility that one manifestation might be in domestic service.

Work of this kind was in an established tradition of Marxist or neo-Marxist scholarship on post-colonial Africa where the character of class formation, economic transformation and state power were central concerns.[3] Tanzania had always proved a difficult case to encompass in classically Marxist terms. Not only did it, from the Arusha Declaration of 1967 onwards, declare for 'socialism' as the only 'rational choice' if social justice was to accompany economic development in a small ex-colonial territory (Nyerere 1973 in Coulson 1979); for almost two decades thereafter it adopted a radical and hostile stance towards private enterprise.[4] Debate in Tanzania therefore ranged around the character of a dominant class which rested on state power rather than private accumulation (Shivji 1976; von Freyhold 1977; Saul 1983).

In the decade since Lubeck's collection was published, the very enterprise of class analysis has been thrown into question: as Shivji notes, Marxist concepts have 'gone out of fashion, have become dirty words' (1991:80). There are many reasons for this: the collapse of communist regimes at the end of the 1980s and an ensuing period of capitalist triumphalism rendered any alternative views of the world suspect for a considerable period. Developed capitalist societies were also said to have changed in ways that made the concept of 'class' redundant: already in 1987 Lash and Urry were insisting that: 'All that is solid about organised capitalism, class [etc] ... melts into air' (1987:313). Postmodernist ways of thinking foregrounded other and pluralistic forms of identity; fragmentation and difference were the motifs of the new age.

This intellectual shift in the North has impacted on scholarship in Africa and perspectives on Africa at a time of considerable social upheaval. Phrases such as 'the transition to capitalism' with its attendant class labels have been generally abandoned as economic growth has faltered and other less appealing dominant groups come to the fore.[5] At the same time neo-liberal economic recipes for economic development (themselves a product of organised global capital) are actually promoting emergent entrepreneurial classes through the discrediting of state economic intervention, the privatisation of state assets and the destruction of state welfare systems ('structural adjustment'). Class divisions are further heightened by the extension of capitalist forms of production in agriculture and the weakening hold of the poorest on the land. This comes at a time when the language of class is discredited and in its place has come an often obfuscating discourse of human rights, democracy and individualism, with ethnicity often seen as the key social division.

Tanzania is not an example where local conflicts and divisions can easily be read as 'ethnically' inspired;[6] nor has it suffered the collapse into anarchy and war that have beset some countries in Africa. It has weathered the collapse of the 'socialist'/ single-party system to re-emerge as a 'multi-party democracy' with a mixed economy. My argument is that class interests were being forged in the period of socialism and have been reworked in the post-socialist phase. In the socialist phase public rhetoric projected an image of 'leadership' in which private accumulation was to play no part, and in which selfless dedication to the people was to elbow out ostentatious show. By the mid-1980s, when the bulk of this research was carried out, the gulf between rhetoric and reality was already well exposed and private accumulation was proceeding apace, but clandestinely, especially amongst those who were functionaries of the state and who could exploit their relationship to the state apparatus. This period legitimised the discrediting of those who had dominated commerce and industry in Tanzania since the colonial period – namely Asian entrepreneurs, whose activities were now publicly denoted as capitalist exploitation, and who were excluded from state patronage (Bujra 1992a). Putting this in another way: older forms of private accumulation were discouraged and disparaged in favour of a new form of public accumulation via the state. At the same time alliances of interest were forged between state functionaries and local agents of international capital through collaboration in joint ventures.

This research highlights the moment when 'socialist' class formation had reached its limits and documents the role of domestic service in expressing and underwriting it. It discloses an employing class whose fractions can be clearly seen to represent the interests of state technocrats, international capital and beleaguered private capital, whilst at the same time these also reflect a historical legacy of 'racial' distinction. Later observations confirm a subsequent process of class consolidation in which accumulated wealth has been put more openly to use and domestic workers have continued to service class privilege and entrepreneurship.

THE EMPLOYING CLASS

One problem in writing about the employers of domestic servants in class terms is that in Tanga (and throughout Tanzania) the predominant mode of discourse in such matters is one of 'race', with the different groupings characterised in terms of colour or originating area. This is particularly true for domestic servants themselves, who are firmly of the belief that employers of different 'racial' origins offer distinctive terms of employment. The term 'race' is a problematic one, often used to legitimate a belief that genetic differences explain social behaviour. This myth is here rejected, whilst acknowledging that in Tanzania it is widely held to be true and socially deployed. The term 'ethnicity' is sometimes used in the same (ideological) way, but more commonly and usefully held to denote the cultural distinctions which groups claiming a common origin use to mark off their differences. In Tanga there were some cultural differences which coincided with named 'racial' groups – Goans were Christian; Arabs Muslim – but in other cases these categories were culturally diverse (the Europeans originating from various countries and backgrounds; the 'Asians' mostly born in East Africa and sharply divided by religion; Africans both Christian and Muslim and speaking a diversity of mother tongues) but they were highly significant groups in terms of how people identified themselves, were seen by others and related socially.

It is difficult to resist racialised stereotypes in this context as there is a marked degree of coincidence between the categories they delineate and the fractions of the dominant class. This can be seen in my Tanga survey of high level formal employers (of servants) in 1986. They fell into five groups based on the economic role of male heads of households (their wives are considered later):

1. High level state functionaries at the executive level, both managing economic concerns (parastatal companies and infrastructural facilities) and in local administration or as directly political agents (high party officials). This category included a Regional Party Secretary, Regional Development Director, Police Commander and Port Manager, all Africans. The category also included a few Europeans representing the interests of multinational companies in partnership with the state such as the managing directors of the Fertiliser Factory (a joint venture).

2. Lower level but still powerful professionals and managers of state enterprises such as bank manager, hotel managers and accountants, doctors, officials of the Regional Trading Company, customs and railways etc. as well as foreign NGO experts servicing aid projects such as the Tanga Integrated Rural Development Plan. Apart from the European foreigners, all of these were again Africans.

3. Private capital, almost solely in the hands of Asians and Arabs, ranging at one extreme from petty retailers living over the shop in the bustling centre of the town, to the owners of small or large companies, in chemicals, transport, clothes manufacturing, printing, cosmetics etc, some of whom lived in large and luxurious suburban houses.

4. Employees of private capital at the managerial, professional and supervisory levels – the only category which included representatives of all 'racial' groups.

5. and 6 are residual categories of those who are either retired or whose income derives from lowly self-employment as artisans (shoemakers, a goldsmith). Also included here is a free-lance auditor.

The degree of coincidence between class position and 'racial' categories is remarkably high here (see Table 7.1), indicating two aspects of the postcolonial phase of class formation. Even twenty-five years after Independence

Table 7.1 The relationship between class fractions and 'racial' groups: Employers' Survey 1986 (male heads of household)

Class fractions	'Racial categories'							
	Africans		Europeans		Asians*		Total	
	No.	%	No.	%	No.	%	No.	%
1. State functionaries (executive level)/foreign collaborators	6	27	2	28	–	–	8	(13%)
2. State functionaries (managerial, professional and supervisory)/foreign NGO experts	13	59	3	43	–	–	16	(27%)
3. Private capital	1	5	–	–	24	77	25	(42%)
4. Employees of private capital (managerial, professional and supervisory)	2	9	1	14	2	6	5	(8%)
5. Self-employed professionals/ artisans	–	–	–	–	4	13	4	(7%)
6. Retired	–	–	1	14	1	3	2	(3%)
Total	22	(36%)	7	(12%)	31	(52%)	60	

* Goans and Arabs are included here, as they fell into similar class fractions as Asians, and only small numbers were involved. African workers make a point of distinguishing them however.

colonial patterns had not been written out – in particular Africans had found no niche in private enterprise in Tanga. Secondly the state was the key employer of African labour at the highest level and their source of politico-economic power. It is worth adding that whilst ethnic/cultural differences amongst Africans (locally described in terms of 'tribe' or 'peoples') were also the subject of local stereotyping, they do not tie in to class distinctions. The same would apply to religious differences within and between 'racial' groups.

The style of life adopted by these various categories set them apart from the rest of the population of Tanga: manual workers and the petty self-employed, who lived largely on the other side of the railway tracks in high-density single-storey housing. The well-off, if not residing in or near the centre of town to protect their commercial property, lived in leafy suburbs, in substantial, often two-storey houses, which were comfortable and well-furnished (though by no means sumptuous in the style of some African countries). African state functionaries had inherited the large and comfortable homes of former colonial officials or houses which had been appropriated from rich landlords by the state in 1971. Such houses often had servants' quarters attached. The usual complement of insecurity with wealth was apparent in night watchmen, occasionally barbed-wire and gates, fierce dogs and the like, though not to the degree that these phenomena manifest themselves in Nigeria, Kenya or South Africa.

Almost without exception they employed servants or were seeking

Table 7.2 Employment of servants by class fraction and 'racial' categories

2a Employment of servants by 'racial' category

	% employing servants	No of servants	Average per employer	% of women servants	% working wives
Europeans	100%	26	3.7	8%	20%
Asians (inc. Goans and Arabs)	76%	49	2	33%	7%
Africans	55%	22	1.8	36%	54.5%

2b Employment of servants by class fraction

	% employing servants*	No. of servants	Average per employer	% working wives
1. State functionaries (executive level)/foreign collaborators	88%	23	3.2	37.5%
2. State functionaries (managerial, professional and supervisory)/foreign NGO experts	44%	17	2.4	60%
3. Private capital	84%	44	2	8%
4. Employees of private capital (managerial, professional and supervisory)	100%	7	1.4	50%
5. Self–employed professionals/artisans	75%	4	1.3	–
6. Retired	50%	2	2	–
Total	73%	97	2.2	27%

* This refers to current employment. All had either employed servants in the past or were presently seeking domestic help.

servants. There were some distinctive differences, however, in the style in which this was done and in Tanga these were again perceived in 'racial' terms. My data (see Table 7.2a) tend to support the view of servants themselves, which was that Europeans employed the most servants and paid them the highest wages. They were also more likely to hire male servants and to support specialists such as washermen or cooks. Africans were seen to pay the lowest wages, to rely on a single general servant, and to hire more women, including poor relations or young people brought from the rural areas whose position was highly ambiguous. They were least likely to be currently employing a formally designated servant although they had done so in the past and were usually seeking to do so again. Asians were perceived, and in general were, somewhere in the middle on all these counts.

These differences do not stem from cultural dictates or from genetics.

They flow rather from differentials in what Veblen identified as 'ability to pay', but what underlies this is the emergent character of different class fractions (see Table 7.2b where the same data is presented in class terms). Both the largely Asian petty bourgeoisie and the African state functionary class are driven by the need to accumulate in order to survive, whereas the European expatriate element is not. Although in all of these groups there is evidence of servants being employed to conspicuously demonstrate superior class position, this is more to the fore with the alien rich than with the locals. Conversely the very visibility of racialised difference creates an issue for African employers who lack these symbolic 'racial' props to power/authority and need to create others to substitute for them.[7]

COLONIAL MODELS

It is the colonial experience which lends symbolic force to the social relations of formal domestic service in Tanzania today. During that period the relationship between servant and employer was one underwritten by very visible 'racial' distinctions: African servants were employed by European, Asian or Arab employers. The exercise of power was reinforced by a gulf of social distance in which the enjoyment of wealth, the mystique of 'colour', culture and language separated the two sides. An old ex-servant summed it up when he said of his wealthy Asian employer in the late fifties: 'I addressed him as "Great Master" (*Bwana Mkubwa*) – that was what was expected in those days: "I hear you Great Master" ... In those days you were constantly at their beck and call, but you didn't question it: white people [sic] had power and you accepted it and obeyed'. Or as a retired European employer described those days: 'all the Boys belonged absolutely to the family'.

The other feature of colonial domestic service, that it was gendered male, is also pertinent here. Veblen remarks that the demonstration effect of servant keeping is heightened where servants are male rather than female, since this practice involves the squandering of a man's more valuable labour (57). This thesis may draw as much on Veblen's patriarchal assumptions as upon patriarchal reality, and in this case, as we have seen, the domestic labour-force simply mirrored the gender composition of wage labour in general in colonial Tanzania. Colonial class relations generally entailed males exerting class power over other males: what was transgressive about domestic class relations was that men became subject to women. The employer a servant had most dealings with was not another man like himself, but the mistress of the house. As a rule it was she who hired him, she who determined his conditions of work, she who supervised him day by day, she who punished him for misdemeanours, and in the end maybe even she who dismissed him.

Until belts had to be tightened in and following the Second World War, it was common for European and wealthy Asian families to have large households of servants. One old man began his working life, aged twelve, as a nurseboy for a European who owned a company and several houses. At his residence he employed several servants – a Headboy, a houseboy, a cook, a pantry boy and a washerman as well as gardeners and probably watchmen as well. All wore uniform, even the young Suedi was fitted out with a white Muslim robe and cap. Not only was this conspicuous evidence of his master's wealth and position but Suedi himself basked in the reflected glory. His pride on being promoted to houseboy was still vividly remembered sixty years later ('then I was a real Boy and I was able to boast!').

Servant-keeping allowed some colonials – or perhaps their wives – to live a private life of relative ease in what were for them difficult physical circumstances. Servants relieved the mistress of the house of many dirty and arduous tasks, and hence might be perceived as simply a utilitarian necessity, were it not that their labour being dirt cheap relative to the salaries of colonial officials, it was conspicuously wasted. Many servants performed non-utilitarian tasks of a distinctively ceremonial character (as Veblen designates them): 'S, my last houseboy, did my husband's uniform and evening kit very well indeed. Also as a waiter he was superb and laid a dinner table perfectly.' 'All our servants were very loyal and excellent workers and maintained the standards of my own senior appointment' (personal communications, ex-colonial officials). Much of their time might simply be spent being 'available' to be called when required. Again Veblen's point is pertinent here: the inefficiency or irrationality of such a practice is beside the point when the point is rather to maintain class position by demonstrating how much labour one can afford to waste.

CONTEMPORARY DOMESTIC SERVICE AS CONSPICUOUS CONSUMPTION

To what extent did the emergent class fraction of African state functionaries borrow from this older model of domestic service as opposed to creating new forms of their own? In Tanga in the mid-1980s the extravagant show of the past was rare, and it was only European expatriates and wealthy local businessmen (Asian) who could afford to be served so ostentatiously. Two examples illustrate this style, one described from the perspective of a servant, the other through the eyes of the employer.

Hassani worked for one of the richest men in Tanzania, an Asian businessman who owned several companies located in Tanga. His house was very large and grand, built in the Spanish style, encircled with a huge garden, and with servants' quarters set to one side. Hassani, unlike many servants who prefer to live out, actually occupied the servant's room allocated to him. He had worked more than twenty-five years for this employer and many of the other six servants were of long-standing. Hassani described himself in colonial terminology as a 'boy' (albeit in his mid-sixties) and the other servants as cook, 'cook's boy', another 'houseboy', washerman, and two gardeners. Almost certainly there were watchmen as well. All the servants, it should be noted, were men, supervised by the woman of the house who did not go out to work. The ceremonial nature of his work is evident. He described his job as to 'flick a duster around, make the place look smart', but more particularly to look after the constant stream of guests visiting the house. His employer entertained lavishly with parties for one to two hundred people. Hassani referred to him as Mzee (elder), 'out of respect', but although Hassani was also elderly, his employer did not reciprocate, nor was this resented: 'He is superior to me. He is rich – he has so much money'.

A European woman, wife of an expatriate manager in a jointly-owned state-multinational enterprise, hired six domestic staff to keep up her very smart and large new house. Two of these were employed as guards to watch her property night and day, one was a 'shamba boy' (her term, i.e. a gardener). The other three worked in the house: one as a 'headboy', one a cook, and one as a 'housegirl'. Except for the latter all were male and she ruled them with a very firm hand and without any intervention from her husband: 'I do not interfere in his work, so why should he interfere in mine?' There were no concessions to egalitarianism here: the servants, 'must know that I am the boss, I am in control'. She conspicuously demonstrated her ability to pay by offering wages almost double the official minimum wage to those who fulfilled her exacting standards. Their membership of her household was advertised to the world by her provision of a basic uniform, with special accoutrements for the cook including a chef's hat brought from Europe. In order to emphasise the difference in status between herself and the servants she determinedly kept a certain distance, and she preferred to forego the constant availability of servants (they did not live on the premises) in order to have a separate 'private life' when they had completed their work and gone home.

Mrs Frau saw herself as struggling to maintain the style of life which servant-keeping allowed: she used to have eight servants, but as the minimum wage crept up she had cut back on numbers whilst determined to maintain standards. The utility of servants was part of her rationalisation for having so many : they had a continuous flow of visitors, and in any case 'why should I do all that work myself? – I wouldn't have time to do anything else'. The leisure time which Mrs Frau purchased by employing servants was spent on 'good works', the Red Cross, distribution of second-hand clothes, helping to organise a kindergarten, etc. But for her, the ultimate goal of the exercise was clearly one of conspicuous consumption: 'My house is the visiting card of myself and my husband. We expect it to be kept up properly'.

The wealth of employers such as these[8] was not accompanied by local political dominance, although they did wield influence through bodies like the Rotary Club (largely European) and the Lions Club (largely Asian), both of which were at the time urgently seeking African membership to justify their existence (African state functionaries – or rather the men of this class, preferred social clubs where drinking and eating roast meat were accompanied by talk about politics and procuring supplies.)

In expatriate and wealthy Asian business households, servants' labour supported the conspicuous consumption of leisure, allowing wives to withdraw from household toil, and to idle time away in resting, visiting friends or in pleasanter pursuits. In rare cases wives had paid employment; often they were engaged in charity work, itself a marker of class differences (Caplan 1978). They were more likely to rationalise their employment of servants in terms of a desire for comfort and their ability to pay for it. Only amongst these employers were servants provided with a uniform (usually shorts and shirt, rather than the elaborate livery of the past such as 'kanzu [kaftan] with cummerbund').

Amongst African state functionaries, and amongst smaller private entrepreneurs (Asians), such examples of conspicuous consumption of service are rare, though not entirely absent. Amongst these class elements lower incomes, and certain other factors to be discussed presently, come to the fore in determining the mode of conspicuous consumption adopted.

The following account of a dinner-party gives some idea of the style in which lower level state functionaries make symbolic statements about their class superiority. The man of the house was an official in the state-controlled retail trade company and his wife a bank official. They lived in a spacious but shabby government flat on the outskirts of the town centre:

> We ate well, with cutlery (which this family did not normally use), and to the music of Jim Reeves. Bottled beer was pressed on the guests, an inordinately expensive luxury in Tanzania at the time and presumably accessible to the man of the house through his work. Two servant girls padded in and out silently on bare feet, placing dishes on the table and removing them after we had eaten. The children of guests and family were very much the centre of attention and considerably indulged, especially the only child of the family, a bright and charming six year old. Much was made of the fact that this little boy was now attending the International Kindergarten, a private establishment, 'where children really learn and are taught in English' (Swahili is the family language here, as well as the official and general lingua franca of Tanzania). Before we ate the children were herded out by one of the servant girls – children and servants ate together on the kitchen floor.

Various elements of ceremonial display were evident here, and the role of the servants was clearly more than utilitarian, but both were very young women. They were paid below the official minimum wage, but lived in, sleeping with the child of the family. They were the silent backcloth to indulgence, shabby and ill at ease.

Amongst Africans, domestic service as conspicuous consumption might be indicated by the size of establishments. Certainly the highest state functionaries employed the most servants (see Table 7.2b) and only one of these officials claimed to have no servants. It was one of these high executives of state who cited the number of visitors as a reason for employing servants. And the house was becoming a common class rationale in itself – Africans, Asians and Europeans all referred to the necessity of having servants to protect one's house, including fittings and furniture. The house itself made a statement about class level that went way beyond utilitarian need. It was a rich owner of a company (Asian) who is described in my notes as having a house 'like an illustration out of Homes and Gardens', but African state functionaries were also investing in home comforts which needed protection. I described the house of one high state executive as 'sumptuous' with carpets, carved doors, beautiful polished furniture, bookcases full of books, glass-fronted cupboards displaying crockery, glasses, carvings and vases, and paintings on the wall. Few others lived so handsomely, and sometimes the large houses they had been allocated were beyond their means to furnish adequately, but most had good furniture, radios, stereo music systems and some decorative effects. Whilst Africans needed watchmen and servants to protect these possessions they were rarely owners of their houses as Asians were – the houses came with the job. The same might apply to most of the Europeans here.

The maintenance of smart and clean clothes fitting to a person's status was not only a colonial imperative. It continued to be a reason cited for employing servants – though from their accounts it was Asians who so frequently changed their clothes that no-one without a servant could manage ('every day there were fifty or more garments to be washed and ironed', complained one servant). This was a period when few, even at this class level, could afford washing machines nor were they freely available. Europeans and wealthy Asians were more likely to have found ways of importing machines, though they then became very possessive of them and were wary about servants misusing them. The only labour saving devices that were common to all these employers were the electric iron and a cooker of some kind. Quite a few also had refrigerators. Such items were as much symbols of status as they were of utility.

Families at this class level were generally larger than most by virtue of their superior position in society. In Asian business families, even limited entrepreneurial success was often accompanied by large households: joint families supporting many dependents. African families at the highest level are also prone to expand according to their perceived means, with hangers-on from the countryside, endless demanding visitors and often many children. A single servant might have to carry much of the drudgery of such a household, with the washing in particular taking a couple of hours a day. In Asian households the women of the household were also hard at work, especially cooking. Servants spoke of how they ate elaborate meals with a dozen different dishes (all to be washed up): 'not like us'. Employers of all colours ate well and saw the labour involved in cooking expensive foods to be an aspect of their need for servants. Giving leftovers to the servants emphasised the class superiority of employers and the lowliness of the serving class.

DOMESTIC SERVICE AND SOCIALIST RHETORIC

The advent of 'socialism' had little direct impact on the practice of employing servants. Rather the opposite: the state might pay for domestic help as a perk of high office – seven servants working for Africans were provided courtesy of employers. The wife of one very high official born in Zanzibar argued that it was difficult to get domestic help in Zanzibar nowadays because: 'the government has forbidden people to use others as servants' – but in Tanga they had three servants and she referred to one of them by the term *mtumishi*, which may be translated precisely as 'one who is used'. An ex-servant explained to me why this term was now locally unacceptable: 'it sounds to us too much like slavery (*utumwa*) – it is offensive'.

Something of 'socialist' ideology had been appropriated by servants in their expectations and accounts of employers. Most would now avoid addressing their employers as '*bwana*' or '*memsa'ab*' (master and lady), preferring instead the pseudo-familial terms of 'mama' (mother) and '*mzee*' (elder). This practice will be discussed further in Chapter 8; the point here is that the respect which such nomenclature carries is rarely reciprocated. One ex-domestic worker claimed that: 'The government has forbidden the use of "houseboy" and "housegirl"', though I could find no evidence of this. Servants who had worked during the colonial period would also say that employers who used to exploit their servants mercilessly were now 'afraid to use them badly' as they used to do – the fear being of the government.

A discourse of class superiority was certainly not tolerated in a period when the term '*ndugu*' ('brother' or 'relative' but here used to mean 'comrade') was employed to address even those in the highest circles. Employers' attitudes were more commonly embodied in a discourse of 'us' and 'them' which varied in terms of their own origins. Europeans and Asians might couch this in the language of 'race'. Thus one European commented critically on how new expatriate arrivals treated their servants, adding 'you need to be firm with Africans. You can't integrate them – they are different'. An Asian Muslim said that many Asians prefer to do their own cooking as they think 'African servants are not very clean in their habits –

they may scratch their heads and not wash their hands'; and it was an Asian employer who expressed her disdain for dirt and manual labour and those who perform it ('We like things to be very clean. We don't like to sweep ourselves'). Another generalised, 'these African chaps – you can't trust them'. These employers were also prone to claim that their class position entailed a higher moral virtue. A European employer commented: 'I know some Europeans when they hear you have servants say "bloody colonialist" ... but it is my duty to provide work for as many people as possible'. Whilst a more saintly Asian employer said piously, 'We must help them'.

African employers must of necessity employ a different discourse of difference – and in this case couched not in racial terms but by comparing urbanity with rural ignorance. Thus an African employer said: 'Care of a house in the rural area is not like here ... I am not yet satisfied with the standards of cleanliness she has achieved – though compared to this other girl that has just arrived ...!'. Another said: 'They forget to wash the cooker; they don't have those things at home'. An air of superiority is evident in comments like, 'They don't have education' or 'The way they live in the villages ... you have to teach them'.

If socialist ideology demands that people be treated equally and with respect, this is confounded by the institution of domestic service in its conspicuous consumption mode where it not only underlines class differentials between employer and worker, but also helps to maintain and demonstrate them to the world at large.

DOMESTIC SERVICE AND 'AFRICAN CULTURE'

If the rhetoric of socialist egalitarianism had little impact, there are other cultural constraints which inhibit the new employing class of African state functionaries from overt display of class superiority towards servants, in particular a hesitation regarding the deliberate rupture of culturally acceptable African styles and their modes of expression. Colloquial Swahili is common to both parties in the domestic service relationship, and cannot be used as a form of exclusion. They may resort to using English for this purpose, or their own local vernacular if this is different to that of the servant.

To assert the social distance necessary for keeping servants 'in order' is sometimes a matter of bridging or avoiding shared cultural assumptions. For example, the buttresses of age and gender might be brought in to reinforce an otherwise unnatural domination. It is culturally acceptable for young girls to be ordered about by older women as well as men, and to play a servicing role, and this was one reason why Africans tended to employ them, despite many disadvantages. Older women cannot be controlled in the same way: 'for we Africans it's not possible'. That it was not completely unthinkable is shown by two African employers who did employ older women, but clearly one of the difficulties that upper class Africans faced in attempting to subordinate fellow Africans was a shared recognition of the respect for age as fundamental to 'African traditions'. One of the older servants, in her fifties, was addressed as 'bibi' (grandmother); whilst in the other case it was 'mama': 'she is older than me so it is a matter of respect'.

To employ men may be even more culturally problematic. If they are also young, then the respect due to age over-rides the gender hierarchy: an older mistress may legitimately dominate adolescent boys. Where government or parastatal companies, as a perk of high office, pay the wages of servants or watchmen or gardeners, all the servants so employed are men, paid the official minimum wage. Otherwise, young female servants predominate amongst those serving African upper class families (see Table 7.2a), even whilst male servants are preferred. Sometimes these girls are poor relations, often they are 'ignorant country girls' who may be procured by way of one's own family in the rural areas. The wife of a Bank Manager, herself a secretary, told me that all her servants were sent from the countryside by her father-in-law, and the advantages were great: she knows who their parents are, and thus 'has someone to complain to if things go wrong'. Another woman had found all her servants through the church choir in her home area, seeing them as God-fearing and obedient.

But for others this solution was more problematic, because complaints can go in the other direction. Such servants may become 'too familiar' and familiarity breeds contempt. One woman described this process in exactly these terms, adding 'if they were working for Indians or Europeans they would be a little bit afraid, but for their fellow Swahili [here meaning Africans] they are contemptuous'. The comment of another woman raises a separate point: 'I brought two girls from home but it was very unsatisfactory. They went home telling all sorts of lies about me – that I used them "like servants" (*kama watumishi*), that I was always ordering them about, that I sat around and didn't do anything – they sent home so many malicious stories!' This comment is telling because the employer behaviour she describes is in fact a 'normal' employer relationship vis-à-vis servants. Clearly it conflicted with more egalitarian village notions of how Africans should treat one another, and in her view diminished her in the eyes of village people who were still part of her social circle.

If the employment of Africans means treating fellow Africans as inferiors, with the impersonal cash nexus as the only bond (or as one woman put it very firmly 'it is a *work* relationship'), then it may be more comfortable to engage those who do not belong to your own particular ethnic group. I found that more than half of African employers and their servants were of different 'tribal' origins. One could assert authority over such people without it having repercussions, because in ethnic terms they were already socially 'distant'.[9] Financial constraints often dictated taking poor relations (usually girls) as servant substitutes, but this was also conceded to be problematic. As one woman said: 'If I could not afford servants I would bring my sister, but it's better to employ someone. If it is your relative they can refuse to do things, get offended, say you are "using" them all the time – it happened when my sister was here before'.

In various ways then, cultural pressures dictate and inhibit the way in which African employers feel able to exploit their African servants.

SOCIALIST AUSTERITY AND PETTY ACCUMULATION

If socialist rhetoric had little impact on employers, the economic and political constraints associated with it had a more direct effect on the capacity of many to employ servants. The 1980s were years of hardship, shortage and restrictions which hit particularly hard at two of these class fractions – private capital and medium level state functionaries.

Asian private capital

The political onslaught on private capital and the creation of alternative forms of state-sponsored accumulation such as the Regional Trading Company or state-owned control of tourism and banking hit many Asians hard. Many emigrated and others were leaving, seeing no future for themselves. Others were too poor to go. They were now hard-stretched to pay servants' wages especially at the official minimum level. Even servants conceded this, noting that domestic workers found it harder to get work: 'The Indians say they have no money'. 'They used to employ so many, but now they cannot afford to pay'.

Images of impoverishment were all around. I interviewed a shopkeeper who sold clothes and had evidently been successful in the past: 'We used to have a Boy, a Girl and a watchman'. They had built a large bungalow with servants' quarters attached, but the rooms had now been rented out to Africans. They used to have three cars but the garage was now empty: as the wife explained, 'my husband goes to work on a bicycle nowadays'. 'Since [the government] began to import second-hand clothes people don't buy new clothes any more and they just stay on the shelves. We can no longer afford servants. Also we live in mortal fear of being robbed – we cannot afford to be robbed'. They had employed a young woman but she left and they were unable to replace her. Having to do their own housework, their standards had slipped: 'we don't polish ... we only wash the floors once a week'. Another Asian shopkeeper employed no domestic help at all; his shop was almost bereft of goods. Another man had owned a company making pasta but was arrested and imprisoned during the Crackdown of 1983. Now he was reduced to being a driver for others and they could not afford to pay a servant adequately. Several young women had stayed briefly and then left. One asked for Sh400 (the minimum wage was Sh810) and the wife said: 'I told her I could only afford Sh300 a month and she said "I can't even buy a wrapper for Sh300"'. So now they had no help.

Local accounts of the Crackdown (which in government terms was a justifiable attempt to stamp out economic sabotage) described early morning swoops on individual homes of suspected persons: 'a "black list" had been drawn up and many on it were Asians'. Some were said to have been found with stashes of foreign currency as well as hoarded sugar, rice, flour and illegally imported goods. They were detained and some were imprisoned (see also Maliyamkono and Bagachwa 1990:121–3). Other Asians threw property out in terror, money and goods were secreted in caves at Amboni nearby. Significantly it is said that servants were bribed to hide or dispose of goods. In the case of the family above it was two African workers in the pasta factory who assisted the family whilst their employer was in prison. They came to work as 'houseboys' but in fact went on producing pasta for sale. Given a ban on imports of pasta this family was able to keep going whilst the man of the house was imprisoned.

In their attempts to find cheaper domestic help these employers came up against government regulations and were always afraid of being caught out. It was Asians who mentioned trouble with the Labour Department more than any other group, though my impression was that they were also targeted. One man, who had first denied having any servant, later told me openly how he attempted to cheat the system: 'Actually I do keep a houseboy but I can't pay them this government salary – I tell them how much I can afford and if they agree I make them sign blank payment vouchers which I fill in afterwards with the government wage'.

Hard times also meant that servants became crucial to freeing the labour of women in these households to help out in the shop, or run small money-making concerns of their own. Only two Asian wives had wage employment so there was a premium on making money from home. This suggests class pressures were culturally constrained, with Asian husbands often exerting strict control over their wives. Not only did servants' labour free wives and others for more profitable enterprise, but servants themselves were often drawn into them – indeed their labour was often indispensable. One example was described in Abu's story in Chapter 2; another was a man with a transport business of six lorries whose wife ran her own business making and selling icecream and raw sugar from home: this required a large refrigerator and an additional 'boy' to assist and go out selling.[10] In some Asian households it was almost impossible to see domestic workers as an unequivocal service category, with no productive role. Servants ran errands for the shop, delivered goods, and on occasions might be taken on as apprentices in craft workshops such as shoemakers or goldsmiths. Conversely there were factory workers 'called upstairs' to wash clothes and clean, shop assistants asked to sweep up their employer's house.

African state functionaries

By the mid-1980s African state functionaries were also facing hardships. A genuine effort had been made to keep income differentials within limits in socialist Tanzania. The gap between the incomes of the highest level state personnel and the lowest (manual) workers was reduced from 70:1 in 1961 to 15:1 in 1975 (President's Office, quoted in Yeager 1989:77). To prevent private enrichment and ostentation 'leaders' (who included all state employees) were forbidden by the Leadership Code of 1967 to own businesses or shares, earn two or more salaries, or own houses rented out to others, and by 1971 they were told that it was also impermissible to be 'arrogant, extravagant, contemptuous and oppressive' (cited in Coulson 1979:38).

The executive fraction of this class could usually find ways around these restrictions but those immediately below them had a harder time. Salaries failed to keep pace with the cost of living at this or any other class level and it was said that 'nobody could live on a government salary'. A civil servant commented on her own case: 'She and her husband were required to sign the Leadership Code which forbade them from supplementing their income by a secondary job or business'. Their joint income fell far short of covering their expenses and they bought land so that at least they could eat. 'They were unable to buy a car as had their predecessors' (Mwingira 1989: report on paper presented to a seminar in London). At the same seminar another Tanzanian 'hinted that District Officers had "other ways" of supplementing income. Everyone had to find a way'. In 1990 it was reported that: 'Nearly a hundred lecturers have resigned [from the University] since 1977 and those remaining are having to moonlight as taxi drivers, farmers or consultants to aid donors in order to feed their families, as monthly university salaries cover less than one week's needs' (*Guardian*: 14 May 1990).

This was a class fraction which could not afford to abandon its hold on land to grow food whose prices increased daily. In Tanga many employers interviewed were cultivating food crops in their gardens as well as having other farms, teachers truanted from classes to attend to their land and most officials had to have some 'business' on the side if they were to bring in enough to support their existence. In addition life was becoming increasingly hard, with severe shortages even of basic commodities and the purchase of household supplies a constant problem requiring hours of searching or judicious manipulation of contacts. Officials were often absent from their offices searching for sugar or rice. Maliyamkono and Bagachwa note that 'only the rich in urban areas would get access to essential commodities' but even for them such procurement was becoming increasingly difficult and time-consuming in the mid-1980s (1990:96; also 93,95).

The contradictory effect of all this in relation to the keeping of servants cannot be over-emphasised. On the one hand, given the cash squeeze there was a constant temptation to pay the lowest wages possible, unless the government were guaranteeing the payment. Some aimed not to pay at all but to exploit the labour of poor and unpaid relatives to carry out the essential work of the household. In the house of the Police Commander I was told there were 'no servants', but the two sullen adolescent girls evidently dressed in cast-offs and minding the children, clearly played the same role, at a lesser cost. In return for their keep and promises of school or training fees, even children as young as nine years old were being press-ganged into such a role. Conversely such a practice had no advantage in terms of displaying class privilege; it had to be disguised because it was against the law.

On the other hand, without servants at all, standards of living would plummet. Who would keep an eye on children while both employers were out at work or searching for essential supplies? Who would stand in queues? Who would help to do all the arduous washing and the cleaning and the cooking in large houses/households, without any labour-saving devices, convenience foods or television to act as child distractor, and where even basic amenities such as electricity and water supplies were uneven and uncertain? And given the prevalence of thieves roaming the better-off suburbs, neither life nor property would be safe if it were not constantly guarded. Servants were a necessity, then, according to many of these employers, despite the cost.

Socialist austerity had two contradictory effects then. On the one hand it made the keeping of servants at this class level a functional necessity if even the ordinary work of the household was to be completed, never mind any 'show'. For Veblen, the employment of servants for mere utility consider-ably undermined their value as props to social position. At the same time socialist austerity forced households to find ways of economising, either by not employing servants at all, by employing the cheapest servants or by finding additional sources of income.

Each of these features had a gender aspect (see Tables 7.2a and 7.2b). On the one hand the cheapest servants were young female servants[11] and it was Africans who employed the greatest proportion of these. On the other hand it was African wives who were most likely to be employed outside the home and it was medium level state functionaries who were most likely to have working wives. It was not simply class need which led to this outcome, as Asian private capital was similarly pressed. Almost certainly the relation of this class to state power gave African women the opportunity to gain employment, whilst gender relations in their own households allowed them to do so. All of them were in state employ at a slightly lower level than their husbands – they were nurses, secretaries, cashiers and teachers. The key role that servants played here was to release wives from domestic labour for relatively high-paid employment.

In these households servant-keeping had also become an adjunct to petty accumulation, though it is sometimes impossible to see this as anything other than a desperate struggle for class survival in impossible circumstances. The Port Manager's house in Tanga was a very substantial one, set in an enormous garden, with a sweeping drive. Each bedroom was self-contained, with its bathroom and balcony. The reception room was around 40ft square, dwarfing the four sofas and eight other easy chairs ranged around the edge. The house was very clean and neat, but sparsely furnished. Walking up to the house, cow pats were noted splattering the drive. The household was very large, containing approximately eighteen people, of all ages, two of whom were living-in servants, although the distinction between them and a few rather distant relations was somewhat blurred in the account of the Port Manager's wife. One servant was a 'housegirl', whilst the other living-in servant was a young herdsman, whom she needed because she kept cows and goats at the bottom of her garden. There were also two watchmen paid for by the Port Authority. Whilst the girl and the herdsboy had specified tasks, there was also a good deal of flexibility here – everyone helped out on the domestic scene. The day watchman was sometimes called in to do the washing, young male 'relatives' did the ironing, and the women, including her own two daughters, helped out with the cleaning and cooking. Everyone ate together, though in groups according to age, where the servants were not treated differently. Besides the livestock, this woman had purchased some land on the outskirts of the town, and at weekends everyone, family and servants, turned out to cultivate there with a young man she employed as a farm worker – she showed me her calloused hands. None of her private employees were paid the official minimum wage, although she justified this in terms of the food and free accommodation with which she provided them. Her attitude towards her workers was strictly utilitarian: young men were more useful as servants because they would work both inside and out, and she would like another : 'Maybe when my cows calve I will be able to employ extra help'.

In another family house a pile of household durables was accumulating in one corner – sanitary ware especially, which the man of the house was able to buy due to his privileged access to official channels of supply. The items were destined to furnish a new house which this man was slowly constructing in a new and attractive part of the town. Again, easy access to very scarce building supplies was a function of his office. To have removed from his government-owned house to live in the new house would have been entirely legal; what he was planning to do however was illegal – to rent out the private house, and continue to live in government-rented property. In the meantime, these valuable goods were an invitation to theft. The importance of having a servant living in, and guarding them and the family's other property was vital. They had been robbed a couple of times, when even foam-rubber seat cushions were taken.

Private enterprises on the side were a common feature of life for African state functionaries, and income from the employment of both husbands and wives, and the expropriation of surplus value from the labour of servants, allowed for savings to be accumulated for investment. Aside from building or purchasing rentable property (which of course had to be done very circumspectly) and buying land, chicken and egg production or the setting up of small retail outlets was common. In the case of domestic production the labour of servants was often necessary to prosper (the domestic worker looked after the chickens, or went around selling the eggs after his/her other work was done). Servants could even be used as cover for a private sideline business, the licence made out in their names, their labour on the front line and so on. These are all classic instances of class formation consolidated through 'straddling' different modes of production: in this case petty accumulation built on a basis of secure income from state employment.

SUMMARY AND CONCLUSIONS

Many have argued that domestic service is a class phenomenon but they have not always explained how. What I have tried to show here is that domestic service is a device both to display and to perpetuate class divisions. I have done this through analysing its role in conspicuous consumption and petty accumulation whilst also exploring the most usual rationale for its existence in Tanzania – i.e. mere utility.

In the early days after Independence fears were voiced amongst some Tanzanians that the extravagant styles of living of those at the top were enjoyed at the expense of the masses: 'The ministers and top civil servants had stepped into the shoes of the colonial officers ... They were nicknamed Wabenzi which means those who drive in Mercedes Benz cars. It was a state of exploiters fattening up on people's sweat' (quoted in Peter and Mvungi 1985:163). If this was somewhat exaggerated, certainly by the 1980s it was a world away. I have shown that both state policies and economic crisis had combined to inhibit such public displays of opulence, whether on the part of state functionaries or on that of alienated local private business. But whilst the state attempted to take over the role of developmental accumulation and to prohibit or undermine private initiatives, its personnel responded both to opportunity and to a serious deterioration in their personal economic circumstances by subterranean private accumulation. Domestic service was caught up in this shift.

When it was later given the opportunity, with economic liberalisation pressed by the IMF and the official abandonment of the Leadership Code in 1991, the African dominant class would expand its scale of petty and not so petty accumulation. This chapter shows that the barrier was in no sense a lack of the appropriate ethic and practice of discipline, thrift and frugality which has underpinned many an emergent bourgeoisie. Tendencies towards opulent and conspicuous consumption were not the problem either, for these tendencies were held in check both by the severe constraints of state policy and economic decline, by cultural inhibitions, and by a preference for saving and investment rather than spending on display. All of this is illustrated in their employment of servants.

African state functionaries also shouldered the cultural task of differentiating themselves from the mass of the population by adopting various marks and signs of relative wealth and position. They were immediately distinctive by their collective appropriation of the houses of colonial officials and local rentiers which set them apart from the common herd living in crowded urban dwellings. Such houses made their own demands in terms of upkeep; and the dependents who followed the promise of their apparent riches imposed further domestic burdens. A certain cultural style was beginning to emerge which rested on the work of domestic servants. Conversely, the appearance of an African upper class in these straitened circumstances was leading the occupation of domestic service to become increasingly feminised and down-graded. Contrary to Johnson's experience (1992:146) I noted no particular mutuality between African servants and their employers. African mistresses were more likely to be out at work than cooking or cleaning with their female servants. It was as exceptional for servants to eat with the adult members of African families or to share their lavatory as it was in Asian or European households. Young female servants had a high turnover rate (mostly less than a year), and none had been with the families for years, building up relationships with children or other members. It was male servants working for wealthy Europeans or Asians who became 'faithful' family retainers, some of them having more than ten years of service.

I have shown in this chapter that the keeping of servants, and the way they are employed, is relevant to the process of upper class formation. Servants are an adjunct to the petty accumulative mode of this dominant class, whilst at the same time the very persistence of the institution, and the way in which service speaks of class inequality in various conspicuous forms, is evidence of its symbolic role.

8

CLOSE ENCOUNTERS: THE MICRO-POLITICS OF DOMESTIC LABOUR

In the micro-politics of the home as workplace, the key struggles are over control of the labour process and its outputs and the conditions and terms on which labour is provided. If, in these struggles, employers have the upper hand (and the most potent control is exercised by those with the most class, gender and ethnic power) servants are not without their own stratagems to resist and manipulate the relationship to their advantage. Whilst one of the key features of the workforce in domestic service is that it is atomised rather than concentrated in the labour process, the same applies to the employing class – or rather to the female employer who has the most dealings with servants and is exposed in her lonely attempt to extort the maximum effort from them.

Something of the complicated tale of manoevrings is illustrated in Mrs Frau's comments: 'You must pay them well and treat them well. But they must know I am the boss. I am in control. Over the years they become a part of you. They should not feel you make profit out of them'. It is also illustrated in a very contradictory discourse of 'familiarity' – which on the one hand is seen to 'breed contempt' but on the other to 'render familiar', to subsume as 'one of the family' and subject to its rules. Servants *and* employers subscribe to this discourse: it offers advantages to both sides whilst simultaneously courting danger.

Some telling examples of the struggles which go on within homes as workplaces have already been offered – the stories of Sara and Abu contained several. Here I focus more specifically on the resources each side can bring to bear in this charged relationship. The approach adopted here, and its conclusions, highlight some surprising similarities and contrasts between the micro-politics of domestic service and wage labour of a more conventional kind.

Adesina's study of an oil refinery in Nigeria aims to show how, within the constraints of exploitative capitalist relations of production, workers challenge and subvert the workings of the system even as they are 'bought' by it.[1] Adesina's key concern is with what he calls 'the complex, contra-dictory character of work relations' and the way in which 'people express themselves as active human agencies, rather than as simple objects of relations ... as active subjects who attempt to redefine their positions in the production process and rescue their subjectivity' (1990:115). The outcome is that value relations (i.e. the overall motivation in capitalist production for the creation of wealth through exploitation) are challenged and 'deconstructed' – to a degree – in the context of work. One of the key groupings through which this is negotiated is the work group, where workers devise an alternative morality which may deny the capitalist ethos, and which has a degree of effectivity: 'while workers are adapting to work they are also adapting the work to themselves' (118).

Although the key relations in this process of creative adaptation are lateral ones of solidarity between workers, Adesina also reconsiders 'vertical' (hierarchical) relations. Supervisory staff are not simply 'agents of capital', he argues: 'the primary value relation is redefined in the process of empathic interaction between supervisor and the supervised' (126). The supervisors in the oil refinery had often been workers themselves, and in the process of sustained interaction, both workers and supervisors come to 'know each other as human beings' (129).

Finally Adesina writes about the 'corporate collective', by which he means an ethos which is cultivated of the whole enterprise as a 'team', working together, of which all can be proud. He argues that whilst management have a clear interest in promoting this view, workers themselves may also subscribe to it on occasion: 'the family spirit ... nourishes a sense of belonging' (124).

The relevance of much of this for the quite different and generally non-commodity producing arena of household employment is striking. Whilst some household workers may be engaged in petty commodity production, domestic service is generally a setting where consumption of surplus value takes place, rather than its production. It is also distinctive from factory production in its scale and in the way that the unit of production is privatised, so that workers are isolated one from another. Despite this, there are clear parallels between Adesina's account of the factory and my own study of domestic service. This has little to do with capitalism or commodity production per se, and more to do with the complexities and contradictions of the labour process in any situation where it is characterised by hierarchy/inequality. Adesina's argument may usefully be taken as a template against which to assess the data of domestic service, highlighting difference as well as similarity.

SEEKING THE BEST EMPLOYER

Workers have little alternative but to find work or another means to livelihood, but they do choose which employers to work for. The discourse of choice is here largely couched in racialised stereotypes, with a preference for European over Asian employers, and Asians over Africans. But what these designations express has little to do with culture or colour; it speaks rather of expectations about the material position of employers.

It is not just views of Others which are expressed here but also gendered and racialised evaluations of Self. Whilst both men and women resisted employment by Africans, I concluded from my difficulties in finding men so employed that they were more able to put this into effect. They chose other employers, believing them to pay more and offer better conditions, but also I sensed, because to be employed by one of your own in such work was galling. Amongst the few who did, one said that he worked for African employers only 'because I can't get anything else. People don't like to work for Africans because they pay little and there is so much work ... they are mean-spirited'. He complained in particular at having to do degrading jobs like washing and de-lousing the dog. He preferred to work for Indians. It was enough to be doing a job which 'at home is done by women' and to be subject to the woman of the house; to be doing it for another man who, given different circumstances, might have been you, was too much to accept. This was especially the case for older men, for whom it would have meant working in a personalised capacity for much younger people. All the time-honoured proprieties were transgressed and dislocated in such a relationship and men avoided it if they could.[2]

Women, by contrast, are used to being subordinates; they were more willing to accept working for fellow-Africans, less discriminating in their selection. Having said this, they expressed the same racialised views about the best and the worst kind of employers. 'Indians use people badly – they have no fixed times of work'. 'Europeans are really good people – when they see you are tired they say "go home and rest"'. On one occasion an elderly ex-servant was holding forth about Goan employers (I did not solicit such views!): 'There's nothing like Goans for being mean! They don't give you clothes unless they are really worn out. And if they are not, then they cut your wages to pay for them ... Food? None! What they cooked for themselves was carefully weighed out with nothing to spare!' Two younger women were listening in and a veritable competition of racialised epithets was brought into play:

> 'Indians give you food, but not Goans ...'
> 'But not Bohoras! They are bad people, they give nothing at all. Other Indians perhaps, but not Bohoras!'

Women were less likely to be employed by those they aspired to work for, given employer preference for male workers. Skilled men could afford to be more choosy. Although most of the men I interviewed had worked for Indians, and continued to seek Indian employers, their view of them was often contemptuous. One man who was particularly bitter said:

> Indians – especially these shopkeeper types – discriminate against us stupid people [note the Self-denigration enclosed in condemning the Other]. They give you left-overs, sometimes tea, but never in their

cups or plates, only in old tins. They think you are too dirty to go in their kitchens – you have to wash your feet first. You certainly couldn't use their lavatory – you have to go outside to the municipal latrine. Abuse, abuse, the whole time.

Another summed up: 'too little money; too much work'. Conversely the 'kindness' of Europeans was often a point of comment. One present-day servant recounted how, as a watchman, he had been caught sleeping by his European employer, but she let herself in quietly without waking him and said nothing in the morning. 'Europeans don't like quarrelling and scenes – not like these Indians, always shouting at you'.

Although the accounts were racialised, it would appear that the greater the munificence and social distance of employers, the more likely they were to be 'respected' and sought after, irrespective of 'race'. Very rich Asian and European employers would not only pay well, but each servant would have their allotted task so that work and hours were ordered and appeared as 'fair'. Some of the glory rubbed off onto the servants and their distant employers were seen in a very favourable light, as generous and just. One old man told me how as a child (in the 1920s) he had left his village just to come and gaze at Europeans and did not rest until he had found the chance to work for them. Their generous gifts on departure were the stuff of myths.

In the end 'race' is a way of challenging employer definitions of the work, talking about degrees of felt exploitation and of one's own standing in relation to the exploiter.[3]

STRATAGEMS AND SPOILS[4]

If servants sought those employers who were most culturally distant from them, it was because they perceived them to be the most likely to pay well. Once in employment both sides executed complicated manoeuvres to control the situation to their benefit, at times distancing themselves, at others edging closer. At the extreme each feared the other: servants feared losing their jobs or their reputations, being mercilessly exploited or being punished. Employers not only feared being unable to get 'value for money', but also the intimate knowledge that servants accumulated and which might be used against them to rob or sabotage their family life. Two examples illustrate the instrumental ways that each side adopts to protect its interests.

The first is related from the employers' side. A Goan family had a male servant who had worked for them for several years. They saw themselves as good employers and contrasted themselves with Africans, who

treat their servants so badly! – pay them only Sh3–400 [a month] or even less, expect them to work all hours – there are no fixed hours … sometimes they beat them … when the man comes home drunk he expects the servant to be there waiting with his food. They really exploit them! They don't like to work for Africans – they prefer to work for people like us who treat them well.

This family's servant, Amos, lived in the servants' quarters attached to their house. He had a wife and six children and was Catholic like them. On Sundays I sometimes saw the employer taking Amos' children to church with her. Although they paid Amos only the minimum wage they pitied him and understood that he needed to augment his wages in order to survive. They suspected petty stealing to subsidise his family's food and he would often disappear in order to sell bread-cakes that his wife made, but they turned a blind eye. He had been arrested for selling without a licence and they sympathised with his anger about government regulations. What was important to them was that he or his family were around all the time, so their house was not deserted and a temptation to thieves. His employer also knew that her kindness would be rewarded by his willingness to do extra work on occasions – if she had sudden visitors for example. When he had errands to do they let him use their son's bicycle, even though the son objected: 'if he doesn't go by bicycle he stays away for hours'.

This account underlines that the degree of control employers can exercise over servants is limited to the time they are actually standing over and supervising them. If they did this full time the whole point of having a servant would be lost. Meanwhile servants look for ways of reducing their input and maximising their returns. When sent out they dawdle, combine errands with visits to friends or relatives or with their own errands. Employers aim to engage their loyalty in a variety of ways, through gifts, favours or advances (Amos was generally receiving advances on the coming rather than the current month's wages). Having the servant live in with them (in the house or in attached quarters) was often presented as a perk of the job, but most servants knew better – indeed as the family above acknowledged, there was a free security built into the arrangement as well as constant accessibility of service. The appeal to commonality of religion in this case was unusual, but a useful device nonetheless.

My second example is presented from the perspective of the servant involved. A young woman, Salma, got a job with an Asian family, a situation that at first appeared rosy. Salma's aunt (with whom Salma lived) was delighted. She expressed her feelings by visiting the employers and presenting 'mama' with a gift of rice from her farm. She exulted when the gifts started being reciprocated – leftover food, a cast-off dress, some old material to make another: 'these people are very rich' she said, anticipating more. But then the relationship began to sour. The employer pressed Salma to come earlier in the mornings, to extend her hours to more than ten a day and to increase her work load. Salma complained to me:

Each day I had to sweep and scrub every room, dust out all the cupboards, sweep out and scrub their shop, wash piles of clothes – and if there were only a few clothes she would whip all the covers off the furniture to make more! Then iron, then make juice ... on and on and on without rest. Before I left she would have me sweeping the whole house again, and preparing the rice for next day, kneading the dough.

Salma in her turn begged to take a bath at the employer's house after work – and this was at first graciously conceded. Both sides jockeying for position, they then began to fall out. One day the employer complained that the water bill would be too high, and that if Salma expected a bath she should live in. Salma told me that if she lived in she would be 'used all the time'. A row after Salma failed to arrive 'on time' one day led to loud words and Salma left in disgust. In telling me the end of the story Salma's final thrust was: 'These Asians! They are our fellow Muslims but they think they are much better than us'. Her argument was about social distance, rather than moral community.

Both sides wish to play the game of 'closer encounters' but they want contradictory rewards. Servants try to extend their privileges within the family setting in which they live, whilst maintaining a social distance which allows them to resist overwork. Employers seek more work for the same money but they also want the work to be done willingly. Gift-giving is normally a means by which employers buy loyalty, but it can also be a device that servants use to secure patronage.[5] Cultural differences and similarities are drawn on as symbolic capital in arguments about control and exploitation in work. In this case, as in the previous one, points were scored by reference to common religious adherence – but with opposing punch-lines.

Living-in

Class power and gender were both reflected in where servants lived. Most servants resisted living in as it allowed them no free time and no end to their work; and less than half of all employers were able to impose it. That in most cases they would prefer to impose it, seems clear. 'They would always be there', said one employer. 'And some mornings it rains and they are delayed'. Another pointed out that, 'if they are living in then they find it less easy to steal'. One admitted that servants preferred to go home after their work: 'if they are here you can't help calling them – you get lazy'. Others used accommodation as a lure: 'We gave him the rooms on condition that he worked in the garden'. If servants in general resisted, it was men who were more able to resist than women. Only 19 per cent of male servants lived in, and most of these lived in servants' quarters where they enjoyed free accommodation for themselves and their families, but provided their own food. Forty-four per cent of women lived in, but this generally meant sharing a room with children or younger relatives in their employer's house so that they were available night and day, with hardly any being allocated servants' quarters.

There was a hierarchy of outsiderness, with men who lived in their own accommodation in the town the most free from employer control, whilst young women were often trapped as involuntary insiders, provided with food and clothing by their employers in lieu of proper wages. It was young girls from the countryside who were forced to accept these conditions, taken in as pseudo-family members, usually by African or poor Asian employers who exerted a tight moral and physical control over their lives.[6] Such girls had little room for manoeuvre, though they were constantly seeking ways. Employers claimed that they would wait until they were given clothes and then disappear. One girl complained bitterly that her employer gave her no soap and not an item of clothing. She had secretly approached a sympathetic neighbour who agreed to send her to work for her own daughter in another town.

Sometimes this exploitation occurred within real families. One girl was 'asked for' by her aunt when she was twelve. She found herself in Dar es Salaam looking after three young children and doing all the housework as her employer-relatives both worked. She claimed that although she was paid (around a quarter of the minimum wage), 'my money was cut any day I was unwell, and my aunt refused to let me leave the house'. She waited until they came back on a visit to Tanga and she could enlist her parents' support in not returning. Both parents agreed that she had been badly treated: 'I didn't know my own sister would be like this – she treated her like an animal'.

Familial discourses

Many writers on domestic service have written about the spurious familialism which pervades the institution. At all levels in Tanga employers were heard to say. 'I treat her as one of the family', and servants to say, 'They treated me as their child'. This is symbolised in the familial nomenclature that is used to refer to employers and occasionally to servants. Domestic service reflects ordinary life in that 'mother' and 'father' are normally used as terms of respect by younger people to older people. Naming carries power. Where there is an age gap between servants and their employers such a transfer is unexceptionable; but where servants are older than their employers there is a status contradiction between class and age. In an unusual case a female employer (a Goan) had chosen, 'out of respect' to call an older female servant 'mama' rather than use her first name. The servant reciprocated as the employer drew the line at being addressed by her first name: 'I would not allow her'. Servants must accept the common use of their personal name by a younger person, which would be insulting if this were not a work relationship. African employers are more aware of this than others and will sometimes encourage, or be unable to prevent servants from addressing them as familial equals or joking partners ('brother', 'sister' or 'mother's brother').

More generally, however, servants call their employer 'mama', and where there is more than one woman in the house, such as a mother-in-law, this may be extended to 'big mother' and 'little mother'. There is more ambiguity about nomenclature applied to the man of the house, who is in any case usually more distant. Servants may address him as 'father', even 'grandfather', but the more generalised 'elder' is equally common. One Asian employer noted that, 'They used to say '*bwana*' [master] but now it is '*mzee*' [elder]'. This indicates that employers do not have it all their own way, and that all are seeking appropriate terms to describe an ambivalent relationship: as another employer said of his servant: 'She is a member of our family but she is still an outsider'.

If familial terminology serves largely to underline the direction of control it also carries certain expectations about treatment. Servants would like to be allocated the privileges and material rewards of 'belonging' and they are prepared to go along with, even cultivate, familial nomenclature if this brings forth the appropriate response (compare Bunster and Chaney 1985:30). After all, these people are 'rich' and can afford to be generous. Generally servants are disappointed: 'They asked me to call them "brother" and "sister" ... and then they told me to delouse the dog', was one account. Another case shows that exceptionally servants can be adopted as 'one of the family' but still perceive themselves as outsiders.

A Kenyan who had been involved in Mau Mau in the 1950s hid away in the forests during the Emergency clamp-down. He made his way to what was then Tanganyika and found work with an Asian family. He looked after the children and did the housework and they referred to him as 'babu' [grandfather]. One of these children told me the story:

> Now he is old and he hardly does anything, but he still lives with us as he has no wife or family. He eats with us, occasionally he goes to the market. He bosses us around a lot, especially if my father is not around. He bought a piece of land near Korogwe and he says that my younger brother is to have it when he dies. If we ask him to go on an errand at night he says: 'would you send me if I were really Babu?'. So we go ourselves.

Familialism may be a more solid foundation on which to build aspirations than borrowings from other relational forms. In one exceptional case an employer was eager to tell me how her servant and she were on first-name terms and that 'she is like a friend. I do not treat her as an inferior'. But later on in the conversation she confided that 'I have noticed my rice starting to disappear – especially this last few weeks, and I'm thinking of kicking off this woman at the end of this month'. At the end of the day the employer, even as 'friend', has the greater power.

Gift-giving

Servants hope that if they play their roles according to the rules they may enjoy rewards of a kind unheard of in more impersonal settings. In some cases they did. Servants would tell me of the gifts they had received from employers who were satisfied. One man had worked for seven years for an Asian who owned a hardware shop. When the man left for Canada he gave him a bicycle, a radio and a large money bonus, and still keeps in touch with him, sending him clothes. This man was remembered with affection as well as respect – he was '*mzee*' (elder) but he also joked with his servants and was always cheerful, 'you didn't notice the time passing'. Servants often talked of how European employers had built houses for their loyal servants.

Amongst the European employers I interviewed, several saw themselves as benefactors to servants who had given unstinting service. One spoke of the bonus she would be giving her cook when he retired, but added that she would not give it in cash – 'they would just spend it' – but would open an account for him. Another told me how she had paid for her servant to have driving lessons and given him large bonuses for his annual leave – adding that the young man in question 'had become like my third son'. She was devastated when he disappeared to work for another employer as a driver. Asian employers sometimes had servants who had worked with them for a lifetime and more than one had given materials for housebuilding, or continued to employ an old person despite their incapacity to work: 'we feel we must provide for him'. Some African employers were also eager to play the role of patron. In one case a young man was rewarded for several years work as babyminder and cleaner by being set up in a business selling roast meat.

The role of such success stories was potent in keeping servants' hopes alive and their 'willingness' flowing; at the same time it allowed employers to demonstrate the power of patronage as the ultimate giving or withholding of rewards. Servants should never be allowed to presume on their employers' goodwill, for this would be a mark of over-familiarity.

Resistance to work

Whilst it was generally the case that the employer had the power to set the tasks which servants were to carry out, we have already seen that servants could legitimately resist certain tasks. For many it was washing underwear; and most employers were aware of this. A young female servant put her resistance in familial terms: 'She is my mother, I will feel shame!'. Other tasks might also be the subject of manoeuvrings. I was surprised at the extent of resistance to ironing with an electric iron by both male and female servants, such that many employers gave in and sent out clothes to a washerman, thus occasioning extra expense. The resistance to the job might be expressed in terms of fear of the electricity or lack of knowledge, or simply a show of 'stupidity' – 'she was keen to learn to cook, but showed no interest when I tried to show her how to iron'. The employer fears the damage that might be done to family clothes. Another example was the female servant who said she couldn't possibly sweep outside the house – it was shameful as she would be seen by passers-by. The employer had to get the gardener to do the job. In negotiating what work they would do, servants could play either on what had become accepted practice through generations of servant resistance or they could take advantage of employer reluctance to invest more time in finding another worker.

Where servants had worked for many years in one household they might enjoy a degree of autonomy in their work, almost to the extent of dictating their terms of work. Knowing what to do and getting on with it without being ordered around were prized. One employer said that his servant of more than a dozen years 'does as he wants to'. A European employer told me that her old servant sometimes tried to tell her what to do. In these cases there is almost certainly a gender aspect to the reluctance of elderly males to be at the bidding of a female employer. They aim to negotiate a separate sphere – usually the kitchen – which is their domain and where the woman of the house may be made to feel unwelcome or uncomfortable. One European employer described how his skilled cook of many years was fine, until his own wife came on the scene and began 'interfering'. The old man was very resentful and 'it was hell'.

It was for this reason that, despite the female employer exercising day to day control over servants in Tanga households, the man of the house was an important element in the power equation. Usually the wife recruited the servants and set up the hours and the tasks of the job. But when it came to the wage it was nearly always the husband who paid out, thus underlining his superior status in the household. Given the degree of social distance maintained by the man of the house, the question of pay was one where there was least room for negotiation. Otherwise, men had little to do with servants, unless 'there is trouble'. One woman described how a cook who had worked honestly for many years suddenly began stealing. It then became a matter for her husband. The cook admitted his guilt. 'My husband told him, "you are an old man – like my father! [note] – how can I call the police to you?" In the end he agreed to leave'.

A female employer, especially one with whom some of the work in the household is shared, can be 'worked on' in a way that is impossible with a man. Male employers may also avoid female servants, knowing that their wives are ever vigilant on this score. With male servants they can afford to be more friendly, though this is usually where an age difference allows for them to act as natural patrons.

NEGATIVE EXCHANGES

The games that servants and their employers play are facilitated by positive forms of interaction expressed in demeanour and in material exchanges. These are backed up by a shadow world of negative sanctions which may be brought into play when the relationship does not bear the anticipated fruit for either party. Both of these aspects display the domination of servants by employers, but also a degree of manipulation by both sides.

Social distancing

Whilst both servants and their employers may initiate forms of familiarity which suit their ends, most employers are aware that their power is precarious and must be continually reasserted. Social distancing is one device which has long been recognised by sociologists as a way of creating and maintaining inequality. Because the unknown is more intimidating than the known, distancing constitutes an unspoken threat. Social distance is easier to organise where the parties are physically segregated; it is harder in the close confines of everyday domestic life. Two attempts to impose it effectively illustrate the problems.

Mrs Frau paid her servants well and consequently they were eager to hold on to their positions. In return she expected total control, which was maintained through a stategy of minimising both lateral and vertical interactions. For example, she told me that a rule of silence was enforced at work: 'if you once let them start talking you can't stop them'. She supervised their work closely but also critically by being '*kali*' (fierce) with them and insisting that everything be done '*haraka*' (promptly). She had a 'Headboy' and transmitted her orders for the day through him rather than directly. Her servants must knock before they entered a room. She was careful to dress properly in their presence – she would not let them see her in a swimming costume for example. They took their food separately from the family – indeed each one ate 'separately with his bowl'. In these ways she did not allow them to get too close or friendly with her or with each other. Despite the rewards of conformity to this regime she had suffered various robberies and petty stealing. If her servants misbehaved they were punished by docking their wages or by dismissal. She was conscious that she needed some back-up, and she told me proudly that the servants were 'afraid' because she knew a lot of big people (Police Chief etc.).

We have seen that this household was exceptional, both in its grandeur and its number of servants. Such resources lent weight to the insistence on distance, whilst distance underlined control. But less wealthy employers could also attempt to keep servants in their place. One extreme version of this was encountered in an Asian household where the employers had a very derogatory view of servants – 'they' were ignorant, all potential thieves, not to be trusted. This was manifested in a regime where the servant did all his work in the courtyard – he was only allowed to come into the house to clean the lavatory. The man of the house said he would not have servants in the kitchen: 'We are vegetarians' and 'They are dirty'. He was careful not to employ any man who could speak Gujerati so that the family preserved their own domain of private speech and commentary. I noted with amusement that their present servant was of two days standing only, whilst the previous one, who had worked for other families for twenty-five years, had complained of a hernia and left the job after a month.

There are many themes in these two examples which were echoed in interviews with employers of all ethnic groups and confirmed by stories from servants, even though few were so excessive. Employers sought ways of distancing themselves from servants even when they worked together in the same confined spaces. Working together was redefined as 'supervising their work' to make sure they did it 'according to schedule' or to 'our ways', and to ensure that they did not steal. Servants were normally expected to use different toilets to those of their employers, often expected to go to municipal latrines rather than use those in the house. It was very rare for them to eat with employers, although it was not uncommon to find them eating with the children. They might be told to use only special dishes or cutlery. They were often excluded from certain inner rooms either because these were bedrooms (and thus redolent of intimacy) or because they were repositories of household valuables. Cupboards, refrigerators and pantries might be kept locked. Language differences were exploited to ensure they did not learn family secrets.

All of these exclusionary stratagems could misfire or be counter-productive. Rooms that servants could not enter had to be cleaned by family members; access to locked cupboards entailed the constant presence of the employer. Insisting that servants relieve themselves at the municipal latrines provided them with a good excuse for disappearing. A cold indifference rarely induced enthusiastic hard work. A servant who spoke your language could be useful – taking telephone messages or orders from family members who did not speak Swahili. One servant told me that Gujerati-speaking employers did not want servants to learn: 'This is their language for business. When you go to their shops they discuss how they can overcharge you whilst pretending to give you "a good price"'. He also described how servants used cunning to acquire the knowledge:

> The key is when they have a child and you are told to take him out – you practice on him. If he understands, you know you've got it. Or he will correct you ... Eventually your boss begins to suspect ... She asks: 'You hear?' and you say 'Me no hear' and when the child speaks to

you, you remain silent. That way you can understand what they say without them knowing.

Fear and punishment

Fear in servants is seen in a positive light and is given as the reason why many employers seek out young girls raw from the countryside as domestic servants. It is not only that such girls are the cheapest labour: they are also 'frightened, still young enough to learn' (African employer); or as an Asian male employer put it, 'we prefer people from the village – they are afraid of you, afraid of doing wrong, they do as they are told'. Fear can also be instilled – in the case of Mrs Frau by servants' knowledge of the big people she knew; in another family explicitly by the keeping of fierce dogs. Dogs may be taught to discriminate – as a child in one family put it innocently: 'our dog is fierce with black people, but otherwise he's really a pet'.

Control could also be exerted by punishing servants for failing to come up to expectations. When I asked about punishments most employers said that they went no further than telling servants off or shouting at them (tellingly one African employer added 'like you would with your own child'). I occasionally saw such confrontations: servants would generally argue back and try to justify themselves. Such unedifying spectacles almost always involved the woman of the house, as the servant was more afraid to contradict a male employer. Men will then say that their wives are partly to blame for losing their tempers and shouting, and they may intervene to sort matters out. It was evident that a cost-benefit analysis was expressed in employers' decisions: the costs of finding another servant, the investment already made: as one employer said 'we had to dismiss her as bras and panties went missing', even though 'she could cook everything'.

Those who offer higher rewards evidently calculate that servants will be more amenable to punishment, fearing their greater loss. Some spoke of docking pay for absenteeism or breakages. Another reported a collective punishment – she told all her servants that there would be no food until some stolen clothes had been returned. However, she lost this round as the clothes were not returned, and after a week she was forced to resume her provision of food. Another told me proudly how, when a knife went missing she docked Sh40 from the cook's wages. Eight years later the knife turned up and she returned the money! Employers who pay less are more nervous. Punishing someone can stimulate resentment and a desire for vengeance against the family. Given the intimate access of servants to their persons and possessions, employers prefer to dismiss the offender, though a fatalistic acceptance of 'poor service' or of petty pilfering seemed the safest course of action to some. As one man put it: 'you can't do anything. Better the lion you know than the one you don't'. Even when servants are caught stealing red-handed, threatening the police is intended to shame them into admitting their guilt, and as one employer said: 'I didn't dismiss him. Servants are thieves and we are afraid of getting someone even worse'.

Trust, betrayal and violation

Servants were seen as potentially dangerous[7] and employers faced a dilemma. They employed servants to protect them and their property – as nightwatchmen, as ayahs to their children, as people trusted to look after the house in their absence. And yet they feared the violation of that trust by the very same people because of their 'insider knowledge'. The problem was how to engage the loyalty of servants through an *appearance* of trust, whilst at the same time maintaining a constant vigilance. Fear of robbery and of personal violence from servants was high amongst some families I interviewed – even whilst their 'evidence' was rarely first-hand. There was a terrible story of an Asian family (in Dar es Salaam) who told off their servant for burning a sari whilst ironing. Next time they left her at home she stole everything and put the baby in the oven. This is probably an 'urban myth', or what Hansen (1989: 250) calls 'the folklore of domestic service' but it has secure purchase in employers' imaginations. Actual incidents were also recounted. One woman had a trusted ayah who ran off with clothes and jewellery, leaving her children all alone.

Some people go to great lengths to protect themselves – watchmen day and night (never allowed in the house), houses like fortresses and so on. I visited several like this. One family was said to have wired up their house – and electrocuted the servant when he arrived for work the next morning (but again, this was 'long ago', 'a friend of a friend' ...). When thefts are discovered it is usually servants who are blamed first. They are often accused of conspiring with others to rob – and usually dismissed. One employer described how two robbers had come with a pistol and a crowbar whilst they were out. Their servants were threatened into opening the gate and fastening up the dogs, but one ran to give the alarm and the thieves fled. 'The police told us to dismiss the two shamba boys as they were probably accomplices. These days you don't know who to trust'.

Servants fear such accusations, and will often, as Sara put it, 'make a big show' of honesty, to allay suspicions and for fear of losing their livelihood. They acknowledge that others steal, though they do not admit to doing so themselves. Certainly for some the opportunity to augment the meagre rewards of work by stealing are too great to resist, and becomes an element in the manoeuvres designed to adapt the work situation to their own interests. For employers these tales of betrayal feed into a generalised sense of distrust.

Aside from the threat which servants are held to pose to possessions there is also the fear (not always admitted) of personal violation. There is the literature (discussed by Hansen 1989 and Gill 1994) which implies that this

issue arises primarily in relation to female servants and male employers. We
have already considered the 'sexuality argument' as an explanation of the
preponderance of men in domestic service (see Chapter 5) and found it
wanting. But it also raises a more general issue: employers' fears that the
close encounters of domestic service might lead to intimacy of the 'wrong'
kind, not in keeping with the employer role of control and superordination.
In this setting either male or female servants might be seen as a sexual threat
by employers.

From the perspective of servants such developments are usually also
dangerous and threatening – they may constitute sexual harassment or lead
to dismissal. Conversely such relationships might be turned to advantage, as
an extreme instance of patronage. Gender power and class power are
equally at issue in such encounters.

Though it was delivered with an air of veracity, I cannot vouch for the
truth of the following account from a male servant who, through wishful
thinking or boastfulness, probably put his own part in the drama in the best
possible light. I had known the elderly man in question for three months
before he confided the story. He was describing a period of employment
with an Indian family before Independence:

> One day the woman asked me: 'Do you have a wife?' I said, 'yes'.
> 'How is it that she is not dead?' asked the woman. I couldn't
> understand what she meant at first, but eventually she said that her
> husband had told her that Africans were like donkeys and that if a
> woman slept with them she died. I had noticed that whenever I came
> near to her in the kitchen she drew away ... I told her, 'it's not like that
> – God created all human beings the same'.

This, he told me, was the beginning of what turned into a sexual
relationship between the two of them. He said he was afraid of her husband,
but she told him: '"Don't be afraid, but don't you dare tell him, or our God
with six arms will surely kill you". So ... and she gave me money'.

To lull her husband's suspicions the wife said she would be irritable and
find fault with the servant in front of him. And this she did: 'Why haven't you
washed the floor yet? Where is the water I told you to bring? This is not clean!'
The servant played his part in the deception by 'complaining' to the husband
about his wife – and was told: 'Just ignore her – women are like this'.

In this story the class difference between mistress and servant was clearly
transgressed and to the advantage of the servant (she gave him money –
whether to keep quiet or to denote her pleasure is unclear). The gender
dimensions are more complex, with a collapsing of the two senses of
'mistress' and the husband trapped into involuntary complicity in male
bonding between men of unequal status.

In Tanga the 'sexual argument' as applied to male servants had a curious ethnic tinge, with only Asian employers raising it as an issue, whilst European female employers presented their relations with male servants as ungendered (class and ethnic status rendering gender inequality irrelevant). Amongst African employers, only one woman mentioned that male servants might be 'badly behaved with young girls in the family', and a reason for preferring female servants (she herself employed an eleven year old). In many Asian families, however, both female employers and their husbands spoke of their fears. 'We are afraid of male servants. We fear for our daughters'. 'Young men can rape our daughters'. 'Men servants can attack or rape women in the house. It's not safe for women to be alone with them'. Actual instances of such happenings are hard to come by – there are apocryphal tales of girls becoming pregnant by male servants, even of the families murdering the men involved, but no hard facts. The linking of men's honour to the proper behaviour of wives and daughters would seem to be at issue here, and the 'donkey myth' a means of warning women to behave.

The relationship of female servants to male employers was seen as problematic by a wider range of employers, generally the women. It was not unknown for male members of the employing family to seduce or to violate female servants, taking advantage of their combined class and gender power (see Sheikh-Hashim 1988 for general confirmation). From the point of view of female employers this could be very threatening although it was rare for them to admit it, a too painful admission of their own vulnerability. One African employer said bitterly of young women servants that, 'they can't be trusted – they steal everything, even our husbands', whilst another said that she did not employ girls who came along 'all made-up'.[8] I was struck by one Asian woman's account of why she did not want young women servants – 'they get their periods and don't manage it very well, and I have sons'. They will dismiss a servant they suspect of behaving provocatively.

From the perspective of female servants the situation might be exploitable – if the man is unattached then they think it advantageous to be 'taken up': servants tell stories of other women they know who were taken up by Europeans or Asians and in return got houses built for them, or money given ('You remember Wilhelmina,' said one informant to my female assistant, 'she was lucky! She got taken up by the European and she bore his child and he provided for her'). Where there is a wife to contend with, it is another matter, and in Sara's case (described in Chapter 2), she felt obliged to leave the job before her situation was further compromised. On rare occasions the sexual dimension might lead to marriage. In one Arab household which I knew well, the young African woman who began as a servant ended up as wife to a young male relative of the family. This drama unfolded before my eyes. The family were not pleased – they said to the young man: 'you have all the world outside to choose girls from – and we have difficulty getting houseworkers. Why must you cast your eyes on our girls when we are depending on them?' But it was no use. The family stopped paying her a wage – 'you have been married [by us] now', they told her. After that she 'became lazy and didn't want to help'.

An African employer told me of how her young female ayah disappeared after a visit by her sister-in-law's son: 'the next thing we heard they had got married and she is still with him'. She evidently felt there was some shame in this liaison. During the interview there were two young male relatives with us and she had claimed that the girl was unreliable and that she did not know why she had run off. It was only as she was seeing me off down the drive that she confided the real reason the ayah had left.

When sexuality intrudes into the work relationship it undermines hierarchy and control. Both sides may be intimidated by its threat, in ways which are marked by the gender composition of the central triad – male/female servant: male employer: female employer (other household members may also be implicated). At the same time the impulse to exploit the access which close relations of domesticity offer may be taken up by any of the parties to the triad in pursuit of their own sexual or material advantage.

The threat of sexuality is one amongst a set of negative sanctions which shadow the relationship of domestic service and ensure that neither side is in complete command and must continually renegotiate the terms of the relationshp.

CONCLUSION

The work relationship is supposedly formal, hierarchical, contractual and characterised by instrumentality on both sides. In practice the purely instrumental is creatively pursued, each side deploying both positive goads and incentives as well as negative threats and sanctions to achieve their ends, and both sides subscribing to familial metaphors to rationalise their actions. The potency of familial language is underlined by its extension to many other social settings where its promise can subdue dissent. Along with many others, Adesina makes this clear in his account of the factory setting, and many have noted its deployment as a metaphor for 'nation': 'Nations are frequently figured through the iconography of familial and domestic space' (McClintock 1993:64). The power of the metaphor lies in the way it imprints a 'naturalness' on social arrangements in general and on relations of inequity in particular. It sanctions 'hierarchy within unity', whilst at the same time appearing to exist 'beyond the commodity market, beyond politics and beyond history'. Domestic service can be seen not merely in terms of an extension of these images to the workplace, but also as a process of moral incorporation.

If the attempt to redefine the workplace as a moral community speaks loudly from the data presented here, it is also a setting for political struggle, of competition for power and for the spoils of power. As I have shown, this is a game played out through contradictory stratagems of encouraging intimacy and asserting distance. Servants cultivate 'closer encounters' which might allow for moral pressure to be brought to bear on the employer. This moral pressure in its turn could allow for gifts to be offered and help provided in crises. It might also limit what was demanded in the form of work – the number of hours, the pace of work, the nature of tasks. We have seen that servants often compared servant work favourably with other jobs in that it allowed for personalised relationships, which might be manipulated. 'Pleasing the employer' and entering into intimate confidence with them is a strategy of survival. For some servants this may extend to allowing or encouraging sexual relationships. For employers these intimacies can be challenging to authority as well as putting undue pressure on the relationship. However they may perceive benefits to be gained from friendly interaction and generosity, to be rewarded by loyalty, reliability and willingness.

A degree of distance must also be maintained if they are to assert their authority. If intimacy is coloured by gender, then the assertion of power is also related to gender in this setting. The woman employer has an active managerial and organisational role vis-à-vis servants and it is difficult for her to avoid the physical closeness and personal knowledge which lay her open to manipulation. She must actively exert power in a context where she is susceptible. The man of the house is 'naturally' distanced by his normally limited participation in the running of the household. Paradoxically it is in fact his non-exercise of everyday power, and his more marked social distance from servants, which enhances his authority. It is the anticipation of his response which is telling rather than any actual response. This male power becomes a crucial complement to women's authority over servants in contexts where it really matters (wages and dispute settlements).

Finally back to Adesina. In domestic service as in large-scale capitalist employment, workers aim to 'adapt the work to themselves' as well as to be adapted by it. They may succeed – a good example here would be in their (generalised) resistance to living in, as well as in the way individual servants manage to get good deals for themselves. As far as the employer is concerned the 'value relation' is also not always the last word – or at least it becomes caught up in a web of other feelings and responses. The point at which the capitalist factory seems to part company most clearly with the home is in its lack of a work group of similarly exploited servants. Even where there is more than one servant employed, the personalised nature of the employment may be such as to set them at odds.[9] Conversely one servant may have been brought by the other and owe him an obligation. If solidarity in the workplace is rare, there is a generalised culture of such workers in the urban community which allows them to share strategies about managing employers, finding new jobs and dealing with disputes.

9

MILITANT DOMESTICS?
CLASS, GENDER AND RESISTANCE

Towards the end of the colonial period domestic servants in Tanganyika were in the forefront of an emergent and militant labour movement with clear trade union goals and methods. This deserves explanation, for it challenges many theories of labour mobilisation. In the postcolonial phase domestic servants have been amongst the least unionised of workers, and could accurately be described as apolitical and passive. What could explain this dramatic reversal and where does it leave any conception of a 'class project' pursued through wage labour?

We have seen that in the postcolonial period domestic service is gradually being feminised. Some may be tempted to see this shift in the gender composition of the work-force as the major explanation for the increasing passivity of workers. Theorists in the sociology of work have often argued that female labour is of value to employers precisely because it is more acquiescent and less likely to be unionised than male labour (see debate reviewed in Barron and Norris 1976; and for world market factories in the Third World, Elson and Pearson 1981a). Women have also been seen as constrained by their 'domestic responsibilities' from engaging actively in politics. Feminists have long resisted this thesis of passivity (e.g. for Britain: West 1982, or more recently Lee-Treweek 1997; and for Africa e.g: Mackintosh 1989; Berger 1986; Tripp 1994; Geiger 1997). I argue that in this case the shifting gender composition of the work-force is purely coincidental and has little explanatory power.

Explaining a decline in militancy is one thing: explaining militancy is another. Shivji drew on classical Marxism to explain the emergence of organised labour in colonial Tanganyika – capitalist forms of development brought workers together and in this context they became aware of their common exploitation and organised to confront it (1983:13).[1] He went on to celebrate the activism of domestic servants amongst others. This synergistic linking of structure with agency runs into difficulty when applied to many African countries. Tanzania is a prime example where capital and labour have been concentrated only in a limited way, with the mass of the population still surviving through family production of the necessities of life and/or by petty commodity production of goods and services, rather than as dispossessed wage labourers. Where concentration has occured, it has often been as much an outcome of state intervention as of the expansion of capitalist forms of production (cf. the colonial creation of a physical and administrative infrastructure or postcolonial experiments in nationalising industry or extending control of the market). Under whatever auspices, the concentration of capital generated workers (largely semi-proletarianised migrants), whose subsequent history of labour resistance and activism is on record. We could conclude that it is not capitalism so much as the concentration of exploited workers which sparks resistance into being.

There are particular problems with the case of domestic servants, however. First, domestic workers are not concentrated. Working for private employers, each one is isolated from the others, except in very large establishments (which have always been rare). Secondly, the sphere of domestic labour – within which servants are employed as wage labourers – has an ambiguous and indirect relation with 'capital'. In the domestic labour debate, its 'end product' was seen as the renewal of the labour power of members of the household. The production of surplus value occurs elsewhere (when the labour power is sold) and the producer, whether wage worker or family member, fails to 'see' how she is exploited. It is through the recognition of exploitation that political consciousness is raised. For many Marxists, therefore, the domestic labourer was structurally ill-placed to be a revolutionary: 'While the labour of housewives remains privatised' says Seccombe, 'they are unable to prefigure the new order nor spearhead the productive forces in breaking the old' (1974:23).

At first sight there seems to be no reason why the same argument would not apply to domestic servants. However, if we redefine the 'product' of domestic labour as services directly consumed within the household, quite different conclusions may be drawn, with consumption at high levels of privilege being grossly apparent to those who are excluded from its enjoyment – i.e. domestic wage labourers. A basis for their politicisation in felt injustice might therefore be assumed.

In many accounts of domestic workers (including those written by feminists) servants are assumed to be victims of their situation. Writing of South Africa, Deborah Gaitskell et al. state that: 'Domestic servants, as members of a service sector of the working class, tend to exhibit similar characteristics all over the world: isolation, dependence, invisibility, low level of union organisation' (1984:87). Reviewing work on North and South America, Wrigley asserts that: 'Domestic workers differ from most other workers in being almost unable to organise collectively ... [they] lack the means to create a collective culture' (1991:327, 326). Noting that domestic service was 'almost untouched' by the growth of unionism in Victorian England, Burnett adds ideological constraints to those of structure: even 'in large establishments ... the employer-employee relationship was still essentially feudal [and] a "peasants' revolt" was unthinkable' (1974:169). It then seems common-sense for Mascarenhas and Mbilinyi to argue that in present-day Tanzania: 'The isolated nature of [domestic] work and the availability of large numbers of girls or women seeking wage employment in towns have blocked organised struggles of domestic servants thus far' (1983:19).

A militant organisation of domestic servants would thus seem unlikely, and yet several examples of such militancy can be cited from colonial and postcolonial Africa where domestic servants have shown themselves able and willing to organise against their employers and to ally themselves with other workers to improve their wages and conditions of employment.

In the 1950s all the East African colonial territories manifested organised action by domestic servants. In Uganda in 1945, 'workers staged their first general strike in the history of the country. Beginning with domestic servants ... the strike spread to every urban centre in the country' (Mamdani 1983:15). The Kenya Houseboys' Association with a largely Kikuyu membership was in existence as early as 1947 and pressing to become legally registered. Domestic servants were active in a general strike in 1947 in Mombasa which led to the formation of the African Workers' Federation: 'work stopped at the docks, on the railway and in practically all hotels, offices and banks in Mombasa. Private homes were without African servants' (Stichter 1975:41). In the 1950s domestic servants were said to have been 'ordered' by their Union to take part in the oathing that led up to Mau Mau (Kershaw 1997:223). In Zanzibar in the late 1940s a dockworkers' strike (1948) was supported by many other workers, including 'the great majority of houseservants' (Coulson 1982:128).

It then becomes less surprising to find Shivji incorporating domestic workers into his celebration of working-class heroism in the national liberation struggle in Tanganyika: 'Among service workers, the domestic servant was one of the most important components', who, together with workers in building and construction, transport, manufacturing and commerce, were led by 'powerful and militant unions' (1983:14).

In all these examples of domestic servant militancy, the workers in question were male. Analysts have often assumed an unproblematic link between female predominance in domestic work and lack of organisational capacity; whereas male passivity demands a particular explanation. Most of the work on Latin America, where servants are almost exclusively female, views as 'normal' their limited capacities for organisation (Bunster and Chaney 1985:30–1), though there is evidence from the 1930s and from the 1980s of female servants unionising in Bolivia (Gill 1994:32–5).

That female domestic workers have the capacity to organise under certain circumstances is indicated by Gordon's work on South Africa. Whilst she repeats the view that 'domestic servants have been considered the most conservative members of the working class', three of the women whose life stories she details were active in the formation of SADWA, the South

African Domestic Workers' Association, in the early 1980s (1985:xxvi). The strength of SADWA in a situation where feminisation of domestic service is now complete is striking. In Namibia too a largely female Domestic Workers' Union was formed before independence, even though to be involved in trade union matters was politically suspect and linking potential members a daunting task (Johnson 1992: 140). Such evidence demands further critical research as it puts into question the assumption that it is the gender composition of the work-force which determines its activism.

Several writers raise another thesis: that the organisation of domestic servants is as much a response to colonialism as to the exploitation of wage labour. Domestic servants found themselves empowered as part of a more general struggle against colonial rule. Whilst domestic servants were isolated in their work situation, the growth of colonial urban 'Native Quarters' generated trans-ethnic communities which brought migrant workers together. Albeit unstable and shifting collectivities, their emergent identity was expressed in the idiom of nationalism (Geiger 1997). It could also be argued that the work situation of domestic servants particularly exposed them to the humiliations and oppressions of colonialism. Adesina's general argument seems pertinent here: 'employment relations are shot through with power relations. This is more so in the colonial context' (1992:49).

Something of all this, given a gender inflection, is illustrated in Van Onselen's account of the Amalaita movement in South Africa in the early years of this century. This movement drew in a diversity of social elements, though the majority were young men employed as domestic servants. Their activities could not be described as organised unionism, since they did not directly confront their individual employers, nor voice clear demands regarding pay or conditions. Their association traversed the line between legitimate and illegitimate activities and was fought out on the public stage of the streets rather than the private space of the work-place. Involved in petty crime, and donning a uniform, the Amalaita engaged in competitive fights and music parades. They continually came up against the police in their challenge to restrictions on urban Africans. Whilst many were docile at work (they had references testifying that they were 'excellent houseboys') they were aggressive on the streets, particularly towards their 'perceived oppressors, white women' (1982:59). Van Onselen claims that the Amalaita was essentially: 'a movement of young black domestic servants and their unemployed peers born out of hard times ... a movement which sought to give its members who laboured in alienated colonised isolation a sense of purpose and dignity' (1982:59). He adds a further twist, arguing that in their challenging behaviour the Amalaita movement was 'the "houseboys'" liberation army fighting to reassert its decolonised manhood' (1982:59). The suggestion here is not that militancy derives from manhood, but rather that gendered identity was under threat, both in the occupation itself and in the authoritarian policing of wage labour in South Africa.

I have argued that masculinity was barely dented by the colonial institution of domestic service in Tanzania; more positively I have insisted that it was redefined as 'men's work', and that this remained the view of many workers and employers in the postcolonial phase. The gender argument must always be viewed critically. However, we shall see that Van Onselen's description of the emergence of a self-conscious community of urban Africans, within which domestic servants become politicised, was a feature also of colonial Tanganyika. Did nationalism lend strength to the cause of domestic workers in this case? Does militancy thereby collapse after independence, when nationalist class alliances fall apart, as they did in spectacular fashion in postcolonial Tanzania?

In short, the militancy of domestic servants is as problematic as their passivity, and several modes of explanation are on offer (structural, political, ideological etc.), though in both cases there is an obvious temptation to explain the phenomenon in terms of gender.

DOMESTIC MILITANCY: THE UNION

On the unpromising ground (in Marxist terms) of semi-proletarianisation for a tiny minority in colonial Tanganyika, some surprising developments took place. Iliffe contrasts the emergence of unionism in Britain (where association began with skilled industrial workers), with that in Tanganyika, where white collar workers, service and transport workers combined first and industrial workers were amongst the last to be unionised (1979a:196). Trade unions were first formed by drivers in the late 1920s and shop assistants in the 1930s. There was a rapid expansion just before and after the Second World War. Strikes and boycotts were organised, wage increases for many workers achieved, and the first minimum wage legislation grudgingly conceded by the colonial government (see Coulson 1982:137). On Independence in 1961, Iliffe claims that 42 per cent of Tanganyikan wage workers were unionised (1979a:539).

Amongst the first African trade unions to be registered was the African Cooks, Washermen and Houseboys Association, set up in one of Tanganyika's larger towns (Dodoma) in 1939. Domestic workers at the time had something to defend. Since the skills which Europeans and Asians demanded from their African servants were initially in short supply, they were not to begin with amongst the worst paid of workers, their wages comparing favourably with those of miners, plantation workers and general labourers in the earlier part of the century.[2] As the inflow of migrant labour into towns increased, these favourable conditions began to fade. Combination was one way of resisting the degradation of an occupation regarded by workers as a skilled job.

In Chapter 4 I described the activities of the African Cooks Association as it surfaced in official files and in European-owned newspaper accounts, noting the response to it as symptomatic of a certain kind of 'colonial discourse'. In this chapter I consider the same events as an example of the potential, but also the limitations, of organised labour in the context of an occupation like domestic service.

There were three phases of union activity involving domestic servants in colonial Tanganyika. The first begins in 1939, and continues through the registration of the African Cooks, Washermen and Houseboys' Association as a national organisation in 1945, until its registration was cancelled in 1949; the second covers the period from 1950–3 when the leaders of the union, refusing to disband, sent numerous petitions to the UN. The third period begins in 1955 with the amalgamation of a Domestic and Hotel Workers Union into the newly formed Tanganyika Federation of Labour (TFL) and extends beyond the dramatic strike of 1956 to Independence in 1961.

It is the first period which both Shivji and Iliffe celebrate as one in which clear trade union principles were in evidence. Not only did the union campaign, in public meetings and in petitions to government for better wages and shorter hours for servants (complaining for example to the District Commissioner in Mwanza, that 'domestic servants are left to die of starvation due to inadequate payments': quoted in Shivji 1986:164), they also schooled their members in elementary principles of solidarity: 'Members should not cheapen themselves as regards wages paid to them by their employers ... Each man must remember what befalls another will react on him ... these are the rules of our association of boys' (quoted in Iliffe 1979a:397). Despite their militant language, they did not achieve wage rises, but they may have inhibited some servants from undercutting each other.

In 1949 the union was deregistered for failing to account for 'current expenditure and monies received from up-country branches'. Colonial officials 'explained' to their superiors that it was led by 'a handful of self-seeking office holders of very doubtful integrity'.[3] The judgement of historians such as Iliffe and Shivji is different. Credit is given to the capacity to organise far beyond the capital: branches were set up not only in Dar es Salaam, but in Mwanza, Kigoma, Chunya, Kilosa, Lindi, Dodoma and Singida as well as Tanga. And there is recognition for the union's earliest leader, Saleh bin Fundi, whom Iliffe described as 'Tanganyika's first African labour leader' (1979a:398).

Perhaps one key dimension of Fundi's forceful leadership was a degree of autonomy from domestic service itself. Special Branch files describe him as a night watchman – a job which would have distanced him from the personalised surveillance which 'inside' servants endured.[4] Iliffe also says that he was a 'Hehe resident of New Street [in Dar es Salaam] who had almost certainly been (and perhaps still was) the capital's *Arinoti* leader' (1979a: 397). The Arinoti was the best known of the *beni* (music/dance teams), of a kind common in towns throughout colonial Africa and expressing the trans-ethnic consciousness of urban immigrant workers, here expressed in the lingua franca of Swahili. This was the same milieu from which sprang political activism amongst women who allied themselves to the Tanganyika African National Union (TANU) in the late 1950s (Geiger 1997).[5] These heightened levels of politicisation may be linked to the growing density of civil society (Adesina 1992:54).

There are suggestions that the union's strength also came from its sponsorship by white collar and petty bourgeois elements amongst Africans. There were links between the original founders in Dodoma and the local branch of the African Association (Iliffe 1979a:397). The African Associa-tion was the forerunner of TANU; its origins were in an even earlier association set up in Tanga in 1922 (the Tanganyika Territory African Civil Service Association: Coulson 1982:104). Membership of the African Asso-ciation incorporated the more educated and better off Africans (clerks in government service, traders etc.). Geiger reports a similar cross-class linking in the activities of Mbutta Milando, who, after working as a clerk in Mwanza 'became a trade unionist, leading a group of domestic employees and hotel workers in Mwanza' (1997:93). Such patronage was not uncom-mon. Both of the earliest leaders of the dockers union were non-dockers – the first an 'educated ex-soldier' and the second a journalist and editor of a Swahili newspaper (Iliffe 1975:65, 67).

Such cross-class alliances indicate a generalised anger of Africans against colonial rule, though we have seen that this did not inhibit Saleh bin Fundi from inveighing against better-off Africans whom he thought had the ear of government (see Chapter 4). Such alliances of expediency are to be differ-entiated from attempts by the colonial authorities to co-opt the emergent union movement and to direct it into 'responsible' and apolitical channels. After a bitter but successful dockers' strike in 1947, Labour Department officials intervened to encourage a more 'constructive' approach in the way the union was run (Iliffe 1975:65; Friedland 1969:36–8). Similar expecta-tions were eventually brought to bear on the African Cooks, 'registration of such a union will again become possible only if and when an association is formed showing itself capable of understanding the principles of trade unionism' (V22/37681/5/25, 4 Nov 1953). In an earlier phase the union leaders thought they would be able to bend government intervention to their own advantage. Iliffe describes a public meeting called by Saleh bin Fundi in Dar es Salaam in 1945 where he claimed that 'government agreed to their suggestions [to set up the Association] and ... [the Union] would receive the assistance of a European who would act for them as Chairman and carry out their orders as directed, and a special office would be opened for them in the *boma* [government offices] to deal with matters concerning their affairs' (1979a:398). There is no evidence of any such arrangement being put in place. We have noted, however (Chapter 4), that there was an overlap between union activities and the operations of the Women's Service League of Tanganyika (WSLT) as a labour exchange.

It was in the interests of European employers to facilitate a supply of well-trained servants and to have a recognised source of recruitment. Government was as concerned about influx control as servants themselves were concerned to limit the supply of labour so as to keep wages buoyant. In one branch the Union aimed for a closed shop: non-members of the Union 'may be made to cease to work' (Iliffe 1979b:291). For a time, then, there was a congruence of interest between the two sides, with the union in some areas even ready to police servants on behalf of their employers. Iliffe notes that one branch devised the rule that: 'If a member is employed but does not follow his master's orders, his master has the right to accuse him before the Heads of the Association who will take serious views and punish him' (1979a:399). However, when the union later adopted more confrontational tactics, these 'responsible' parties disappear from the scene to be replaced by alliances with other workers.

From 1949 until 1953 (at least), the central committee of the union refused to disband and bombarded the world with long letters of political complaint, usually signed by Saleh bin Fundi and several other men. I have argued (Chapter 4) that these intemperate and, to a degree, seditious communications represent a form of oppositional discourse embodying a class-based critique of colonial rule. But these union leaders also spoke as men, complaining: 'we have no means at all to feed our fathers, our children and our wives'.[6]

Saleh bin Fundi disappears from the historical record in 1953 after the colonial authorities contrived to prevent him and his commmittee from meeting the UN Trusteeship Committee. In 1955 a new phase began with the establishment of an umbrella organisation to speak for the interests of all Tanganyika Unions – the Tanganyikan Federation of Labour (TFL). One of the ten unions which came together to form the TFL was a more substantial body, the Hotel Workers and Domestic Servants' Union. A contemporary source claimed it had 4000 members in 1956 with 3000 in domestic service and the rest in hotels (*Sunday News* 28 Oct. 1956:5). The link with hotel workers gave a distinctive edge to the new grouping. Hotel workers, though they carry out similar domestic tasks to those performed by private domestic servants, are, from a Marxist point of view, quite differently situated vis-à-vis the productive system. Hotel workers produce a commodity in the form of services which are sold at a profit by the owner of the capital involved (i.e. hotel proprietors). Their exploitation is transparent. They are also concentrated in large establishments as compared to the atomised existence of domestic servants. In Tanganyika at that time, and to a large extent today as well, hotel workers, like domestic servants, were male, and they have always been able to earn higher wages than domestic servants.

DOMESTIC MILITANCY: THE STRIKE

In October 1956 workers at a hotel or hostel in the capital city, Dar es Salaam, were sacked, and the union demanded their reinstatement. When this was refused and efforts at conciliation had failed, the union called a strike of all hotel and domestic workers throughout the country. The strike lasted for approximately three weeks in the capital, though seemingly for shorter periods in the provinces. The original demand for the reinstatement of the sacked men was now augmented by demands for higher wages for all categories of domestic work. In a submission to the government the union pointed out a crucial difference between hotel and private domestic workers, and one which would continue to be significant: 'In the case of hotel workers we have direct contact with the Hotel Keepers' Association with whom we can negotiate for our members ... but it is not easy in the case of domestic servants. This Union therefore considers that some statutory machinery should be established for domestic servants, and ... a Wages Council is strongly recommended' (*Sunday News* 28 Oct 1956:5).

Newspapers soon reported several thousand workers on strike (*Sunday News* 9 Dec. 1956:1). More threatening still, the strike generated a wave of sympathy action amongst other workers, orchestrated by the TFL, as well as boycotts of buses and bottled beer. Contemporary accounts refer to the Commercial and Industrial Workers Union, Building and Construction labourers and motor transport workers as having backed the industrial action (ibid.).

Some accounts state that 40 per cent of workers in private households came out on strike as well as many hotel workers, but the reliability of such estimates cannot be confirmed (quoted by Shivji from a labour report: 1986:197). The European press complained that the strikers' demands had nothing to do with private employers and exulted that: 'Many reported for duty as usual' (*Sunday News* 9 Dec. 1956) . Later they derided the action as a failure; it was an 'abortive strike' (*Sunday News* 30 Dec. 1956). Whilst the actions of servants in staying away from work for a few days hardly affected the economic fortunes of the country, they certainly undermined the comfort of their employers, and generated disproportionate wrath, as contemporary newspaper accounts attested. Europeans expected continuing loyalty from their workers and were often rewarded. My survey of colonial pensioners picked up some of these attitudes. 'My people never went on strike!' recalled one. Another remembered that: 'My own servants did not strike, but I remember being asked "if they could stay indoors" ... fearing that they might be branded "blacklegs"!' Another employer had clear recall: 'Notices calling for a strike were pinned onto trees in Tabora Township. I talked about it to my servants. Their attitude and that of others in Tabora, was indignation at being told what to do by a lot of people they didn't know in Dar es Salaam'. Some Europeans made sure their servants did not join. One who had been in Mtwara said: 'I ... do not think it affected my boys as they lived on the premises. A servant coming [to recruit] from the African quarter would have been stopped'. And the European press reported that in Regent Estate in Dar es Salaam 'vigilante' groups were set up 'when the present series of strikes began. Strike agitators can obviously expect ... swift action if they start any "monkey business" ...' (*Sunday News* 3 Feb 1957).

The European press recommended the dismissal of strikers. Such a response would meet with 'nothing but approval from the loyal servant' (9 December 1956). When the strike was called off by the TFL on 28 December, many workers were laid off in the affected sectors, including domestic workers in homes and hotels. 'At one hotel ... all the strikers rolled up, to be told, "We have already filled the vacancies you left"' (30 December 1956). Commercial, building and motor transport workers were also denied their jobs when they returned to work.

By 27 January 1957 the TFL called for a general strike to reinstate victimised strikers and for a statutory minimum wage to be imposed. Ten thousand union members were said to have held a mass meeting in Dar es Salaam to back these demands, claiming 5000 had been victimised (*Sunday News* 27 Jan. 1957). The government brought severe legalistic pressure to bear on the leaders of the TFL, and the intervention of two British TUC officials (Walter Hood and Albert Hammerton) led to the threat of a strike being called off in early February. The TFL had nothing to show for the hardship strikers had undergone, but a minimum wage was soon afterwards established for Dar es Salaam for which, as Friedland notes, 'the unions were able to claim credit' (1969:22). But the proposed rate of Sh81.90 was to be imposed only in the capital and was limited to adult males over 18 (Shivji 1986:130). It was also only half the demand put forward by the union for the lowliest domestic worker (*Sunday News* 28 Oct. 1956).[7]

Given all the structural and ideological obstacles to the unionisation of domestic workers this period of active militancy is remarkable. The strike in 1956 was a key episode in a phase of union activism which fed into the struggle for national liberation in the period leading up to Independence in 1961. Cutting across ethnicity and religious affiliation, the union was anchored in a consciousness of common class position and colonial oppression. In gender terms, however, it was led and dominated by male workers. This was not so much a statement of male power as a reflection of the fact that domestic service was almost wholly a man's job, a skilled job in which men took pride, and which they were prepared to defend. That some women were involved is suggested by Saleh bin Fundi's comment that 'our sons and daughters are working ... for Europeans and Indians',[8] whilst a union leader in Tanga spoke of recruiting 'ayahs'. But women do not figure elsewhere in the historical record and amongst the few I found in Tanga who were working as servants at that time, none could remember the strike. In this they were no different to men.

UNIONISATION IN TANGA

Tanga was by no means peripheral to these events. It had long been the site of associational activity amongst Africans, with the earliest association amongst educated white collar workers established there in 1922 (TTACSA) and the earliest combination of dockworkers in struggles over casualisation and low wage levels in 1937 (Coulson 1982:104–5). In the surrounding region sporadic localised actions by sisal workers were common (though employers resisted the legal organisation of plantation workers until 1957: Shivji 1986:211).

There is no written record of when the Tanga branch of the African Cooks was established, but oral accounts suggest the same initial flirtation between union, government and WSLT elements as occured at national level. Erasto Matayo, one of the early leaders of domestic servants in Tanga, told how they were helped in setting up their local association by the local Labour Commissioner (Bwana Leba) and by two European ladies 'Memsabu Dimitri and Memsabu Bennett'.[9] He said that these people thought it would be useful to have an association which could represent workers in any dispute with their employers, and they collected money to help them rent an office, to hire a typist and even to buy a sewing machine to teach ayahs how to mend and make clothes. At first the main activity of the union was to assist these three Europeans to arbitrate in disputes which arose between servants and their employers. From 1948 there are archival references to the Registry run by the WSLT in the Tanga Labour Exchange Office in which some servants were involved.[10] A more activist phase would seem to have begun after the formation of the TFL in 1955. A visit to Tanga from the General Secretary of the Hotel and Domestic Workers' Union, Mr T. C. Msumba, led to the recruitment of Erasto Matayo to be their local leader and organiser of domestic workers.[11]

Matayo[12] was a Sambaa Christian born in a village near Muheza in the late 1920s. He had no formal schooling – it was through the TFL and later the National Union of Tanganyika Workers that he learnt to read and write as an adult. His parents were peasant farmers and his first job was as a 'garden boy' for the European manager of a nearby sisal estate. His grandfather was working as a cook for other Europeans in Tanga and he sent for his grandson to become the kitchen boy. After this Matayo worked his way upwards in the domestic service hierarchy to become successively houseboy to the District Commissioner, the Provincial Commissioner and then for the Sisters at the European Hospital. Along the way he also worked for two companies as a domestic servant, one of them the Sisal Estates Association. Finally he became the Head Waiter at the Tanga Hotel.

Matayo became the District Chairman of the Tanga branch of the Hotel and Domestic Workers' Union and later Regional Secretary. Other leaders were John China (secretary), Mzee Shaba and Ali Samponda. The majority of members were domestic servants rather than hotel workers: 'the hotels were very few in those days'. Matayo remembered an initial influx of two hundred members and said they built the union up over the next few years to six to eight hundred members.[13] Members paid two shillings for their membership card and then a subscription of 50 cents per month. He claimed to have been the main recruiter of members; his method was to go round the houses of rich people on his bicycle and to accompany a milk lorry making deliveries. This way it was easy for him to contact cooks, ayahs and shamba boys and tell them about the union. He said that some were afraid to join, and this was confirmed by another ex-servant who told me: 'I remember this Union but I didn't join. In those days employers warned you not to get mixed up in politics or you would be dismissed'. But according to Matayo many were eager and he did not have to do much persuading.

Matayo represented the strike in Tanga as having been a success. Some evidence comes from a letter from the Provincial Secretary of the Tanga branch of the Hotel and Domestic Workers Union (possibly Matayo) to the *Sunday News* on 16 December 1956. This made it clear that alliances with other working class unions were to lend power to the domestic workers' cause. Explaining that the Tanga branch was to begin its strike on 16 December the secretary wrote: 'The reason for the delay in strike action in Tanga of domestic and hotel employees is that it was thought advisable that the day of the strike should at least coincide with the proposed Tanga dockworkers' strike in sympathy'. In the event the dockers in Tanga, like dockers in Dar es Salaam, were warned off collateral action by the Labour Department: 'such a strike being in an essential service would in these circumstances be illegal' (quoted in Shivji 1986:197). But the domestic workers went ahead. Matayo reported that European employers put up with the inconvenience of having no servants, but many Asian employers sacked their striking employees and took on non-unionised workers. The outcome was in line with the objectives: 'our strike was for a minimum wage of Sh80 and this is what we achieved'.

Between 1956 and the time of Independence the Tanga Union seems to have been swallowed up in the TFL and to have handed over to national leaders the responsibility for pressing the government to improve conditions. (Ali Samponda did recall a later strike at the Tanga Hotel for a rise in wages to Sh100 and more security of employment.) After Independence, when the TFL was forcibly disbanded and the National Union of Tanganyika

Workers was established in its place (see below), Matayo became a local representative and relocated to Dar es Salaam.

When I tried to collect oral historical accounts of the events of the 1950s from amongst domestic servants in Tanga thirty years later, I encountered first the fickleness of memory. The details of events so long ago have faded, and incidents which figure large in colonial files may have seemed less significant to ordinary people. Conversely the events may not have been so far-reaching and portentous as they appear in hind-sight. Few may have been directly involved. Moreover, since wage labourers are still largely migrant workers, the composition of the workforce is continually changing. Few of those who are servants today were also servants in the 1950s – most of these have long ago retired to the rural areas. Even amongst those whose memory of domestic service stretched back to the forties and fifties, only one or two could remember a union ('we thought it would help us but it didn't', said one), none except Matayo could remember the 1956 strike, and even Matayo could not remember Saleh bin Fundi.[14] Tanganyika's 'first African labour leader' existed, he has a large file in the colonial records, but he is an unknown hero for domestic workers today.

POSTCOLONIAL MUZZLING OF THE UNION MOVEMENT

After 1957 the Hotel and Domestic Workers Union disappears from the public record of forceful union activity which continued in the period leading up to Independence (1961). Much of this union ferment was seething in the Tanga region itself, as plantation workers in the sisal industry were at last unionised and strike actions in local estates led to violence and massive lay-offs. Both TFL and TANU leaders became involved, with Nyerere himself appealing to Tanga residents to shelter strikers (Shivji 1986:201). Shivji argues that it was union activity in this period which forced a rise in real wages (56 per cent between 1958 and 1961) – and whilst the record is silent on domestic servants their wages could not but have been dragged upwards by the general pressure and by the institution of a nation-wide minimum wage immediately after Independence (ibid.:204). Their passivity in this period still needs to be explained.

Independence raised the expectations of all workers. At first these seemed to be realised as minimum wages were raised and other fringe benefits instituted. In retrospect, however, Matayo and Ali Samponda put these improvements down, not to Independence, but to the solidarity amongst workers achieved by the TFL: 'With the TFL many things began to happen', said Matayo, mentioning the minimum wage and the introduction of insurance for workers. Ali Samponda said that the TFL was 'strong and able to help workers'. For example, he credited it with getting rid of the system of contract labour in the sisal industry and negotiating for severance benefits and annual leaves for all employees.

After Independence the government almost immediately began to curb the autonomy of the TFL and failed to deliver quickly on another urgent demand of workers, for the Africanisation of managerial positions. Strikes continued (in 1962 there were 152), and again the sisal workers in Tanga were at the centre of these actions (Shivji 1986:216, 226, 227). Victor Mkello, the plantation workers' leader, became the President of the TFL after Independence. In this capacity, and as a nominated member in parliament, it was he who mounted the most forceful attack on the government's bid to curb the unions, bring the TFL under control and effectively ban strikes and sympathy action. Not only did his appeals fall on deaf ears but since the sisal workers' union was at that time engaged in industrial action, Mkello himself was 'rusticated' to Sumbawanga for a time (Shivji 1986: 233). Matayo told me of this; he and Mkello were friends.

With Mkello out of the way, the government circulated a plan for incorporating the TFL into the Ministry of Labour (1963). Whilst other unions in the Federation opposed this plan, the Domestic and Hotel Workers' Union, together with the Transport and General Workers Union, acquiesced (Shivji 1986:233).[15] I consider later why this was the case. The final blow to the TFL came during an abortive army mutiny in 1964: the unions were accused of making common cause with the rebellion and 200 union leaders were detained (Shivji 1986:233). Whilst the leaders were in goal the government dissolved the TFL and set up the National Union of Tanganyika Workers (NUTA) as an arm of the state, affiliated to TANU and led by government appointees. It consisted of nine industrial sections, of which one was Hotel and Domestic Workers. As Shivji notes, however, these were 'administrative departments rather than organs representing particular sections of the working class and they had no structural or organic links with the membership' (1986: 235). Many of the appointed administrators were from the TGWU, whilst Matayo became a representative for Tanga hotel and domestic employees.

Although socialism was rhetorically introduced in 1967 in the name of 'workers and peasants', there was no expansion in the rights of workers to organise. But workers did claim government slogans of socialism and self-reliance and they demanded justice and the extension of worker control over industries. With formal industrial action outlawed, spontaneous and localised wildcat strikes to lock out managers or owners became a feature of the 1971–5 period (Shivji 1976; Mihyo 1983). Mihyo records two actions in 1972 in Dar es Salaam hotels, both against expatriate management (Mihyo 1983:100–1).

NUTA's name was changed in 1978 to the Jumuiya ya Wafanyi Kazi wa Tanzania (JUWATA) but its mode of operation remained as before. Officials of the Union were active in repressing industrial action whilst their salaried positions depended upon a legalised system of deducting subscriptions from employers for union membership. A visit to JUWATA headquarters in 1986 revealed that Domestic and Hotel Workers were by now the smallest section, accounting for only 3 per cent of all members (9964 out of a total of 342,468 members overall). Due to the heavy-handed system of checking off subscriptions it could be claimed that more than 55 per cent of Tanzanian workers were 'unionised' at the time, even though JUWATA was but a department of state power. At local level the significance of the industrial sub-sections was lost, and workers, if they joined at all, saw themselves as having joined JUWATA, rather than combining with fellow workers in the same occupation or facing the same employers.

The mood of militancy in other sectors in the immediate postcolonial phase was increasingly out of tune with domestic workers' interests. The causes espoused – the ownership of concerns or the Africanisation of management made little sense in the domestic context servants faced. Indeed servants bemoaned the departure of (European and Asian) employers who had paid well and provided employment,[16] whilst decrying the employment practices of the new class of masters. Their racialised political landscape was transformed. Perhaps inevitably servants became a reactionary element in the union movement, their prospects tied up with the perpetuation of class privilege and neo-colonialism.

JUWATA AND THE POSTCOLONIAL ATOMISATION OF DOMESTIC SERVANTS IN TANGA

Domestic service in private homes, whilst still an occupation dominated by men in Tanga in the mid-1980s, was no longer a job to be defended. Wages were amongst the lowest – few employers paid even the minimum wage. Domestic workers now faced exploitation as atomised workers in a context of extreme economic hardship and state repression of any voices of protest or oppositional groupings. In this context workers 'forgot' their history of collective action. Though there was a culture of individualised complaint and bitterness, few thought of combining against employers and they did not see JUWATA as a friend of such action.

In attempting to understand this situation I took particular note of what servants, employers and the local secretary of JUWATA had to say on matters of workers' rights and how they were to be secured. Another party to the debate appeared to be the Labour Office in Tanga (locally known as 'Leba'). The Labour Officer distinguished his operation by saying that he represented government, whereas JUWATA was an organisation of workers with a degree of autonomy from government. Employees might approach either body to be acquainted with their rights. Employers might also wish for advice. Only the Labour Office had the power to prosecute, however. Small matters could be settled in the office through conciliation, though he recalled no cases being brought to him personally. At most one or two cases a year passed through their office.

I therefore made numerous visits to the local offices of JUWATA in 1986. The local secretary at first made grand claims that he had between one and two thousand local members in the Hotel and Domestic Workers' section of the union, and that amongst these were many private domestic servants. After several months he admitted that, after all, he had only 256 members in the Hotel and Domestic section, with only sixteen of these not working in hotels (probably domestic servants). This tallied with my own counts: amongst the servants and ex-servants I interviewed, I found only one present member of the union, a man whose membership had been arranged by his employer. By contrast, amongst those who had moved on to work in the hotel industry, membership was fairly common.

Domestic servants made a rational calculation in choosing not to join JUWATA. It could rarely help in the lonely day by day struggles with employers. As workers said, in these cases, you 'just had to endure' – or look for other work. In a time of economic hardship servants feared for their jobs. Abu gave as one reason for not joining the union his fear of being branded a troublemaker, not only by his existing employer but in any future attempt to secure work. In a small-scale setting like this, employers passed on warnings about 'difficult' workers (and in this sense atomised workers might be confronted by solidarity amongst employers).

An added dimension in a highly personalised occupation was that servants did not wish to poison the on-going relationship with their employer. The JUWATA secretary himself noted that even after he had explained a worker's rights to a complainant, they were often reluctant to confront their employers. One male servant told me he had worked for an Indian family for several years, but when they left for India he was given only 'a few chairs and things'. He added that 'I could have gone to JUWATA but I didn't want to bring trouble and quarrelling into a house where I had stayed so long'. The 'economy of affection' constrains workers from demanding their due. Employers may be similarly constrained. An elderly European employer was reluctant to call the police when her servants robbed her: 'they had been with me so long'. She sacked them but was then forced to pay gratuities by the Labour Office as she refused to prosecute.

Servants also feared the government and they often equated both JUWATA and the Labour Office with state power. One woman was apprehensive when I asked about union membership and hastened to tell me that she had paid her government tax! An elderly male servant responded by producing his party card and said he had joined the party, 'because I am a citizen and it is our duty, it's the law and it will help me if any problem arises. But I haven't sought any other [i.e. union] card'. In the case of hotel workers it was argued that: 'JUWATA is part of the government and you don't want to quarrel with the government', or that membership 'is required by the government' – more than one worker adding that they had no choice as the subscriptions were cut automatically from their wages. The same applied to the only domestic servant who claimed membership – he worked for a rich Asian employer who deducted his subs at source (more than one of the employers whom I interviewed had put their personal servants on their factory pay-rolls, where subscriptions to JUWATA were deducted as a matter of course). There was a tendency to see JUWATA and the Labour Office as indistinguishable and equally unhelpful. One man, a domestic servant, claimed he had received little support: 'if you go for help you are sent to Leba and then back to JUWATA ... there is no point'.

JUWATA was also seen as a corrupt body. Matayo said that JUWATA was very different to the TFL – officials were dishonest and workers could not trust them with their money. One servant described how he and his fellow domestic workers had disputed the severance benefits paid to them by their wealthy Asian employer in the early 1970s, when houses were taken over by the government and the employer was leaving the country. The union (then NUTA) did not follow the rules about payments but made a 'deal' with the employer: 'there was no law'. Nowadays things were no better: 'the boss will go to the clerk at JUWATA and bribe them maybe Sh1000 when you are quarrelling about Sh400 ...'

Despite the 'realism' of domestic servants' low expectations of union support, they found both JUWATA and Leba useful as a veiled threat or, more often, as an actual end game, where the aim was to rescue something from a relationship which had already failed. Hence the frequent references by employers to JUWATA intervention in the case of severance pay, when the worker no longer has anything to lose, and potentially much to gain.

From the perspective of the union, the issue of low recruitment looked very different. The secretary of JUWATA eventually revealed his difficulties in signing up domestic workers. He complained that many people employed servants without completing an official registration form, and many denied employing servants at all, saying that 'these people are my relatives'. The JUWATA secretary distinguished employers along racial lines: Europeans followed the law whereas Asians were argumentative and evasive and got servants to sign false statements regarding wages they had not received. But he reserved his most virulent characterisation for Arabs and Africans who exploit relatives or others. 'They pay them little or nothing and treat them like slaves'; their money went on 'booze' rather than paying proper wages.

This alerted me to the mode of operation of the union: these were employers who refused to yield up workers for affiliation. Membership was enlarged not by responding to the demands of workers, but by prevailing upon employers to sign up their servants. All the better if this could be done in bulk as was the case with employees in hotels. In this encounter pressure could easily be brought to bear, as the union also represented the government in the eyes of many employers, and Asians in particular have always been vulnerable to such pressure (most of the hotel owners in Tanga were Asians).

The fear of being caught out kept employers on their toes. 'We have to pay what the government says – the minimum wage – otherwise they go to Leba and there is trouble'. 'JUWATA officials come round to ask me why my servants haven't joined'. Abu's case was evidence that JUWATA did approach employers for evidence of workers' contracts – but whilst their intervention led his employers to pay the minimum wage Abu still did not join. Employers were aware that they should pay national insurance for their servants (though very few did), and that failure to pay severance benefits would lead to trouble from JUWATA or Leba. They saw workers as instrumental and calculating and insistent on their rights, whilst behind them lay the state. An elderly European employer with two male servants complained that they did not act out the role of loyal family retainers that she had been used to. 'The boys these days work exactly the hours [according to] the regulations and insist on overtime pay for each minute, even when they themselves take time off for their own interests ... [These days] there is the boss and there is the worker and everyone has his own interests. They are not as familiar as in the old days ... when they belonged to the family'.

Employers were fearful that servants would bring in the authorities. One employer was at first reluctant to talk to me, suspicious that I had come from the Labour Office. A European employer complained bitterly, asking: 'Why do Africans, Arabs and Indians get away with treating their servants so badly? We treat our servants very well, but if there is some little thing they go straight to Leba'. One of her watchmen had been laid off and although he was paid his severance dues he went to the Labour Office and claimed he was owed money for overtime. 'There was no definite proof but we were called two or three times and forced to pay Sh400'. An Asian employer gave as one reason for not employing women that, 'housegirls bring a lot of trouble. They are always going to the Police and to Leba and complaining that you didn't pay them when you did – and you are made to pay a lot of money'.

Another Asian employer had dismissed a servant who refused to explain why he was throwing packages from their yard into the house next door. Next day the servant brought JUWATA officials to the house, claiming he had not had his leave pay. 'But we had the records so JUWATA were not able to fault us at all'. Asian employers felt particularly vulnerable – one said they had decided not to go to the police when their servant was caught stealing and ran off. 'It would be trouble for us, and the police are Africans and will find in favour of fellow-Africans'.

The fears of employers exaggerate the influence of JUWATA on workers. The reality was that an attitude of cynicism and distrust regarding collective action prevailed amongst workers, rather than one of solidarity. JUWATA officials were not engaged in the politics of working-class struggle: state-sponsored unionism did not welcome worker unrest. They strove rather to boost their membership (and thereby their career prospects) by threatening employers – and particularly those whom they viewed as most vulnerable.

If JUWATA does not instigate workers to demand improved work conditions or levels of pay in the workplace, it does have one general advantage to workers in its negotiating role with government vis-à-vis the official minimum wage. In 1986, when times were very hard for wage workers, JUWATA was reported as having put forward a national claim for Sh2500 a month as compared with the existing Sh810.

Whether in a settlement about severance pay or national negotiations on the minimum wage, the solidarity of union members was not part of the equation. In the former case the dispute was settled in an individualistic way, leaving open the potential for corruption and deals between employers and officials. In the latter case domestic servants benefitted by default, without even having to join the union. Here the deals are between the powerful at national level. At the local level the most charitable interpretation of JUWATA's activities in the 1980s was that it policed employment law rather than representing workers.

THE COLLECTIVE WORKER AND THE PRIVATISED WORKER

There was a marked contrast between domestic servants in private homes and collective workers in hotels or other industries in terms of their evaluation of unionisation. Whereas few domestic servants ever considered joining JUWATA, seeing no value in it, other workers had a different view, even when they had joined involuntarily. They commented without prompting on the strength which numbers could give in settling disputes. One man who had been a docker said: 'In the docks we were many and if there was a problem it was quickly sorted out'. A hotel worker compared the social solidarity of working with others to the isolation of housework: 'working in the house you only went to the market and came back again'. Tellingly, however, one hotel worker compared the remoteness of JUWATA to the collective strength of their semi-autonomous branch at the hotel which actually engaged in dispute settlement, dealing with unfair dismissals, non-payment of increments and so on. JUWATA only became involved if there were large-scale lay-offs, whilst wage levels were determined by national agreements. Hotel and other workers saw membership of the union as an insurance policy – if there were problems at work it was as well to be a member. One described an occasion when a man had been saved from dismissal because JUWATA intervened.

This distinction in expectation and consciousness can be regarded as a reflection of differences in the objective structural position of private and collective workers (those I interviewed had experienced both situations). However it also reflects the limited nature of what JUWATA could offer to servants in private homes, given its state-led class perspective. Hotel work being more prized and better paid than domestic service, and still almost totally dominated by men, all the JUWATA members here were male.

Whilst domestic workers shared a negative view of unionisation, women were the most apathetic and least likely to mention JUWATA or the Labour Office or to see themselves as having rights as workers. The young women (and men) who were inching into the occupation as a new tide of green labour flooded into urban areas rarely stayed long enough for JUWATA to catch up with them. Older women were also passive. One woman complained bitterly about her treatment at the hands of Arab employers and described how she had left by using the device of 'being called by my grandmother'. I asked why she had not gone to the Union. 'Ah! in those days we were stupid', she replied. Workers, whether men or women, are not stupid, but they are understandably fearful of bringing down the wrath of employers on their heads when there is no-one else around to protect them.

The situation I found in Tanga reflects that of Tanzania as a whole, and worker apathy in the domestic worker sector continues to the present.

CONCLUSION

This case study throws up some very challenging material for explanation: on the one hand worker militancy in a privatised setting; on the other a growing apathy that seems to coincide with the increasing feminisation of the labour force. Whereas apathy appears unproblematic, given that it is in line with many accounts of the passivity of domestic workers – and especially female workers, whether paid or unpaid; the 'militant domestic' has either gone unnoticed, or has not been theorised. Explaining either activism or passivity amongst workers became a deeply unfashionable venture in industrial sociology as Foucauldian emphases on the discursive nature of power and the subjectivity of social relations rendered resistance either invisible or uninteresting to sociologists (Thompson and Ackroyd 1995: 628–9). More recently it has been argued that labour must be 'put back in' to the debates in order to recognise and evaluate new and older forms of resistance. In this case we must encompass both the petty but perpetual workplace skirmishes described in Chapter 8, as well as the unexpected evidence of combination amongst workers described in this chapter.

My concern here has been with three debates relating to the mobilisation of labour. One, deriving from Marxism, sees structural factors in an over-determining light, but links these to agency, to class formation, class consciousness and class 'in itself'. The second revolves around gender as explanation for the militancy or apathy of workers, though in some versions the focus is on cultural construction and in others on determinant sets of social relations into which each sex is locked. The third debate emphasises political synergy: the facilitating contexts within which combination amongst workers appears or is inhibited. Here the role of the state and of political movements are seen as central explanatory factors.

In the end each of these perspectives offers only a partial understanding. Marxist approaches see the activism of the proletariat as bound up with the progress of capitalism. Capitalism exploits the worker, but in collective ways which form the basis for organised resistance. Given the limited reach of capitalist relations in colonial and postcolonial Tanzania this argument might be applied with more relevance to phases of worker apathy, when one may adduce the semi-proletarianised and mostly casualised and unstable migrant labour force as inhospitable material for institutionalised resistance to the employing class. It is indeed difficult to sustain a union movement in such a setting, but whilst routinisation and stability may be inhibited, spontaneous outbursts of anger at exploitation are not. This can throw up, albeit briefly, forms of leadership and organisation from the bottom, whose impact is the more powerful precisely because they are not constrained within the straitjacket of rule-governed collective bargaining. It was just such a maverick but potent threat which Saleh bin Fundi and his African Cooks represented. The routinisation of this charismatic phase depended on an alliance with workers who in structural terms were powerful as *collective* workers, more clearly exploited within capitalist relations of production – i.e. hotel workers.

The domestic labour debate delineated another version of Marxist reasoning. Privatised or family forms of production, though they might also be oppressive, presented neither opportunity nor model for worker resistance, and domestic labourers would not form the backbone of revolutionary activity. Structure and agency did not resonate in this case. Domestic labourers were bound by ties of personal obligation and were essentially collaborators in their own oppression. I have argued that for domestic wage workers the appearance of 'loyalty' was adopted in the expectation of rewards.[17] It was essentially a game-playing performance, not to be taken at face value – servants did not 'labour for love'.

Whether performance or reality, one might expect these bonds to inhibit organised opposition. And yet it was precisely in the setting of the private household that organised resistance appeared in colonial Tanganyika. Or did it? It is facile to adopt a view of domestic workers as working class heroes without examining the evidence more critically. There is evidence here of unionisation as a national structure with an articulate and class-conscious leadership making demands on behalf of its members. But it was also a union concerned initially to collaborate with employers to maintain its standing as a skilled occupation, and to limit dilution.[18] In order to pressure employers its first resort was not to mobilise members and to threaten industrial action, but to appeal to higher authorities (the UN etc.). The strike weapon was one which only became credible when private domestic workers combined with collective workers in hotels and backed this up with strategic alliances with other organised workers. Even then it was easy for private employers to deny that their workers were 'on strike', to reinterpret the evidence as 'intimidation' of workers by the union, and for their employees to be unable to gainsay this interpretation or to link their absence with collective demands for fear of losing their jobs. Even at the height of political expressiveness of class interests during the 1956 strike it is notable that there is no account of servants confronting employers directly with a statement of their demands. Instead they stayed away or were 'sick' – valour disguising itself in discretion. At the same time bonds of personal knowledge, dependence, identification, gratitude and even affection muddied the waters of straightforward class feeling. The employer was not a remote hate-figure with whom there was no personal contact.

Both classical and feminist Marxist formulations draw attention to structural features of domestic employment which lead us to reconsider the evidence of union militancy – not in order to diminish it or to deny its impact, but to set it in its limiting context.

The second debate derives from feminism, where it is argued that women are particularly vulnerable to exploitation and that this renders them docile and unresisting – an argument that may rely on structural or cultural props. Conversely others assert that women workers are not passive creatures of destiny, but as forceful as men in resisting oppression: 'toughness at work, rather than being a preserve of males, is fundamental to working class occupational sub-cultures, both male and female' (Lee-Treweek 1997:61). This latter thesis alerts us to the way in which the militancy of men may be seen as unproblematic – part of a more general assumption of male activism or of cultural constructions of masculinity. Militant domestics may go unremarked if they are men, or their actions may be interpreted as a response to slighted masculinity. Women's passivity in this occupation is explained in general structural terms (isolation, atomisation, personalised bondage) which, however, should equally apply to men in the same settings.

Clearly gender is not the explanation for a decline in organised resistance amongst workers where the blight of apathy and cynicism spread across the gender divide. Today, it is not only women servants who are unorganised. Men too – and they are still in the majority amongst servants – fail to join the union. The job of servant is now degraded, partly because the supply exceeds the demand, and since few employers amongst the new African dominant class can afford to employ specialists like cooks or washermen, the skills it encompasses have been devalued. Many servants now receive less than the official minimum wage.

With regard to the militancy shown by domestic workers in the colonial period, there is little evidence that their being male was a determining factor. This development is more convincingly explained in terms of the relative privilege of domestic workers compared with other manual workers: the skills which they learnt were in short supply and their wages commensurate with this in the early years. Good servants were not easily replaceable, and for the dominant class to manage without them was unthinkable. This gave such servants a certain leverage, and led to a degree of stability in the workforce, with employers eager to see them return after periods of leave. It also reconciled men to doing a job which at home was 'women's work', and led to their redefining it in male terms, rather than as emasculation.

If workers at that point were also concerned to limit the dilution of their occupation by new green labour flowing in from the countryside, it is worth remembering that this labour would likewise have been male. It is only in the postcolonial phase that men are confronted on any scale by female entrants. Though these new workers may be more easily exploited than men of long-standing in the occupation, they are far from docile. Employers regard young women as more difficult to control than men and this is a factor in their preference for men. Young women appear to be less influenced by an ethic of 'professionalism', or pride in the skills of the job. Unlike older men they are rarely looking for a 'career' in domestic service – and indeed the prospects for such a lifetime job with progression in salary and conditions or transfer to more lucrative hotel work are now more limited for all. And we have seen that the newer African employers feel uncomfortable with employing older women. Young women do not aspire to remain in domestic service, and their attitude to work discipline is one of resistance. The same mind set is increasingly adopted by young men. The job is now not worth defending except as a stop-gap measure, and turnover is high. This leads to a sub-culture of resistance in the workplace, but a generalised cynicism with regard to organised opposition, even were this feasible in the current political climate. This conclusion evens up or negates a gendered interpretation of worker militancy/apathy.

The third explanation of this phenomenon is that worker mobilisation in colonial times was an epiphenomenon of the nationalist movement rather than an indication of class consciousness. A dry analytical dissection of these variables cannot do justice to the way in which nationalist sentiment and awareness of exploitation in the work context fed on each other. Servants were more likely than most workers to experience personal humiliations and racist attitudes at first hand and to link this to support for the nationalist cause; they were also strategically placed to see the chinks in the armour of their colonial masters.

The historical record shows that unionism in general and the particular agitation of domestic servants for better wages and conditions were a powerful contributory factor to the strength of nationalism in Tanganyika, rather than being brought into existence by it. The timing of worker mobilisation, the language in which it was promoted and the pattern of alliances which workers made with other exploited sections of working-class labour all testify to more than a single-issue movement aimed at the overthrow of colonial rule. The degree of autonomy which the TFL claimed as a partner to independence is also notable, as well as its rapid co-option and suppression by a state which could not tolerate autonomous struggles.

If workers became apathetic this can also be understood in terms of the iron grip which the postcolonial state exerted over official union activity. Unions were no longer an instrument for the militant expression of grievance. For local union officials promotion was a matter of subscription lists, and evidently it was easier to achieve the expansion of such lists through pressure on employers than by grass roots activity amongst workers (which might at the time have been regarded as politically suspect). It was not until 1990, and in the run-up to political liberalisation, that JUWATA was separated from the ruling party and the state and transformed into the Organisation of Tanzanian Trade Unions (OTTU), though Shivji argues that this development 'is still a far cry from genuinely autonomous trade unionism' (1994:32). Even if it were genuine, the continuing dire economic situation for wage workers has not encouraged worker militancy in the 1990s, nor, in the process of political liberalisation, the organic expression of worker interests through any of the new political parties created.

It is important to acknowledge the way in which servants became a significant element in an emergent, politically aware and trans-ethnic wage labour class in colonial Tanganyika, which at that point was largely gendered male. The urban communities in which this was nurtured (and in which women were also active participants) formed a unifying context for their transient populations. In the postcolonial period the exploitation of domestic workers is greater than before, but workers are cynical and disorganised. Non-unionised domestic workers still have the potential to resist oppressive employers, but this is in an individualistic rather than a collective form: by their 'unreliability', refusal to live in, by stealing, 'laziness', walking out on the job, and so on. Though it must be regarded as a class response to exploitation, resistance of this kind, leading to high turnover of workers, is antithetical to organised unionism – it is anarchic rather than 'disciplined'.

CONCLUSION

'IT'S BETTER TO STAY AT HOME'?

Servant work? It's a job without honour. These days employment has diminished. Wages are too low to live on and people have to do more than one job. More people are going in for trading now. Some women go as far as Kenya. Now I think of domestic work as a job without prospects. I would have been better to stay at home (bora nyumbani). *I didn't build anything. I improved the house a little but I did not improve my prospects in life. You leave all your money in town*
(Abu, 1997)

Each chapter in this book has problematised the question of domestic service in a different way – as colonial discourse, gender dislocation, labour migration, personal narrative, class statement, household politics, and political struggle. Despite the many angles and a babel of 'voices', one thing comes over clearly: domestic service in Tanzania is 'a job without honour'; and whereas it has always had its compensations, these have diminished over the years. An occupation which seemed so redolent of colonial domination, a practical illustration of white mastery over 'lesser races', survived the transition to African rule and was unremarked even when it underwrote 'socialist' class formation.

Despite this, it has been work through which many have passed and made their own in the bid for everyday survival. And a close perusal of the institution in colonial and postcolonial Tanzania has thrown up some surprises and some compelling questions which we may now state in more general terms.

MASCULINITY AND THE DOMESTIC MODE

What this case demonstrates most effectively is that masculinity can be defined in the domestic mode, as men turn housework into a man's job. Does this 'dislocate masculinity' in any meaningful sense when the same men live out a patriarchal contract with wives and daughters in their own homes? I would suggest that it simply emphasises that masculinity is situationally defined and that gender assertion takes second place when set against the more urgent need to earn a living.

We have become too accustomed to associating 'masculinity' with 'power' – there is a taken-for-granted quality about this equation, despite a long-term recognition that men and their masculinities may be differently defined in different class and status settings. The literature on working class masculinity (from Willis 1979 to Back 1994) implies that whilst these are men subordinate in class power they have other ways of demonstrating potency through work – men's hardness, strength, aggression and bloody-mindedness in the industrial setting are often commented upon. 'Subordinate versions of masculinity validate self-worth and encourage resistance', argue Cornwall and Lindisfarne (1994:5).

Men in Africa did not specifically choose an occupation whose tasks they associate with women. It is rather that masculinity here became strongly bound up with earning a wage in the colonial economy. Masculinity could be equated with externality (leaving the rural areas), with control of cash, with the status of breadwinner. All of these weighed more in the balance than the 'emasculating' tasks which might be the means to these ends. Aside from the 'demeaning' tasks, the work entailed subordination to women employers, although this was hidden within the home and not on public display to other men. Where these were women of another 'race', men could bracket off their gender to some degree; class difference also played a part in rescuing men's self-esteem. There was little scope here for exercising brute strength or male forcefulness in the job, though some men clearly prided themselves on exercising technical skills. At best men might adopt a paternalistic stance vis-à-vis female employers (protecting their interests) or a haughty distance (keeping them out of the kitchen).

Men also made such a job palatable in gender terms by keeping it strictly separate from their own home life. We have seen that they felt uncomfortable when the two were counterposed, with the suggestion that one might be a transformatory model for the other.

With the wage labour 'squeeze' in Tanzania, entailing dramatic declines in the real value of wages and only limited expansion in the opportunities for wage labour, men are rethinking their gendered universe in which they went to towns to earn wages whilst women stayed at home. This is why men say (like one elderly man who had spent all his working life in Tanga) that, 'these days women at home can make more money [selling surplus crops, chickens, eggs] than men who come to work in town'. My own view from researching women's rural lives is that this is overstated, even in the 1990s – married women have little to sell and earn merely enough for everyday survival – at least in the area from which this man comes. But the devaluation of wage work which is bound up with this opinion clearly impacts on those who have made it their life, lowering their self-esteem as men.

Now it is trade which is seen as a means to prosperity and freedom and any man who can scrape together enough to buy trade-goods heads for the market place. Oscillatory labour migration is translated into buying cheap at home and selling dear in town. Wage work is now viewed as fine for the short-term, or as a supplement to mercantile activity, but it is devalued as a sole source of livelihood or long-term commitment. If women begin to drift into men's jobs now (especially that of domestic service), then men are less concerned than they would have been at one time, because they see the work itself as materially devalued: 'No-one wants to be a domestic servant nowadays, especially men ... it has no benefits. Nowadays it is women who are more often seen doing this work ... men would prefer any other work'. Rather than protesting against urban competition, men express concern about the perceived threat to rural patriarchy: in the 'old days' 'men had control over their wives and a husband or father would not allow his wife or daughters to work/go to town'. Whilst a few women have made the same deductions as men about the profitability of long-distance trade over labouring for a wage, men can still delude themselves that most wives go no further than the local market.

FEMINISATION OF DOMESTIC WAGE LABOUR

It is often argued that the most deeply-etched demarcation lines, in men's bid for recognition from other men, are between their work and that of women, and that men cannot handle the entry of women into their domain when these carefully constructed walls begin to crumble (e.g. Cockburn 1983). In this case, men would appear to have shifted the goalposts. Seeing domestic service devalued, the demarcation lines now begin to be drawn in other directions. Pulling up the ladder of 'promotion' out of domestic service into hotel work, men will say: 'Women in hotel work? Never! Work like this needs a "sharp" person. Women are "slow-slow", they panic and tire quickly' [inverted commas indicate use of English words].

It would equally be true to say that wage work always entails resistance to competition: this is a 'class' issue as much as a gender issue. Occupations like domestic labour are particularly vulnerable to dilution by successive waves of green labour in economies characterised by uneven development. In this case men first found themselves in competition with other men; now they face infiltration by women. However, given the long haul to accumulate capital for trading, the scarcity of other jobs and the failure of industrialisation to take off, they continue to hang on to jobs 'without honour'. There is nothing inevitable about the feminisation of domestic wage work.

As Pearson notes, '"green" labour does not exist in nature; it has to be cultivated' (1988:43). The creeping feminisation of domestic wage labour in this case has more to do with economic and social transformations in the rural areas than with the demands of employers for particular kinds of labour. We have seen how it is linked to state intervention in rural areas and the extension of capitalist forms of land ownership. At the same time female migration is evidence of struggles between men and women for control over women's labour (productive and reproductive) and for rights to the product of that labour. Generational inequities are implicated in the outcomes of these rural domestic struggles as well as gender.

In so far as domestic service is being feminised, it is by a new generation of younger women who do not see it as anything but a temporary sojourn. Earning a wage may be a way of improving their chances for marriage (as with young men) or of passing time whilst other possibilities are considered – other kinds of wage employment, trading or selling goods from home. These new entrants do not see domestic work as a life-time career, and they are resistant to its disciplines, its constant surveillance, its mode of incarceration ('inside'). They would prefer the freedom and pleasure of interacting with others of their own age; consequently they are, as workers, 'difficult', unreliable, skittish.

In this case then – and probably in others, feminisation of an occupation does not equate with increasing docility or malleability of the workforce. Employers who can afford it know the value of an older man – or to put it another way: whilst employers did not originally see housework as a man's job, they are now ambivalent about its feminisation.

THE CLASS RELATIONS OF DOMESTIC SERVICE

In addressing domestic service, 'class' is a crucial organising concept, even in this situation where class formation reflects an economy only partially subject to processes of capital accumulation. The phenomenon of class needs to be disclosed in its myriad guises of inequity, struggle, solidarity, exploitation, identity and culture as they operate within private homes and in the linking of homes with the wider political economy.

Investigation of domestic service in this postcolonial setting uncovers some unexpected features of class formation. One example of this emerges from engagement with Veblen's view of domestic service as conspicuous consumption. It becomes clear that this is dependent on the nature of the employing class. Where that class is in the process of establishing itself or is impoverished, domestic work, whilst never losing its value as a symbolic marker of class status, can be directed into servicing petty accumulation.[1] This may be seen as a 'reversion' to household-based production systems or a transformation more in line with capitalist relations of production. It puts in question any notion of a linear transition of modes of production.

Our attempt to document the contested relations between servants and their masters confirms other accounts of class struggles in the workplace. In an occupation which involves cleaning up the dirt made by others, domestic servants strive to wrest their own job satisfactions – whether pride in the practical skills learnt, or self-congratulation in outwitting the employer on her own ground. In the private home as workplace the employer does not have it all her own way. The management of employers by their servants is almost as pronounced as the control of servants by their masters.

Perhaps least anticipated in this study was the discovery that domestic servants can, within limits, organise themselves as unionised labour, making class-conscious alliances with other workers. The constraints on such action are acknowledged – in structural terms privatised workers are not assembled for exploitation in a context where their consciousness of grievance leads to solidarity with fellow workers. Even demonstrating militancy is problematic in a private setting. Against all the odds, domestic servants here and in other parts of Africa combined to protest their lot, becoming a significant element in the creation of a trans-ethnic and politically conscious urban working class. That class project could not be realised within the backward terms of Tanzanian capitalist development. If degraded wage workers now define success as independent trading, this reflects the neoliberal discourse of individualised expression through the market and consumption which has been adopted as state ideology. It is diametrically opposed to a discourse of collectivity or solidarity built on production relations.

DOMESTIC LABOUR: IS IT BETTER TO STAY AT HOME?

Domestic labour still prompts urgent questions for feminists and labour activists and analysts. Investigating its transformation into wage work offers a window of analytical opportunity. We note, for example, that at the same time that domestic labour is commoditised women become aware of their labour power as a commodity. Indeed these two processes are often intimately connected and demand framing in class as well as gender terms. That domestic labour can be sold for a wage offers limited liberation to women who may have little else to sell. That domestic labour can be purchased offers liberation to other women at higher class levels: for better paid work, philanthropy, leisure.

The purchase of domestic labour also deflects domestic struggles which might have potential for more far-reaching liberation. A Brazilian feminist noted that:

> The domestic worker is like a buffer between the husband and wife who employ her, keeping the conflicted situation of who is to do what domestic chores from exploding. It is this contradiction that is the origin of the feminist movement in those countries where domestic workers have practically disappeared. (quoted in Pereira de Melo 1989:262–3)

There is little debate amongst articulate and better-off feminists in Africa about the issue of housework. Rather than confronting husbands to share the work (which might lead to divorce or domestic violence) they off-load the dirtier, heavier and more tedious aspects of it onto servants. At best their consciences are quietened by reference to the desperate needs of those seeking work, or stirred to the effect that 'some women mistreat their maids'.

Can domestic labour be organised in other ways? Is it a politically acceptable solution to employ others to do the work if they are paid at a rate and on terms more equivalent to that of wage labour in general? Does it make the institution more or less acceptable if the labour force is male, rather than female?

Although the 'technological fix' may eventually reduce the dirt, the strain and the tedium of household work, there is little evidence that it either transforms gender relations or reduces the exploitation of domestic workers: its overall effect is to raise the anticipated standards of domestic work rather than to question who does the work or for what remuneration (Bose on USA, 1979; Shindler on South Africa, 1980). In a situation such as that in Tanzania, the calculation that technology was more expensive than labour has yet preempted its wide adoption, and made employers wary of letting servants tamper with devices such as washing machines. And where 'service' rather than 'efficiency' is to the fore, technology cannot substitute.

Even if 'socialism' was nothing but bad news for domestic servants in Tanzania and did very little to question the gendering of domestic work, it did have an impact in other places. In Cuba after the revolution an attempt was made to address the issue of the exploitative and oppressive situation of housemaids by 're-educating' them to become workers in occupations such as clerical work. Once they had achieved other jobs they left their domestic employment. What this account fails to record is how their previous employers then managed their domestic tasks, or whether another wave of domestic labour took their place (Izquierdo 1989).

In some 'socialist' societies (China, Russia) there have been half-hearted attempts to socialise domestic labour, to make it a community responsibility rather than one of private households (see e.g. Croll 1976:76–7; Myrdal and Kessle 1970:113). Such attempts have foundered on the 'opportunity costs' of this provision in the context of developing economies, but more tellingly on the exclusion of women from decision-making, the marginalisation or silencing of women's organisations. They have also stumbled on the rock of privatised living arrangements and familial relationships to which both men and women cling as a buffer against the world. As communism has given way to state-sponsored economic liberalism, even the women's movement in China now endorses domestic wage-labour.[2]

In the end there is no conclusion to this debate, as the cross-cutting conflicts of interest between servants and their employers, between workers (men or women) and bosses (female or male), between green labour and established workers, between men and women in families and in the wider world cannot be finally resolved – these struggles must continue. Only one thing is certain – there is no escape by staying at home.

APPENDIX:

THE PROCESS OF RESEARCH

Research began in 1986 with an attempt to document domestic service as an historical phenomenon. My first excursions into the National Archives were frustrating. The preservation of records was a very hit and miss affair, with material often missing from files and access to what was available dependent on the Archives Landrover having petrol to fetch material from distant stores and there being torch batteries available for search in dim rooms. These were signs of the time, a period marked by severe shortages.

In later phases of the study historical data was sought in reminiscences and life histories. In Tanga servants and ex-servants' narratives of life offered a way of assessing servants' social origins and their typical 'careers' as well as their subjective take on this. In Britain I contacted a group of ex-colonial employers who also reflected on their experience. Oral history yields invaluable accounts of the past which speak as much of today as yesterday, as people reflect on and evaluate their past in terms of who they are now.

Defining the subjects of my research was a foundational problem. Although the title 'domestic servant' might seem to be unambiguous in meaning, it soon became evident that the job title was a contested one. The usual Swahili word for servant (*mtumishi*) was not employed here. Instead servants referred to themselves as 'house workers', 'inside workers' or 'househelpers' (*wafanyi kazi ya nyumbani* or *wafanyi kazi ya ndani* or *wasaidizi wa nyumbani*). Employers often (and servants occasionally) used the colonial terms 'houseboy'/'housegirl', no matter whether they were speaking English or Swahili.

A second ambiguity inhered in the task boundaries of the occupation. In the end I chose to count as servants both 'inside' and 'outside' workers: gardeners and watchmen as well as cooks, cleaners and washermen (themselves ambiguously both 'in' and 'out'). The similarities in their terms and conditions of employment made this valid, and it was not unusual for domestic workers to be expected to cross these boundaries in their work.

A third and more confusing factor was the pervasiveness of 'servant-like' relations throughout society. As I soon discovered, even servants might employ servants! For generations Africans in Tanzania have taken non-relatives into the household to assist with domestic labour. In precolonial times this sometimes took the form of domestic slavery; or it was embodied in arrangements that we might call fostering or adoption; it could also be an extension of mutual help between neighbours or friends; sometimes (perhaps more often in the coastal areas where trading had commoditised some relations) it involved the outright purchase of labour.

Except for overt slavery all these forms of domestic help clearly persisted and were employed by Africans at all class levels. In some cases domestic help could be considered as a mutual exchange of equal benefit to both parties, but for the most part it was evident that the partners were very unequal to begin with, and the terms of the relationship did nothing to erase that inequality.

In this study my focus was on domestic service at higher class levels, where the employment relationship is more formal and impersonal and where servants receive wages for carrying out tasks in and around private homes. When I surveyed employers it was at this class level, although in the collection of life histories and in participant observation I covered the broader canvas of domestic service at all levels of society. It is at the higher class level that domestic help is more evidently a matter of conspicuous consumption than it is a utilitarian necessity. As symbolic statement, its class character is most sharply edged at this point.

I determined not to interview servants at their place of work as this would have required the prior permission of employers, whose ally I would then appear. Servants would have been unable to speak freely in such a setting; I would also have felt inhibited. Moreover I wanted to set the experience of service in the context of servants' lives. This required more than a hurried interview under the suspicious gaze of the lady of the house.

The validity of this instinctive feeling was underlined for me later when I read what Cock had to say about her field study: 'fear was expressed ... by the domestic workers. Several refused to be interviewed at work without their employers' permission, and others were reluctant to be interviewed at all for fear of repercussions from their employers' (1980:19).

Cock was forced to arrange interviews with servants without their employers' knowledge. My attempt to avoid this difficulty was not without cost, for it meant that I could not match the interviews of employers with their own servants, and had to seek some other way of gaining access to servants and ex-servants.[1] The method adopted could best be described as 'networking'.

Wishing to study both male and female servants I looked for assistance from those with direct knowledge of each sex's experience. Amina Hemedi and Bakari Mtangi, both in middle years, had been employed as servants in the past. Largely through them I began to trace others who had been similarly engaged, these leading to a further set and so on. In this way we were never entirely strangers to those interviewed – there was always some 'known other' linking us together. Women I visited with Amina, whilst Bakari accompanied me to interview men. These interviews were complemented by others with servants I traced directly as I wandered round Tanga or had dealings with my neighbours.

Some of the men and women we interviewed had been employed many times as servants, others only once. Some were still servants or looking for servant jobs whilst for others service had been an incident in the past. They had worked at all class levels, from formally-employed lifetime servants with specialised skills, to drudges on a casual basis for other poor working families. A curious contrast between interviews with men and those with women expressed much about the different conditions of men's and women's lives. Women were invariably interviewed in their own homes, and I found this a revealing backcloth to their accounts of themselves. One could see at a glance the material hardships they faced, the children they were struggling to raise, even the meals they were preparing. Without giving it much thought I assumed that the interviews with men would follow a similar pattern. But men, it seemed, did not expect to be visited at home; indeed they hardly spent time at home.[2] These interviews were thus more public, either in cafes, at work on the verandahs of houses where they were carrying on a business of some sort, on a few occasions in servants' quarters, or literally in the street. It was thus impossible to match the man against his claimed domestic circumstances.

Amina and Bakari became skilled in putting people at their ease, and helping to explain our objectives. Some of my best material emerged when my assistants were addressed as the 'audience'. Some servants/ex-servants found it perplexing that I wanted to talk to them about their lives – it was the first time that an outsider had taken an interest in them. Once having got over their initial shyness they warmed to the subject. A few stonewalled all the way through, suspicious of the outcome. Once we had introduced ourselves, I did most of the interviewing in Swahili, whilst my assistants joined in as the mood relaxed. Wanting the interview to flow like conversation I did not fill in a written questionnaire. I had a set of mental guidelines around which we ranged quite widely to uncover the circumstances which had led them to leave home and seek work in town, the range of jobs they had tried, the detail of their work as servants, the general development of their lives and their expectations of the future. Many of the interviews lasted over an hour, after which I immediately committed the data to paper, often in the company of the interviewee so that points of detail could be checked.

Using this method I was eventually able to trace 44 women and 34 men who had worked or were working as servants (total 78). They were diverse in their ethnic backgrounds and origins, and they lived in rooms and small houses scattered all over Tanga (a few in servants' quarters, though this is not a common practice here). The material was often rich in quality, but it could make no claim to be representative in any statistical sense. My survey of 60 formal employers (in the course of which I asked for details of their present domestic workers) was aimed partly at assessing the typicality of the servants whose life histories I was collecting. It was also an attempt to create a profile of that social group at the highest class level who would be most likely to employ servants on a formal basis.

Given the lack of any pre-existing data base from which to devise a sample of this social category, I drew on that most visible manifestation of class in ex-colonial towns like Tanga, namely housing. I therefore carried out my survey in two low density areas of Tanga, and in the town centre. Old Nguvumali is the suburb where most Europeans used to live, though it is now more racially varied. It consists of large houses with spacious and beautiful gardens. The area stretching out towards Ras Kazone on the other side of town has housing which used to accommodate European administrators in the colonial period; with the transfer of power after Independence the self-same houses had been appropriated and re-allocated to African state functionaries. There were also new houses being built here by Arab and Asian businessmen. In each suburb I randomly selected three-quarters of the houses on the central road, interviewing altogether 38 potential employers, only two of whom had never had domestic workers.

The town centre is still largely occupied by Asians, and indeed Asians tend to live here rather than in the suburbs. Whilst they were major employers of domestic servants few had come into my sample. In the town centre the streets were short and arranged on a grid system, and residential quarters were mixed in with public buildings and commercial and industrial premises. Four flats/houses were selected from the six main blocks of houses, the aim being to include representatives of all the Asian religio-ethnic groups (Muslims, Hindus, Sikhs and smaller subdivisions). No Europeans or Africans were encountered here, and 22 further interviews were conducted, only three of which were with people who had never employed a servant.

Most of the interviews with employers I did alone, although in the town centre Asian sample I had the help of a Muslim girl who could speak Gujerati. In each case I asked for 'the woman of the house', and consequently (by choice) interviewed mainly female employers. There were a few cases of single male employers, whilst in Asian households men seemed to feel that their wives/mothers would not be competent or confident enough to deal with outsiders and hence, in spite of my protests, often took over interviews begun with women. Each interview lasted from between fifteen minutes, where no servants were presently employed, to over an hour. I had no outright refusals, though some were evidently sparing with the truth. My presentation may have helped. I explained that I was interested in the problems of employers hiring domestic servants, and that 'I had heard that these days it was difficult to get good servants …' Rarely did I have to say more.

Table Ap. 1: Employer samples

| Ethnic group | Sample Area | | | | Total | |
| | 1 Nguvumali/Ras Kazone | | 2 Town Centre | | | |
	No.	%	No.	%	No.	%
African	22	58	0	–	22	37
Arab	2	5	1	4	3	5
Asian	4	10	21	95	25	42
Goan	3	8	0	–	3	5
European	7	18	0	–	7	11
Total	38	100	22	100	60	100

Table Ap. 2a: Servants in Employer samples/Servants and ex-servants in Life history sets: Contrasts and similarities (by Sex)

| Servants in Employer samples | | | | | Servants/ex-servants in Life history sets | | | | |
| Women | | Men | | | Women | | Men | | |
No.	%	No.	%	Total	No.	%	No.	%	Total
27	28	70	72	97	44	56	34	44	78

Table Ap. 2b: Servants in Employer samples/Servants and ex-servants in Life history sets: Contrasts and similarities (Age/'Tribe'/Religion: by Sex)

| Variable | Servants in Employer samples | | | | Servants/ex-servants in Life history sets | | | |
| | Women | | Men | | Women | | Men | |
	No.	%	No.	%	No.	%	No.	%
Age:								
10–15	2	8	0	–	3	7	0	–
16–35	18	75	34	56	25	57	17	50
36–55	4	12	17	28	8	18	9	26
over 56	1	4	10	16	8	18	8	23
Age unknown	2	–	9	–	–	–	–	–
Median age		20		30		33		35
'Tribe':								
Sambaa	12	55	31	53	24	54	28	82
Others	11	45	27	47	20	45	6	18
Unknown	4	–	12	–				
Religion:								
Muslim	13	52	42	66	28	64	29	85
Christian	12	48	21	34	16	36	5	15
Unknown	2	–	7	–				

These 60 employers had between them 97 servants, from which I was able to derive a contemporary profile of domestic workers against which I could match my collection of life histories. Tables Ap. 1, Ap. 2a and Ap. 2b list the major characteristics of servants and employers from the various sets of interviews.

The ethnic origins of employers were significant in terms of the way servants were recruited and employed, and there was a large degree of coincidence between ethnicity and the varied class fractions at this highest class level. Census data from 1967 indicated that Asians formed a much larger category than Arabs or Europeans in the total population of Tanga (see Chapter 1). This is reflected in my sample of employers (Table Ap. 1).

Table Ap. 2a provides evidence for statements made several times in the course of this book – that domestic service is still predominantly a man's job in Tanzania. The life history sets were not intended to mirror this, but rather to provide comparable information on the experiences of both sexes in this occupation – with an emphasis on women about whom nothing was known.

In Table Ap. 2b the weightings of age, ethnic origin and religion are compared for the two sets of servant data: the domestic workers in the employer sample and the life history sets. It can now be seen that the latter were 'biased' in various ways, though fortuitously they also reflect some of the characteristics in the employer sample (particularly for women). My life history set included more older people than those uncovered by the survey as I particularly sought men and women who had worked in this occupation for some years. Both my assistants were Sambaa Muslims and this is reflected in a bias in the life history sets towards people 'like themselves' (particularly marked in the case of the men) – ethnicity is still very much a factor determining the social networks of urban Africans. Nevertheless it is notable that Sambaa/Muslims are the majority amongst servants in the employers' sample too.

The life history sets were not created as a statistical sample; in so far as they reflect the population of currently employed servants exposed in the survey of employers, this is helpful, but fortuitous. One other bias needs to be reiterated: whereas the survey dealt with servants formally employed at the higher class level, the life histories covered a wider range of experiences of domestic servitude. Nevertheless the majority had been formally employed at one time or another, mostly by Asians, but with substantial minorities who had experience of European or African employers.

Finally, Table Ap. 3, drawn from the employers' sample, shows the distribution of men and women servants in particular domestic jobs. The job titles used here are those most common in local parlance. It can be seen that whereas there is a very distinctive sexual division of labour in domestic service, men outnumber women even in domestic work done inside the

Table Ap. 3: Distribution of servants by task and gender (Employers' designations from employers' sample)

	Women		Men	
	No.	%	No.	%
Headboy	0	–	1	1
'Houseboy' (msaidizi wa ndani)	0	–	31	44
'Housegirl'/nursemaid (ayah)	27	100	0	–
Cook (mpishi)	0	–	3	4
Washerman (dhobi)	0	–	1	1
Gardener (boi shamba)	0	–	14	20
Watchman (askari/mlinzi)	0	–	20	29

house. However, it should also be noted that a small majority of the men employed here are working in 'outside' tasks (gardening and guard duties). Gardeners and watchmen are most likely to be allocated specific tasks and not to be allowed 'inside', but many 'inside' servants have to extend their work 'outside', to cultivation and watching over the house in the absence of employers. Not many inside servants nowadays are employed in specialised tasks (cooks, laundrymen, headboys) – most are expected to be general servants and to clean, wash, iron, help in cooking and watch over children.

Qualitative data, in the form of stories, conversations, interruptions and asides were embedded in the outcome of more formal survey procedures. On frequent occasions tangential material proved more interesting than that which we had formally requested. One interview with a servant in a rather wealthy area (for once breaking my own rule of not interviewing servants at work) was brought to an end as his employer unexpectedly drove up the drive, graciously waved aside my apologies and went into the house, cool, dignified and distant, leaving our informant to hastily bid us goodbye and collect her shopping from the car (thus casting doubt on his account that after seventeen years his employers had become 'like family').

Studying the relational aspect of domestic service using methods of participant observation (rather than survey and interview techniques) is a tall order and subject to more than the usual caveats regarding the relationship of researcher to researched. Several of those who have researched in this area (probably more than openly state this to be the case!) have joined the ranks of employers. They are thus direct, if unwilling, participants in one side of a very unequal relationship (see e.g. Armstrong 1990).[3] Few have become servants (though see Rollins 1985 for the distinctive and challenging slant this gives to analysis).

My experience of employing a servant was invaluable in research as well as domestic terms. During my first month in Tanga I endured the same hardships and vicissitudes of domestic labour as experienced by ordinary people (women at least). Together with my two children I lived in a crowded sociable house in the high density area of Tanga, in a single room, with space for little except the beds we slept in. We ate and I cooked, washed clothes and tried to write notes in this one room. This was a useful initiation[4] even though half my time had to be given over to domestic tasks.

When we moved into a larger place in Chumbageni (the other side of the tracks, but a very mixed area by the 1980s) I needed domestic help if I were to have time to work at all, and to leave my children safely. In the best local tradition, a woman was recommended to me by a previous employer. She was around fifty years of age, bright-eyed and wiry, talkative, tough and hard-working. In employing Sara I gained one of my best friends locally, one who had a fund of knowledge and experience of life as a servant. Having said this, I remained an employer on whom a worker depended for wages and from whom she calculated to receive extra-economic perks. Here I had an 'insider's' view, as one partner in a contractual power relationship.

In Tanga I was not seen as a typical employer, but as an 'outsider'. I did not fit the stereotypes of the distant or demanding European/Asian employers which ordinary people recognised. On visiting my own servant's previous employer, whilst she was also there helping out, I was struck by how different her demeanour was with them. She served at table in 'respectful' silence, whereas at home she ate with us (admittedly under protest at first, that this was not 'proper') and chattered non-stop.[5]

My assumptions about childcare also differentiated me from most other local employers of domestic help – at least amongst Africans. One day I mentioned to a teacher that I could not leave my children without someone at home in charge. She eyed me pityingly:

> I can ... it doesn't matter if I'm home or not ... I tell my friend I'm going out and she makes sure [the children] are fed and so on. Even if there is an accident she will take responsibility and get them to the hospital. Sometimes I go to Arusha for a few days and I think nothing of leaving them at home.

My 'difference' was also noted in another respect – that I employed an older woman to work for me. On a visit to me the same woman said to the friend that accompanied her: 'For Them, people like this really work hard. But not if they come to work for Us! You would just find them idling about'. And she added that 'for me to tell an older woman "do this", "do that" – for we Africans it's not possible'.

As a researcher I was indebted to Sara for many insights. She led me to other women who were or had been servants and with whom I was able to establish friendly relations outside of more formal data collection procedures. Another link which generated its own network was through Abu, whose name I was given before coming to Tanga, and which in later years took me to his home village in Lushoto. Networks generated in this way are crucial if one is to go beyond the more calculated accounts that people give of their circumstances in interviews, and to see the vicissitudes of their lives at first hand.[6]

The other challenge was to achieve informal access to a range of employers. It is all too easy to be taken over by one group who will strain to socialise the newcomer into their own view of local custom and practice as employers of servants – what should be paid, how not to 'let them get away with things' or 'become too familiar'; which applicants for the job to favour and which to turn away (often couched in ethnic and gendered stereotypes). Fearing encapture I cultivated a range of friends and acquaintances amongst African, Asian, Arab and European employers, whom I visited regularly and who also visited me. The earliest of these contacts were with the African owners of our first home in Tanga.

My friends knew that I was studying servants; I doubt if they appreciated the extent to which I learnt from them as individuals. As well as insider views of the experience of employers and servants, I wanted to observe at first hand their interactions and to follow through the drama of their relationships. The minutiae of daily intercourse between servants and their employers was easily viewed – commands given and responses made, the division of labour, responsibility accorded and trust or distrust displayed. One could rarely be around when furious quarrels or dismissals took place, and when the often contradictory assumptions of employer and employee regarding the nature of the relationship were laid bare. Employers and servants, like the rest of us, wished to be seen in the best light and not in their moments of anger or loss of control. If the more tempestuous scenes took place out of sight, one could be a party to accounts of incidents not observed, which whilst undoubtedly self-serving in their tone, nevertheless betrayed attitudes and feelings both general and idiosyncratic.

In this study, then, 'participant observation' may be taken to include all of the above activity. I also lived in Tanga with my two children as 'normally' as any social researcher can, given the peculiar nature of her occupation. We made friends, entertained and visited; my children went to the nearby primary school and were rapidly accepted into local street life. Having previously been married to a Kenyan made a considerable difference to the way I was treated – women in particular assumed a complementarity of experience in matters relating to marriage and family, and felt free to put me right or to share intimate stories. A white woman with two black children has little chance of being invisible - we quickly became famous and popular and strangers would call out 'Mama Nana!' as I passed. I had no transport except my own feet, so the sight of me walking from one end of the town to another became familiar. Whilst I was evidently a *mzungu* (European), I confounded the expectations people had of Europeans. I had spent a decade of my life previously living in East Africa (including a period spent teaching at the University of Dar es Salaam). I therefore spoke Swahili and conducted all my work in this language, except that with Asians and Europeans.

The researcher's self-presentation and the construction that is put on this by others has a definite effect on her ability to collect data, and on the quality of the data collected. There are painful contradictions here, thrown up by the history of colonialism and imperialism, and focusing on questions of 'race', class, power and representation. Feminism itself has not been free from the contradictions here, nor could it be: indeed this debate added a new twist to a preceding feminist challenge to masculine representations of women. At the same time these very terms – gender, class, 'race', colonialism – have been subject to the challenge of deconstructivism and de-essentialism.[7] In the course of this debate, writing ethnography has sometimes become an exercise in displaying 'innocence' or 'guilt' (Haraway 1991; Nast 1994) and the 'ethnographic enterprise' as one of 'inescapable "othering"' (Babcock 1993:63).

A useful contribution has been made here by Kobayashi. Noting that an insider/outsider distinction is always relative to time, place and situation, she criticises the erection of 'barriers of difference' leading to the formulation of 'hierarchies of oppression'. She calls instead for a seeking out of commonalities in both fieldwork and ethnographic analysis – 'recognising that commonality is always partial' (1994:76). This view echoes Presnell's plea for strategies of 'co-production' between researcher and researched (1994).

Whilst the researcher cannot control the varied ways in which they are perceived, they can be in charge of how they present themselves and how they relate to others. Social research cannot be done convincingly unless both parties are genuinely seeking a degree of common understanding through mutual respect. In one sense research is always 'co-production' in which even the party with more privilege and power (the researcher) is dependent on the other to speak, to explain, to describe. And whilst the researcher must also speak, question and disclose, listening is more important to the enterprise. When I began this research my aim was to document rather than to challenge the institution of domestic service, even whilst my own political sense was that it was a demeaning and exploitative occupation. I discovered through listening and observing that it had many other facets, even for those who were subjected to servitude. Hearing their voices, I hope I have then faithfully represented their views: I cannot claim to speak on their behalf.

NOTES

CHAPTER 1 SIGNS OF THE TIMES

1. From Ngugi's play *I Will Marry When I Want*, quoted by him in 1983:40.
2. See Nyerere 1968. His successor as President, Ali Hassan Mwinyi, reaffirmed the goal of an egalitarian socialism aimed at preventing 'the growth of a class society' (speech on the 20th anniversary of the Arusha Declaration, December 1986, quoted in *Bulletin of Tanzanian Affairs* 27, 1987:23).
3. The inadequacy or lack of official statistics on domestic service is encountered also in Zambia (Hansen 1989:221). Sanjek struggles with the same problem in relation to maidservants in Ghana (1990:48–52); whilst Rollins refers to the 'gross underreporting' of domestic workers in contemporary America (1990:74–5).
4. Domestic servants are excluded from the annual Employment and Earnings reports, for example, which are based on responses to a postal survey sent to businesses. Labour Force surveys, which use a sample of households and individual questionnaires, do not list domestic workers separately though they may be encompassed within the very large category of 'service workers' (Bureau of Statistics 1994:12).
5. Domestic slavery was a pre-colonial institution amongst some African peoples (Bigilimara 1963) and both Arab and African slave traders expected women slaves to provide domestic services (Wright 1993:9).
6. For example: in 1945 officials calculated that there were 1836 juveniles employed as servants in the six largest towns of Tanganyika. Excluding Dar es Salaam, where no distinction was made between employers, 28% of these were said to be employed by Africans (Archives V14/30136: Employment of Children in Domestic Service, 1941–). For the context of this statistical exercise, see Chapter 4.
7. Memo from Labour Commissioner, 9 Oct. 1949 (National Archives file on Domestic Servants V14/32744, 1949).
8. The Annual Blue Books are cited in Shivji 1986 (Table 1.3:20) where their reliability is noted to be 'doubtful'; for 1947 Census of Native Labour see Archives, file V14/32679; for 1948–50 Labour Department sources see Shivji 1986:119; the Tanganyika Statistical Abstract for 1951 is cited in Mihyo 1983:12; the East African Statistical Abstract for 1952 by Sabot 1979:22. For NUMEIST (National Urban Mobility, Employment and Income Survey of Tanzania) see Bienefeld and Sabot (vol. 3), Tables 9/10, 1972:26–7.
9. This conclusion is drawn from Shivji (1986:20). Estimating the wage labour force in colonial times produces rough approximations at best. But by the end of the 1940s it can be guessed at around 12% of the population of working age. (Shivji 1986:17 calculates a total of 457,221 wage labourers drawing on Tanganyika Labour Enumeration figures for 1949, at a time when the Census counted a national population of the order of seven and a half million.)

10. The Census of 1988 confirmed that sex ratios were evening up, with some towns now having a preponderance of females (see report in the *Bulletin of Tanzanian Affairs*, 37, 1990:26–7). Women accounted for only 3.3% and 3.4% of the wage labour force in 1945 and 1947 (Archives V14/32679: Census of Native Labour). By 1965 they constituted 4.5% of those counted in the Employment and Earnings statistics and the proportion rose every year thereafter to 18% in 1984 (Selected Statistical Series, 1951–91, Table 5.2:15). By 1992, based on more inclusive labour force statistics, women were 25% of the wage labour force (Statistical Abstract, 1994).

11. In 1949 formally accounted total wage employment was 457,221 (Shivji 1986:17 based on the 1951 East African Statistical Bulletin). By 1965 it had fallen to 283,753 and it continued to fall, rising briefly in the early seventies and falling again in the mid-seventies. From then on it rose gradually year by year (Bureau of Statistics 1994, Table 5.2).

12. A complete switch had occured in the first twenty years of independence. In 1961 only 26% of wage employment had been in the public sector, but by 1984 this had risen to 73% under state socialism (Bureau of Statistics Table 5.1, 1994:14).

13. Summarised in Coulson 1982:177–8: 'leadership' was defined to include all the higher and middle-level state and party functionaries and their spouses. The Leadership Code was not repealed until 1991: the Zanzibar Declaration then stated that leaders were permitted to earn more than one salary, buy shares, take up directorships in private companies and build houses for renting. The Party's General Secretary 'admitted that many leaders ... had been involved in corrupt activities and dubious accumulation of wealth contrary to the "Ujamaa" (socialist) policy. Many ... had started poultry schemes and housing projects in order to improve their economic conditions'. The Party was now bowing to 'common-sense' in legitimising these activities (quoted in *Bulletin of Tanzanian Affairs* 39, 1991:12–13). Sarros and Tinios argue that during the whole period 1976–91 'much of the economic activity in Tanzania ... went underground and was hence unobservable' – or at least went officially undocumented (1995:1401).

14. This should be compared with Sabot's comment of 1972, when the urban population constituted only 6% of the total: 'Tanzania remains one of the least urbanised countries in the world' (1972:18). Urban growth rates increased rapidly from the mid-'70s, and by 1988 it had an urban population which was 30% of the total population (World Bank 1990:238).

15. World Bank 1994:200. This is the first insertion of Tanzania in these listings of income distribution. Though of doubtful accuracy they suggest that Tanzania now has one of the most unequal distributions in the world. In the 1970s it was Nyerere's proud boast that egalitarianism was becoming a reality, with elimination of gross income disparities (quoted in Yeager 1989:77 and fn30:165).

16. There is an echo here of the immediate post-Independence phase when the newly promoted African ruling class was derided by those of the Left as '*Wabenzi*' (owners of Mercedes-Benz cars): Peter and Mvungi 1985:171.

17. Mbughuni 1991:25. More specifically: Wage employment in urban Tanga was estimated at 5000 in 1946 (Archives:45/1738); in 1967, 13,029 (36% of the adult population aged 15–64); by 1978, 31,958 (54.5% of the adult population aged 15–64 (calculated from census figures for relevant years). This should be compared to the national decline in wage employment from 1948 up to the late 1970s and is to be accounted for by industrial development in Tanga. Ethnic statistics: The non-African population of Tanga in 1952 comprised 34% of the population of the town (Molohan, Appendix III, 1957). By 1967 many

Europeans and Asians had left the country and the non-African population now comprised 12% of heads of household (2068 in all). Amongst these, 66% were Asians, 15% Arabs, 7% Europeans and 13% 'others' (calculated from Census 1967). 'Racial' categorisations were abandoned in census enumeration after 1964 in favour of 'citizen/non-citizen' categories.

18. Cited by Sabot (Table 1.3, 1979:22 from the East African Statistical Department 1953). This is the only published count, so far as I know, of the number of domestic servants in the Tanga region, and would have included servants in the houses of large farmers, and in Lushoto town and other smaller settlements as well as the city of Tanga.

19. Archives: V14/32679, Census of Native Labour, 1944–7.

20. Archives: File 967.822, Native Affairs (1937); V14/25918, Complaints against Malungu Sisal Estate (1938); V14/25956, Labour disturbances at Lanzoni Estate (1939); 4/172/4, Commission of Enquiry into Tanga Dock Strike (1939).

21. Archives: V14/30136 Employment of Children in Domestic Service (1941–4); V14/25971, Labour Conditions in Tanga (1940);4/172/4, Commission of Enquiry into Tanga Dock Strike (1939).

22. Archives: V14/32744 Domestic Servants: Memo from Labour Commissioner, 1 Sept. 1948.

23. Archives: File 967.822, District Officer's Reports, Tanga, 1933–7; V22/37681/5/25, UN Visiting Commission 1951: Petitions -African Cooks, Washermen and Houseservants' Association, Dar es Salaam.

24. Archives: File 45/1738, Africans in Urban Communities.

25. On the sisal industry in the eighties: *Statistical Abstract 1992* (1994); on textiles: *Selected Statistical Series* (1994, Table 9.2:26).

CHAPTER 2 BRIEF LIVES: A TALE OF TWO SERVANTS

1. An earlier version of this chapter was published in the *Review of African Political Economy* 56, 1993. Correspondence with Abu and Sara seeking permission to tell their stories elicited simple approval from Abu; Sara wrote to tell me the sad news that her eldest daughter had died ('Out of my three children one has now departed this world'). She added that the article 'was not a bad idea ... I think you must have thought for a long time about the problems which your sister Sara has faced'. It was she who offered the pseudonym adopted here.

2. A recent Tanzanian example is Caplan 1997. Acknowledgment is also made here to the pioneers in feminist, social and labour history such as Rowbotham 1974; Burnett 1974; Thompson 1988; Personal Narratives Group 1989 et al.

3. Many have noted the significance of the 'breadwinner' discourse to underwriting conceptions of masculinity (e.g. in Britain, Willott and Griffin 1996:86, 90; in India, Sweetman, 1998:16–17). In rural Africa, it is often women who have been the major breadwinners, whilst men have been the managers of this.

4. The notion of 'genres' in oral history is borrowed from Werbner's stirring and provocative account of family history in Zimbabwe (1991:68).

CHAPTER 3 A TOUCH OF CLASS – AND GENDER

1. In US society the employment of domestic servants dropped by two-thirds between 1900 and 1950 (Bose 1979:30); whilst in England 'servants were the largest single occupational group up until the 1900s' (Laslett 1977:35). By the mid-twentieth century they barely figured in occupational statistics, only to reappear in the 1980s (Gregson and Lowe 1994; and for a more sceptical view, Bittson et al. 1999)

2. Geiger 1997; Mbilinyi 1989; Iliffe 1973; Ngaiza and Koda 1991; Wright 1993.
3. Note Tellis-Nayak's description of how employers' children in South India, 'at an early age begin to note and assert their superior status. They issue commands to adult servants in vocabulary that betrays status consciousness', whilst parents warn them to maintain dignity and keep their distance from servants (1983:70). Winifred Foley, a general maid in 1930s Britain wrote afterwards of how she hated the two children of her employer with 'their toffee-nosed attitude of looking me slowly up and down ... I detested them, but ... it was the way they had been brought up. Their mother was quite aware of ... their antics, but as it was only the maid she turned a blind eye' (Burnett 1974, 233). The ambiguous role of 'governess', stranded between servants and masters, underlines the problem of class as a socialisation process. Some of those brought up by servants remember this as a formative experience: Ronald Fraser, brought up in an English Manor House by a nurse: 'No-one could have known me better than you' he tells her, years later. 'In many senses you brought me up', and even more tellingly he reports his early awareness of social differences: 'to me they were very real ... the servants were the real human beings in my childhood. Of course it was an ambiguous alliance because I knew I was the little master' (1984:82,111). Similar experiences were and are unusual in Tanzania, where the high turnover of servants inhibited long-term intimacy with children.
4. The apolitical nature of postmodernism has been noted many times. Harvey asks: 'If, as the postmodernists insist, we cannot aspire to any unified representation of the world, or picture it as a totality full of connections and differentiations rather than as perpetually shifting fragments, then how can we possibly aspire to act coherently with respect to the world?' (1990:52). In relation to feminism it has recently been reasserted that there is a 'palpable sense of commonality [amongst women] in spite of great differences' (Baden and Goetz 1997:20).
5. Iliffe 1979a:397, quoting the constitution of the Association of African Cooks, Washermen and Houseservants in colonial Tanganyika, 1944, drawing on Tanzania National Archives.

CHAPTER 4 COLONIAL DISCOURSES

1. Foucault's views were originally published in May 1968 (*Esprit*, No. 371, 850–74) but the reference is to a later revised version translated into English (1991).
2. See Althusser and Balibar, 1979:13–69, 88. Their *Reading Capital* was also originally published in 1968. On why feminists (and Marxists) must ask *who* speaks, see Ramazanoglu 1993. On anti-Althusserian Marxist cultural analysis see E. P. Thompson 1978. Perhaps the key distinction between Foucault on the one hand and feminists and Marxists on the other, is that for Foucault social power is constituted through discourses, whereas for Marxists and feminists power has generally been regarded as lying in social relations themselves, though significantly *expressed* through discourses. E. P. Thompson breaks with Althusser by decrying the structuralist reification embedded in the work of the latter and emphasising *agency*.
3. Any attempt to contextualise these modes of representation requires us to concede that (as E. P. Thompson puts it, 1978:220) 'evidence is witness to a real historical process', and should not preclude us from the view that this process is characterised by (in Marxist terms) an interactive relationship between social being and social consciousness (Thompson 1978:201).

4. The official files are most complete for the late 1930s and the 1940s. Barely any derive from the 1950s, in the period leading up to independence. Maybe these files were regarded as too sensitive and were destroyed by outgoing officials? There is therefore no official record of the domestic servants' strike of the mid-fifties, and reliance had to be placed on contemporary media accounts, whose conditions of existence were different. File V14/32824 (1949) on the 'African Servants' Association, now African Cooks, Washermen and Houseservants' Union' existed, but was empty, as had been noted by several previous researchers.

5. Manuals and books of this kind were produced in all parts of the Empire, usually by colonial women. Strobel discusses several other examples (1991:17–18).

6. Two such women were Miss M. Pelham Johnson who was the Assistant Director of Education for Women and Girls in the 1940s and '50s and Margaret Ellwell-Sutton who was an Education Officer in Tanga in the fifties. I am grateful to both of them for their help in my research.

7. My analysis is based on archival work at the British Library of Newspapers at Colindale, where a limited selection of Tanganyikan newspapers is preserved. My sample was of issues of the weekly *Sunday News* over the period 1956–7 when a strike of domestic workers took place. That Africans saw this paper is demonstrated by an occasional letter from an African writer; on 25 Nov. 1956 they published their first picture of an African wedding. Other papers reviewed briefly were issues of the *Tanga Post and East Coast Advertiser* (a virulent outlet established in 1919 but closed in 1921 during the Depression) and the daily *Tanganyika Standard* (described by Shivji as a 'mouthpiece' of settler-employer interests: 1986:189) of which only two sets, each covering six months in the mid-1950s, were available. There were also some copies of newspapers in Swahili whose target audience was African and which were decidedly of a propagandist nature – e.g. *Mambo Leo* (Today's Affairs) published by the government's Public Relations Office, and *Kiongozi* (Leader) addressed to adherents of Catholicism. Their representation of colonial reality was, to say the least, economical with the truth. Shivji writes of the strict colonial censorship which excluded the development of an indigenous press (nd: 1993?), but there were Swahili newspapers addressed to more politically conscious Africans which flourished for a while (e.g. *Kwetu* (Our Place) produced by Erika Fiah in the fifties: see Coulson 1982:104) but to which I had no access.

8. This is illustrated in a press report reproduced in an official file (4/172/4: Commission of Enquiry into Tanga Dock Strike, August 1939) when 'local boys' (not domestic servants) were said to be amongst the strike leaders. 'Local boys' are here distinguished from 'alien natives' (ex-sisal workers who had swelled the ranks of casual labour in Tanga and were said to be threatening jobs). By the 1950s this general usage of the term 'boy' is no longer acceptable – it has become almost unsayable.

9. The term 'growing pains' is used in relation to 'political development' (Archives: V22/23886, Government Policy towards African Associations, 26 June 1936) and to labour matters (Archives: 967.822, Tanga District Officer's Reports, 1937).

10. This was not simply Tanganyika parlance: a Colonial Office document of 1948 (East African Office) lists wages appropriate for house, kitchen and garden 'boys'. The WSLT booklet on domestic labour also refers at one point to African males in general as 'boys' (1948:4). When talking about juveniles, it then becomes necessary to refer to them as '*young* boys', rather than simply 'boys' (5). In the European press of the 1950s the term 'boy' is used with more specific

reference to domestic or hotel servants. Bates' book (1962) makes considerable play on the word 'boy' (see pp. 65–6).

11. The file concerned a pamphlet to be sold to the public and apparently to be printed by the government (Archives V22/41713: Information regarding the employment of native servants, by Mr Broadhead Williams, 1951). Its coverage is broader than domestic service, as is the relevant statute: The Masters and Native Servants Ordinance. Discussion flitted around the name of the pamphlet as well as of the ordinance, with the latter settling doubt about the former.

12. The *Tanga Post* in 1919–21 had no such compunctions – it was then quite acceptable to write of 'evil smelling natives' (25 Oct. 1919), to claim that the African native, 'in spite of education' remained a 'free and indolent savage' (19 March, 1921) and to assert that 'the amount of grey matter under the kofia [cap] of the nigger is lamentably inadequate' (13 Dec. 1919). The context of the last statement is telling – it provides backing to an argument that only through white immigration could skilled labour be provided in what the *Post* called 'The Conquered Territory' (this was after the German defeat and before the League of Nations mandate came into force). Class interest as much as cultural denigration is here in evidence, and was underlined in their last issue when they spoke up for a 'reduction in wages' of African employees (21 June 1921).

13. Reported in Labour Board minutes of 25 Sept. 1944 (Archives: V14/30136 Employment of Children in Domestic Service, 1941–5).

14. Archives 4/652/28: Tanga Labour Dept: Employment of women and young persons (1937–48).

15. Archives V14/30136: Employment of Children in Domestic Service (1941–5).

16. Labour Board minutes of 25 Sept. 1944 (Archives: V14/30136 Employment of Children in Domestic Service, 1941–5). Efforts to reduce juvenile labour were ineffective. In 1947 there is discussion within the files as to the advisability of publishing the 1947 Census of Native Labour as it showed 22,000 juveniles in employment contrary to UN rules (V14/32679: Census of Native Labour).

17. An unconventional version of the moral consequences for children of employing servants was reported in the press in 1940. In a speech day address, the Headmaster of the Arusha European school complained that, 'Much of the constructive work of the school is – with all respect to parents here in Tanganyika – undone during the holidays. Late nights, drinking parties, unwholesome dependence on 'boys' for even the lightest of tasks, all militate against the building up of discipline' (quoted from the *Tanganyika Standard*, undated, 1940, in 'Fifty years ago', *Bulletin of Tanzanian Affairs*, 36, 1990). That parents sometimes depended heavily on servants (though not always male) to care for their children is confirmed by an advert which appeared in the *Sunday News* of 21 Oct. 1956: 'Wanted immediately a Goan or Seychelloise Nanny ... to look after two children of a Greek family in Tanga ... *Parents mostly on safari*' (my emphasis:7).

18. WSLT 1948:5. It was big news in 1956 when GEC brought an exhibition of household appliances to Tanganyika (*Sunday News*, 21 Oct. 1956:2).

19. The same point is made by Hunt in Hansen, 1989.

20. The NIH also produced a short 'journal' called *The Houseworker*, full of uplifting platitudes. Two issues, from 1948 and 1949, are enclosed in the file.

21. Archives: V14/11625, Native Labour in Tanganyika Terrritory: General Information: memo from Provincial Commissioner, Dar es Salaam, 9 March 1928.

22. An indication of the life that European women hoped to lead can be gleaned from the WSLT pamphlet of 1947, *Notes for Newcomers to Tanganyika Territory*. It was not to be wholly domestic; there were 'outbursts of hospitality' (9), as can be seen from recommendations on suitable clothing: 'afternoon frocks [for]

sundowner parties and going to the Club' and 'a few dance frocks' – 'in Dar es Salaam, Tanga and a few other places one can do with quite a number'; but also 'trousers or dungarees' for travelling, gardening etc: 'Even people [the reference is to women's clothes] who do not usually wear them will find one or two pairs almost indispensable' (4).

23. The issue of votes for women also bracketed European women with those of other 'races' as 'Tanganyika housewives' (*Sunday News*, 30 Dec. 1956). African women were also reported (12 Feb. 1956) to have petitioned for the vote whilst its main proponent in the Legislative Council was one Mrs S. Keeka, described as 'a Vice-Chairman of the UTP' (the multiracial party formed 1956) and also as the 'diminutive Representative Member for Central Province' – one of only two women in the Legico (ibid. 8 Jan. 1956/30 Dec. 1956). The vote was lost when a slight majority of men voted against 'housewives' achieving the vote.

24. Note however that in April 1951 the leader of the African Cooks wrote to the Colonial Secretary in London, complaining about the seizure of the Association's mail. And in a communiqué to the Governor listing various petitions from the African Cooks and others (1 July 1953), UN officials drew attention to one of their complaints: 'about the condition in which their mail is received' – presumably after its perusal and reseal by Special Branch officers (see p. 69).

25. The fears of Europeans, particularly of servants, in the period of Mau Mau are noted by Lonsdale in Kershaw (1997): 'the black savagery that lurked under the sunny servant surface' (xxiii).

26. Most of the letters were signed not only by Saleh bin Fundi but also by several other men, not always the same ones.

CHAPTER 5 MEN AT WORK IN THE TANZANIAN HOME

1. An earlier version of this chapter was published in Hansen 1992.

2. In what follows I draw on the reminiscences of a small sample of European ex-colonial residents of Tanganyika, now retired in Britain, as well as on the memories and reports of past and present servants. Data from formal interviews is supplemented by that gleaned from everyday observation. All names are pseudonyms.

3. Both one of the oldest (74) and the very youngest (16) male servant whom I interviewed had taken care of babies or very young children when they were barely grown-up themselves. The old man had started his servant career in this way, working for Europeans, whilst the youth had done the same for an Indian family. This is not unusual in Africa: see Hansen on Zambia, 1986a:22; Van Onselen on South Africa, 1982:27–9.

4. She used the Swahili word *mvulana* meaning teenage boy/young man. *Msichana* is the female equivalent, also used for young servants. This nomenclature does not have the derogatory implications of the terms 'boy' or 'girl' used in English, although these English terms may also be used by Africans.

5. This is almost certainly to be explained by the earlier entry of men into wage labour in the colonial period, as well as parental acceptance of formal education for boys compared to their resistance to girls' education. Both work and school were places where smart clothes, clean and pressed, were insisted upon.

6. Hansen (1989) documents the argument meticulously, and it may have more purchase for the Zambian case. Evidence which could point to a 'supply-side' explanation is not excluded: that initially women were 'hardly available' for this work, given a distinctively male pattern of labour migration (86). By the 1930s

and '40s women were moving into towns on a larger scale, though it is implied that the majority were wives of male workers rather than single women (note the early and considerable urbanisation of Zambia through copper mining). The argument that white householders could have recruited servants from amongst them (86) had they not been beset by 'sexual anxiety' (106) is not convincing, especially when we are assured that women were not seeking such work. That males who sought domestic work aimed to hang on to it and to exclude women, especially in times of economic recession, is also a factor (129). And since some women were taken on as nannies it is difficult to see how this can be squared with the sexuality argument – were nannies not equally a sexual threat to female employers' peace of mind?

CHAPTER 6 GREEN WAVES: THE SUPPLY OF DOMESTIC LABOUR

1. Explaining the gendered basis of domestic service in terms of the supply of labour out of rural areas originates with Boserup (1970), and was pitched implicitly within the evolutionary perspective of 'modernisation' theory. Arguing that paid domestic work appears in the phase of transition to modern industrial society, she insists that it is eventually replaced by services 'commercialised outside the household' (103). We have seen that there are problems with this thesis (Chapter 3; and more specifically on Boserup's thesis, Beneria and Sen 1981). At the same time the gender of domestic servants is related to the level of economic development: 'the whole domestic service sector grows with economic development and ... tends to become more exclusively feminine' (104). It is in the more industrialised areas of the Third World that women dominate the labour force in domestic service. Industrialising South Africa is contrasted with Kenya, for example, the former having a predominance of female domestic workers (78 per cent), whilst in Kenya 90 per cent of servants were men (102). It was not merely the level of industrialisation which explained the gender of workers but gendered patterns of labour migration. Boserup links patterns of male migration to 'female farming systems' which are characteristic of Africa and other low population density areas, whilst female migration is associated with 'male farming' which is predominant in Latin America. The example of domestic service confuses the point, as both Kenya and South Africa are within the female farming system and should thereby generate male servants. Many critiques of this oversimplified correlation (Guyer 1980) have suggested that a more critical analysis of the nature of economic development and the complex and diverse effects which it has upon indigenous patterns of agricultural production and gender relations are required (Gaitskell et al. 1984:89; Bozzoli 1991).

2. Bozzoli's work again has resonance, for the men of Phokeng also tried to prevent women's departure in the 1920s and '30s: 'keeping the girls at home meant that the bulk of agricultural and indeed other labour continued to be performed' (1991:89).

3. Sender and Smith claim to borrow from Marxism in their analysis, arriving at a conclusion few would find palatable. They argue that the expansion of rural wage labour and the squeezing out of 'microholdings' would be the single most valuable contribution to rural women's welfare, despite the fact that only the desperate want this low paid work.

4. The involvement of the state in controlling waves of green labour is noted by many. Strobel recounts how in South Africa between the 1890s and the 1920s the entry of white working class women was encouraged so that African men could be pressed into the mines, rather than into domestic work (1991:26).

Influx control was still being practised in South Africa in the 1980s (Shindler 1980) and in Tanzania, particularly against young women (Shaidi 1984).

5. A Sambaa Burial Society, set up to collect funds to transport home the bodies of those who had died in town, had been established by at least 1942.

6. As early as 1931 reports on the ethnic composition of Tanga District (the town and surrounding area in which several sisal estates were situated) indicated that amongst Sambaa residents there were 3850 adult men, but also 3200 adult women: an unbalanced sex ratio, certainly (120 adult men to every 100 women), but one which emphasises that women here were never absent from towns and have always been part of the migratory flow (Archives 4/183/2 Native Census, 1931). It is possible that many of these women were on temporary visits to resident husbands.

7. One Sambaa man described the learning process. As an adolescent he went to work as a 'garden boy' for a European farmer. This was in the late 1940s and he was paid Sh10 per month. 'I put up with it until I heard that in Tanga you could get Sh40 a month'. He did not go directly to Tanga, however, but spent a month working as an agricultural labourer in the Amani tea plantations: 'When I saw my first pay – it was Sh25 – I thought, this is not much better than at home', and he left and went to Tanga.

8. The precarious nature of peasant survival was brought home to me in the 1990s on visiting the Usambara area. Three years of semi-drought had led to near famine conditions and people were relying on relief supplies from government.

9. My data on how much land these men claimed to possess was not complete, but of those who had individual holdings, more than half claimed less than five acres, much in line with the average holdings for this area: TIRDEP:1975. Just under a quarter had between 10 and 15 acres, though this was often after many years of work. Only one man was landless: an Ngoni from Songea in the far south who had left home as a twelve year old, never returned or married, and was still working as a laundryman in his late seventies. Without land he had no choice.

10. Evidence of the increasing migration of women into urban areas comes from Tanga town, where sex ratios have evened between 1967 and 1988: from 118 to 105 men to every 100 women. Evidence from one village in the Usambara area in the 1990s indicates the continuing practice of oscillatory migration with men predominating. Out of a sample of 100 adults (half male, half female) 62 per cent of the men had spent time away as migrants; only 8 per cent of the women had done so. Of the 34 married women in this sample, 26 per cent had husbands currently away.

11. Exceptional circumstances generate exceptional responses. One woman could not survive on what her husband sent her and migrated independently from Mlalo. 'Hunger drove me to it', she insisted. Her mother's brother was working in Lushoto town, and he got her a job as a servant to an African couple. She abandoned their land and moved into town, taking her three children with her. She worked for this family for fifteen years, until they were transferred elsewhere, and by now her children were grown up. Meanwhile her husband had managed to construct a small house in Tanga and to let out rooms, so she went to join him.

12. She added 'And then she might find a young man for herself. Nowadays women are taking these pills so they can get away with it ... Our mothers did not know such things.' By the 1990s women feared men's philandering in towns even more because of the threat of AIDS; conversely they may be less inclined to take risks themselves, and press harder to be with their husbands in town.

13. The parallels between this case and the account which Bozzoli offers of young

women from Phokeng in South Africa are very striking. There too, young women migrants are described as 'wilful' and 'rebellious' by their families, especially men. Nevertheless their longer term objectives, achieved through domestic wage work for whites, were to settle down with husbands in the urban setting (1991: 89, 110). Domestic servants in this case made the same favourable comparisons between domestic service and factory or other manual work that are made in Tanzania.

14. In the rural areas in the 1990s it is said that young girls who return are infected with AIDS and thereby unmarriageable. However young village women are still sought as servants by urban employers and in one such case I witnessed the marriage of the girl in the year following her return to the Lushoto area.

15. My life histories showed that women with experience of domestic work were marginally more educated than male servants – just over half of the women had completed primary school compared to 45 per cent of the men, and there was a larger minority of men with no schooling at all.

16. Strobel describes how, after the abolition of slavery in Kenya in the early years of this century, many female domestic slaves in Mombasa moved into the more lucrative area of petty trade, whilst their place as domestic servants was taken by men, almost certainly unskilled migrant labourers, who would command only the lowest wages (1984:127).

17. Van Onselen's account of service in the Witwatersrand during the Depression confirms that at this period, 'African women were simply no cheaper to employ than black men. Despite the Depression, black women sought virtually the same wages from employers as other groups of servants on the Rand' (1982:17). It was only when a life-threatening drought forced a flood of women off the land and into the towns in dramatically increased numbers that wage rates for female domestics fell relative to those for men – but in the longer term this depressed male wages in this occupation as well (21).

CHAPTER 7 SERVING THE DOMINANT CLASS

1. Similar patterns may be found elsewhere. In Bolivia, domestic service plays one role (status enhancement and display) amongst rich white aristocratic families; and quite another for mixed race Chola families who are striving petty entrepreneurs and where the servant is an aide to production (Gill 1994). Sanjek argues that in Ghana the labour of young female household workers 'is the basement supporting capitalist investment and surplus realisation in the upper storeys of the Ghanaian economy' (1990:58).

2. There is an immense literature on this topic both within sociology in general and within the field of development studies. For a recent critical comment on the latter see Slater 1993.

3. Examples could be found in Alavi 1972 or *The Review of African Political Economy*, 8, 1977. A sympathetic and more recent usage is provided by Adesina 1992.

4. Hartmann (1990) argues that both the Nyerere period and that of his successor were characterised by inconsistent and contradictory policies with regard to private capital despite the commitment to 'socialism'. Towards the end of the 1970s: 'The political climate which prevailed was hostile to private capital' (243), but these elements were never totally excluded. One Asian industrialist, Somaiya, even had some official approval as 'Tanzania's only socialist millionaire'.

5. The issue of characterising ruling groups and analysing their forms of politico-

economic management is still pressing, even whilst the terminology may have changed, with the use of terms such as 'militariat' (Sierra Leone), 'kleptocracy' (Zaire under Mobutu), 'spoils regimes' (Somali, Zaire) etc. (*Review of African Political Economy*, 72, 1997). The same issue of *RoAPE* discloses that orthodox Marxist terminology is still hotly in debate in the most industrially developed country of Africa: South Africa.

6. Cultural differences amongst Africans have not generally been politicised in Tanzania. (For a critique of the general argument see Szeftel 1994.) 'Racial' differences are another matter (see pp. 115–19 and p. 127).

7. Cf. Rollins' description (1985) of a 'cross-cultural pattern of the darker domestic serving the lighter mistress' (7) with the implication that this is universal and that power derives from colour rather than symbolising its achievement in other ways. It is precisely the taken-for-granted linking that is problematised by a case such as this.

8. The fragility of their wealth is also notable. By the mid-1990s the Asian magnate's business empire had collapsed, largely due to the import of secondhand clothes, and the fertiliser company which allowed Mrs Frau to live in such style had been closed down, with considerable pollution of the area around. Class reproduction foundered on hard times.

9. As cooking styles differed from tribe to tribe, employers then spoke of having to teach servants how to do 'our cooking, as we like it'. Cultural adjustments might also have to be made by those who worked for Asians: 'he had to be shown how to cook for us – he made the pilau too oily – like Sikh cooking'. Apart from the issue of ethnic distance or ease of recruitment, African employers were rarely interested in the 'tribe' of their employees – like other employers they would say 'the main thing is that they do the work properly'. Occasionally Asians would express ethnic preferences – Muslims for other Muslims, or at the extreme: 'we ask what tribe they are because we have been here a long time and we know the tribes. The Chagga we would never employ – they are dangerous and they could even kill you. Sambaa are mostly all right – they work hard'.

10. Comparison can be made with practices amongst the Muslim Hausa, of employing children, especially males, to sell goods produced by women restricted to home (Schildkrout 1978).

11. The differential in wages between men and women servants at the time was marked. Even taking into account employers' overstatement of wages paid, women were earning on average 70% of men's wages.

CHAPTER 8 CLOSE ENCOUNTERS

1. There is an older literature on the workings of capitalism in the Western world which speaks to similar views – e.g. Nichols and Armstrong (1976), Beynon (1973), Burawoy (1979), Willis (1979) – but its application to contemporary industrial relations in Africa is unusual. This literature displayed an often unacknowledged marriage of Marxism with interactionist/interpretivist perspectives derived from Weberian inspired cultural studies. It noted the scope for worker resistance within the 'rules of the game' – recognising that the 'rules' are continually being renegotiated in the interaction between labour and employers. A current revival of such approaches is notable (Durrand and Stewart 1998; Thompson and Ackroyd 1995).

2. Similar attitudes were displayed by domestic workers in what was then Southern Rhodesia (Weinrich 1976:Ch. 4). Workers preferred employers who did not know their culture, language or habits, as this intimate knowledge would allow

them to 'scold us by our clan name'. Conversely Rollins produces evidence of American black domestic workers preferring to work for Southern white women rather than Northerners because the 'Southern black and the Southern white understand each other – whether they like one another or not' (1985:221). Domestic workers and their employers can be alike in one respect and different in another, of course; the relationship forces a close-up view which can be both comfortable and unsettling.

3. Chin's work on Malaysia (1998) shows that the significance of 'race' can be strikingly different. The Malaysian state pursued a distinctive ethnic policy which involved favouring the emergent Malay middle class and facilitating their import of the cheapest domestic servants from Indonesia.

4. I borrow this useful phrase from Bailey's study of the social anthropology of politics (1969).

5. Whisson and Weil (1971) argued that domestic service in apartheid South Africa was rewarded as much by gifts in kind as by wages and that: 'to pay more in cash would be to admit the greater worth of the servant; to give more in kind retains the servant as a dependant whilst reducing his moral worth' (43). The whole point of gift giving (vide Mauss) was that such gifts were unreciprocated, thus placing 'the recipient in the position of a child or a beggar' (41). My observations suggest that even subordinates may give gifts in the hope of initiating reciprocity.

6. Whisson and Weil (1971) and Tellis-Nayak (1983) make similar points about the relative manageability of young female servants, Whisson and Weil add that such an arrangement demonstrates most effectively the higher status of the employer; my own data suggest that the employment of older male servants speaks more convincingly of higher status. Here manageability is contrived through better wages and conditions.

7. Chin shows that where the control of servants is policed by the state and there is little opportunity for legitimate resistance, servants may resort to personalised sabotage such as deliberate pollution of food or environment, e.g. with menstrual blood (1998:163–4).

8. Mokake describes a similar response in Dar es Salaam. In an account of a young woman who became a prostitute she describes her initial intention to 'look for a job as ... a housegirl, but she had bad luck. No-one wanted her. The woman is very beautiful, housewives were afraid to take her, thinking she will break their marriages' (1997:4).

9. One example of this was related by an employer. Lia was marginalised when they employed an extra male servant who agreed to live in and watch over their property as well. Whilst on leave Lia had an accident, leaving a gash on her foot which took weeks to heal. She went to a traditional doctor to discover the cause of her bad luck. He told her that someone at her workplace had bewitched her. Lia wrote to tell her employers. Apprehensive about what they interpreted as dangerous jealousy between the two servants, they decided it would be safer if Lia only worked whilst 'mama' was around: she thereby lost her full-time job.

9. MILITANT DOMESTICS? CLASS, GENDER AND RESISTANCE

1. Marx's passionate thesis was that: 'there is a steady intensification of the wrath of the working class – a class which grows ever more numerous, and is disciplined, unified, and organised by the very mechanism of the capitalist mode of production' (1930:846).

2. Evidence of this is to be found in the archives and in Shivji's invaluable work (1986). Although the wages of kitchen and garden 'boys' might be as low as any,

houseboys, cooks and dhobis fared much better and usually enjoyed wage supplements in the form of cast-off clothes, housing and left-over food. A telling account is that of Mzee Mhemedzi (cited in Mlagala 1973) who, whilst looking back on domestic service as the most humiliating job he had ever done, nevertheless spoke well of its wages. In 1934 when economic depression had led to the halving of wages in some sectors, he was earning Sh15 per month – more than the Sh6–10 which gold miners earned through the 1930s (Shivji 1986:48). Trying to improve his position he took a job as a veterinary guard, only to find that he was paid no more than as a servant. Reverting to his domestic job he earned Sh80 per month by 1943, and 'with this he was able to support his family well' and brought his wife to live with him (1973:127). Few other migrant workers earned enough to live with their families at this time.

3. Archives: V22/37681/5/25 UN Visiting Commission: Petitions from the African Cooks, Washermen and Houseservants, 14 April 1951.

4. Archives: V22/37681/5/25, 21 October 1953. Saleh bin Fundi was then 53 years old.

5. The parallel with Amalaita activities should be noted here; see also the pathbreaking account by Mitchell (1956). Geiger argues that men were more afraid than women of political involvement – as wage labourers they had more to lose, where women had an independent anchorage in urban petty commodity production (1997).

6. Archives: V22/37681/5/25, 14 April 1951.

7. Leslie's *Survey of Dar es Salaam* (1963) claimed that many servants were laid off after the minimum wage legislation came in, as Indian, Arab and African employers were unable to pay. This may be true; it is equally likely that with legislation in place, employers were denying that they employed domestic servants (1963:5, 126).

8. Archives: V22/37681/5/25, 14 April 1951.

9. Interview Tanga: 31 July 1986.

10. Archives: V14/32744, File on Domestic Servants: 26 August 1948; 1 September 1948.

11. Matayo interview, 31 July 1986. He said it was in 1954, but it must have been the following year after the TFL was set up.

12. After searching unsuccessfully for anyone who could remember the strike in 1956, my meeting with Matayo in 1986 was accidental – he was on a brief visit to Tanga and I was about to leave. I had only a short interview with him which could not be followed up. (Enquiring a few years later, I learnt he had died.) I located Ali Samponda (see p. 163), still working at the Tanga Hotel, who told me that Matayo could explain the circumstances of the 1956 strike, which he did not remember himself. I was sent to find Matayo through a path of social linkages: go to one of the outlying neighbourhoods of Tanga town, ask there for Victor Mkello (see p. 165) and then enquire for a neighbour of Mkello's ('a Mzigua from Tuliani') with whom Erasto was staying.

13. Since the memory of others was blank I have no way of checking Matayo's recollections of union activity in Tanga. He may have overstated the enthusiasm and the numbers involved.

14. Matayo was able to reel off the names of other Dar es Salaam leaders of the earlier Union, only one of whom was listed in the fearless band of letter writers to the UN: Edward Tumetika – presumably the same Edward Mwitike/Tumitwike (V22/37681/5/25). Matayo also mentioned Abdallah Kidevu, Hassan Haji, Juma Seng'onda, Edward Siyambo, Mzee Suleimani and Bakari Yale amongst Dar es Salaam leaders. At least two of these were hotel workers.

15. In 1962 membership of the Domestic and Hotel Workers Union was at its height, numbering some fifteen and a half thousand, though the plantation workers, local government, teachers and railway workers formed bigger unions (Friedland 1969).
16. This puts in quite another light Saleh bin Fundi's demand (in his petitions to the UN), that Europeans, Indians and Arabs be sent home (V22/37681/5/25: 1 Sept. 1951).
17. The same argument is now applied to query the efficacy of new management models in capitalism – those which rely on cultural manipulation, ideological incorporation and self-discipline of the worker – e.g. TQM (Total Quality Management). Even in these settings the workers find ways to resist whilst appearing to comply (Durrand and Stewart 1998).
18. Compare the exclusivity of the female cooks' association in 1930s Bolivia: concerned to raise their wages and improve working conditions but also to consolidate their privileged and superior specialised role as cooks working in high class families ('I wasn't just anyone, I was a society cook': Gill 1994:34).

CONCLUSION

1. The ever-present potential of domestic service to display class position was reiterated recently in Tanzania's Political Leaders Retirement Bill (1999). 'Retiring presidents will ... be given a house, nine servants and health insurance. Vice-presidents will get six servants' (cited in *Tanzanian Affairs*, 63, 1999).
2. By 1995, one of the most startling indicators of the reversal in political ideology and practice was reported with pride: 'The Beijing Federation of Women has set up a "March 8 Family Service Company" which offers service to some 180,000 Beijing families, through recruiting thousands of house maids for them from the impoverished rural areas ... Such a development has also helped in resolving the unemployment issue for the rural Chinese women' (*Chinese Women are Getting Ahead*: one of a series of booklets produced for the UN Fourth World Conference on Women in Beijing, China Intercontinental Press, 1995:39).

APPENDIX

1. One solution to this problem was adopted by Hansen (1989 Ch. 4). She interviewed employers herself, whilst an African assistant simultaneously interviewed their servants. I would not have wished to exclude myself from the latter interviews; I would also have worried about employers pressing servants to reveal what they had been asked, and servants' fears of information being passed to their employers. This underlines that there is no ideal way of doing research on this topic.
2. Being 'not-at-home' may be a more general index of masculine identity – it is also noted by Willott and Griffin in a study of unemployed men in the English Midlands (1996:82).
3. Hansen deliberately avoided this role: 'I anticipated that I would be an unsuccessful madam ... lacking the firmness that household manuals suggest madams exhibit. Keeping my own servant would have taught me nothing about other people's servant-keeping practice" (1989:206–7). See also Gregson and Lowe: 'This book was written without the assistance of any waged domestic labour!' (1994).
4. My stay in this household was instructive in other ways. There were several young people living here, distant and not so distant relatives of the residents (the owner of the house and her tenants), who were helping with household tasks as

well as studying or looking for work. We were also entertained by the unfolding saga of one tenant, a man on his own whose wife had left him with two small children. His attempts to have them cared for by a succession of female skivvies whom he did not always pay and whom he abused roundly when drunk (frequently) were illuminating.

5. Note, however, that this woman had worked for her previous employers for many years and had called one of her children after the man of the family. She also saw them as depending on her; it was by no means a one-way hierarchical relationship.

6. Accessing the subjective aspects of servant experience requires direct and sensitive contact. Cooke is open about her lack of contact with servants themselves (1990:72); Tellis-Nayak (1983) describes how employers intervened in interviews with servants and sometimes took over; for Cock's account of the difficulties (1980), see p. 183.

7. From Tanzania there have also been contributions to this debate – e.g. Nkhoma-Wamunza (1987) and Mbilinyi (1989).

BIBLIOGRAPHY

Adesina, J. 1990. 'The construction of social communities in work: the case of a Nigerian factory', *Capital and Class* 40.

Adesina, J. 1992. *Labour Movements and Policy Making in Africa*. Dakar, Senegal: CODESRIA Working Paper.

Aidoo, A. 1970. *No Sweetness Here*. Harlow, Essex: Longman.

Alavi, H. 1972. 'The State in Post-colonial Societies', *New Left Review* 74.

Althusser, L. and E. Balibar 1979. *Reading Capital*. Original 1968. London: Verso edition.

Armstrong, M. J. 1990. 'Family household workers in industrialising Malaysia', in R. Sanjek and S. Colen (eds), qv.

Attems, M. 1969. 'The Shambala system of agriculture (Usambara)', in H. Kraut and H-D. Cremer (eds), *Investigations into Health and Nutrition in East Africa*. Munich: Weltforum Verlag, 179–218.

Babcock, B. 1993. 'Feminisms/pretexts: fragments, questions and reflections', *Anthropological Quarterly* 60 (2), 59–80.

Back, L. 1994. 'The "White Negro" revisited: race and masculinities in South London', in A. Cornwall and N. Lindisfarne (eds), qv.

Baden, S. and A. M. Goetz 1997. 'Who needs (sex) when you can have (gender)? Conflicting discourses on gender at Beijing', *Feminist Review* 56.

Bailey, F. G. 1969. *Strategems and Spoils: A Social Anthropology of Politics*. Oxford: Basil Blackwell.

Barron, R. D. and G. M. Norris 1976. 'Sexual Divisions and the Dual Labour Market', in D. Barker and S. Allen (eds), *Dependence and Exploitation in Work and Marriage*. London: Longman.

Bates, D. 1962. *The Mango and the Palm*. London: Rupert Hart-Davis.

Beechey, V. 1987. *Unequal Work*. London: Verso.

Beneria, L. and G. Sen, 1981. 'Accumulation, reproduction and women's role in economic development: Boserup revisited', *Signs* 7 (2).

Berger, I. 1986. 'Sources of Class Consciousness: South African Women in Recent Labor Struggles', in C. Robertson and I. Berger (eds), *Women and Class in Africa*. New York: Africana Publishing Co.

Beynon, H. 1973. *Working for Ford*. London: Allen Lane.

Bienefeld, M. and T. H. Sabot 1972. *NUMEIST (National Urban Mobility, Employment and Income Survey of Tanzania) 1971*: Report. Dar es Salaam: University of Dar es Salaam.

Bigilimara, R. 1963. 'The history of a family emerging from slavery', *Swahili*, the Journal of the East African Committee 33 (2). Dar es Salaam, 12–18.

Bittson, M., G. Matheson and G. Meagher 1999. 'The changing boundary between home and market: Australian trends in outsourcing domestic labour", *Work, Employment and Society* 13 (2), 249–74.

Bose, C. 1979. 'Technology and changes in the division of labour in the American home', *Women's Studies International Quarterly* 2, 295–304.

Boserup, E. 1970. *Women's Role in Economic Development*. New York: St Martin's Press.

Bozzoli, B. 1983. 'Marxism, feminism and South African Studies', *Journal of Southern African Studies* 9 (2).

Bozzoli, B. 1991. *Women of Phokeng: Consciousness, Life Strategy and Migrancy in Southern Africa 1900–1983*. New Hampshire/London: Heinemann/James Currey.

Braverman, H. 1974. *Labour and Monopoly Capitalism*. New York: Monthly Review Press.

Bujra, J. 1990. 'Taxing development: why must women pay? Gender and the development debate in Tanzania', *Review of African Political Economy* 47.

Bujra, J. 1992a. 'Ethnicity and class; the case of the East African "Asians"', in T. Allen and A. Thomas (eds), *Poverty and Development in the 1990s*. Oxford: Oxford University Press.

Bujra, J. 1992b. 'Men at work in the Tanzanian home: how did they ever learn?' in K. T. Hansen (ed.), qv.

Bujra, J. 1993. 'Gender, class and empowerment: a tale of two Tanzanian servants', *Review of African Political Economy* 56.

[Bulletin of] Tanzanian Affairs. The Britain-Tanzania Society.

Bunster, X. and E. Chaney 1985. *Sellers and Servants: Working Women in Lima, Peru*. New York: Praeger.

Burawoy, M. 1979. *Manufacturing Consent: Changes in the Labor Process under Monopoly Capitalism*. Chicago: University of Chicago Press.

Burnett, J. 1974. *Useful Toil: Autobiographies of Working People from the 1820s to the 1920s*. London: Allen Lane.

Callinicos, L. 1975. 'Domesticating Workers', *South African Labour Bulletin* 2 (4).

Caplan, P. 1978. 'Women's organisations in Madras city, India' in P. Caplan and J. Bujra (eds), *Women United, Women Divided*. London: Tavistock.

Caplan, P. 1997. *African Voices, African Lives: Personal Narratives from a Swahili Village*. London: Routledge.

Centre for Contemporary Cultural Studies (CCCS) 1982. *Making Histories: Studies in History-writing and Politics*. London: Hutchinson.

Chin, C. B. N. 1998. *In Service and Servitude: Foreign Female Domestic Workers and the Malaysian 'Modernity' project*. New York: Colombia Univ Press.

Cliffe, L., W. Luttrell and J. Moore 1969. 'Socialist transformation in rural Tanzania: a strategy for the Western Usambaras'. Economic Research Bureau paper 69. 24. Dar es Salaam: University of Dar es Salaam.

Cock, J. 1980. *Maids and Madams: A Study in the Politics of Exploitation*. Johannesburg: Ravan Press.

Cockburn, C. 1983. *Brothers: Male Dominance and Technological Change*, London: Pluto.

Cohen, R. 1987. *The New Helots: Migrants in the International Division of Labour*. Aldershot: Gower.

Colen. S. 1990. '"Housekeeping" for the green card: West Indian household workers, the state and stratified reproduction in New York', in R. Sanjek and S. Colen (eds), qv.

Collinson, D. and J. Hearn 1996. '"Men" at "work": multiple masculinities; multiple workplaces', in M. Mac an Ghaill (ed.) qv.

Connell, R. 1987. *Gender and Power: Society, the Person and Sexual Politics*. Stanford: Stanford University Press.

Cooke, M. T. 1990. 'Household workers in Nyishang, Nepal', in R. Sanjek and S. Colen (eds), qv.

Cornwall, A. and N. Lindisfarne (eds) 1994. *Dislocating Masculinity*. London: Routledge.

Coser, L. 1973. 'Servants: the obsolescence of an occupational role', *Social Forces* 52, 31–40.

Coulson, A. 1979. *African Socialism in Practice*. Nottingham: Spokesman.

Coulson, A. 1982. *Tanzania: A Political Economy*. Oxford: Clarendon Press.

Cowen, M. and K. Kinyanjui 1977. 'Some problems of income distribution in Kenya'. IDS Discussion paper, unpubd, Nairobi.

Croll, E. 1976. *The Women's Movement in China*. London: Anglo-Chinese Educational Institute.

Davidoff, L. 1976. 'The rationalisation of housework' in D. Leonard Barker and S. Allen (eds), *Dependence and Exploitation in Work and Marriage*. London: Longman.

Donaldson, L. 1993. *Decolonising Feminisms: Race, Gender and Empire-Building*. London: Routledge.

Durrand, J. and P. Stewart 1998. 'Manufacturing dissent: Burawoy in a Franco-Japanese workshop', *Work, Employment and Society* 12 (1).

East African Office. 1948. *Cost of Living in East Africa*. Information sheet (April). London: Fosh and Cross Ltd.

Elson, D. and R. Pearson 1981a. '"Nimble fingers make cheap workers": an analysis of women's employment in Third World export manufacturing', *Feminist Review* 7.

Elson, D. and Pearson, R. 1981b. 'The subordination of women and the internationalisation of factory production', in K. Young et al. (eds), *Of Marriage and the Market*. London: CSE Books.

Enloe, C. 1989. '"Just like one of the family": domestic servants in world politics', in C. Enloe, *Bananas, Beaches and Bases: Making Feminist Sense of International Politics*. Berkeley: University of California Press.

Feierman, S. 1974. *The Shambaa Kingdom*. Madison: University of Wisconsin Press.

Feierman, S. 1990. *Peasant Intellectuals: Anthropology and History in Tanzania*. Madison: University of Wisconsin Press.

Foucault, M. 1980. *Power/Knowledge*. New York: Harvester Wheatsheaf.

Foucault, M. 1984. *The History of Sexuality*, Vol. 1: *An Introduction*. London: Penguin.

Foucault, M. 1991. 'Politics and the study of discourse', in *The Foucault Effect*, G. Burchell, C. Gordon and P. Miller (eds). London: Harvester Wheatsheaf.

Fraser, R. 1984. *In Search of a Past: The Manor House, Amnersfield, 1933–45*. London: Verso.

Friedland, W. H. 1969. *Vuta Kamba: The Development of Trade Unions in Tanganyika*. Washington: Hoover Institute Press.

Gaitskell, D. 1986. 'Girls' education in South Africa: Domesticity or domestic service?'. Unpubd paper presented to ASAUK conference.

Gaitskell, D., J. Kimble, M. Maconachie and E. Unterhalter. 1984. 'Class, race and gender: Domestic workers in South Africa', *Review of African Political Economy* 27/8.

Gaskell, J. 1986. 'Conceptions of skill and the work of women', in R. Hamilton and M. Barrett (eds), *The Politics of Diversity*. London: Verso.

Geiger, S. 1997. *TANU Women: Gender and Culture in the Making of Tanganyikan Nationalism 1955–1965*. New Hampshire: Heinemann.

Gill, L. 1994. *Precarious Dependencies: Gender, Class and Domestic Service in Bolivia*. New York: Columbia University Press.

Glaeser, B. (ed.) 1980. *Factors Affecting Land Use and Food Production: A Contribution to Ecodevelopment in Tanzania*. Saarbrucken: Verlag Breitenbach.

Gordon, S. 1985. *A Talent for Tomorrow; Life Stories of South African Servants*. Johannesburg: Ravan Press.

Government of Tanganyika. 1930. *A Handbook of Tanganyika Territory*. London: G. F. Sayers.

Government of Tanzania. 1967/1978/1988. *Census*. Dar es Salaam: Bureau of Statistics.

Government of Tanzania. 1994. *Selected Statistical Series 1951–1991*. Dar es Salaam: Bureau of Statistics.

Government of Tanzania. 1994. *Statistical Abstract 1992*. Dar es Salaam: Bureau of Statistics.

Gramsci, A. 1957. *The Modern Prince and Other Writings*. London: Lawrence and Wishart.

Gregson, N. and M. Lowe. 1994. *Servicing the Middle Classes: Class, Gender and Waged Domestic Labour in Contemporary Britain*. London: Routledge.

Guyer, J. 1980. 'Food, cocoa and the division of labour by sex in two West African societies', *Comparative Studies in Society and History* 22. Cambridge: Cambridge University Press.

Hansen, K. T. 1986a. 'Household work as a man's job: Sex and gender in domestic service in Zambia', *Anthropology Today* 2 (3).

Hansen, K. T. 1986b. 'Domestic service in Zambia', *Journal of Southern African Studies* 13 (1).

Hansen, K. T. 1989. *Distant Companions: Servants and Employers in Zambia 1900–1985*. Ithaca: Cornell University Press.

Hansen, K. T. (ed.) 1992. *African Encounters with Domesticity*. New Brunswick: Rutgers University Press.

Haraway, D. 1991. *Simians, Cyborgs amd Women: the Reinvention of Nature*. London: Free Association Books.

Hartmann, J. 1990. 'The rise and rise of private capital', in N. O'Neill and K. Mustafa (eds), *Capitalism, Socialism and the Development Crisis in Tanzania*. Aldershot: Avebury.

Harvey, D. 1990. *The Condition of Postmodernity: An Enquiry into the Origins of Cultural Change*. Oxford: Blackwell.

Hunt, N. R. 1992. 'Colonial fairy tales and the knife and fork doctrine in the heart of Africa', in K. T. Hansen (ed.), qv.

Iliffe, J. 1969. *Tanganyika under German Rule*. Cambridge: Cambridge University Press.

Iliffe, J. 1973. *Modern Tanzanians: a Volume of Biographies*. Dar es Salaam: East African Publishing House.

Iliffe, J. 1975. 'The creation of group consciousness: a history of the dockworkers of Dar es Salaam', in R. Sandbrook and R. Cohen (eds), *The Development of an African Working Class*. London: Longman.

Iliffe, J. 1979a. *A Modern History of Tanganyika*. Cambridge: Cambridge University Press.

Iliffe, J. 1979b. 'Wage labour and urbanisation', in M. Kaniki (ed.), *Tanzania under Colonial Rule*. London: Longman.

Izquierdo, E. 1989. 'Sharpening the class struggle: the education of domestic workers in Cuba', in E. Chaney and M. Castro (eds), qv.

Johnson, C. 1992. *Women on the Frontline: Voices from Southern Africa*. London: Macmillan.
Johnson, M. 1984. 'Domestic work in rural Iceland: a historical overview', in N. Long (ed.), *Family and Work in Rural Societies*. London: Tavistock.

Kandiyoti, D. 1991. 'Islam and Patriarchy: a comparative perspective' in N. Keddie and B. Brown (eds), *Women in Middle Eastern History*. Yale University Press.
Kershaw, G. 1997. *Mau Mau from Below*. Oxford: James Currey.
Kitching, G. 1987. 'The role of a national bourgeoisie in the current phase of capitalist development', in P. Lubeck (ed.), qv.
Kobayashi, A. 1994. 'Coloring the field: gender, "race" and the politics of fieldwork', *Professional Geographer* 46 (1), 73–80.
Koda, B. et al. 1987. *Women's Initiatives in the United Republic of Tanzania*. Geneva: ILO.
Kristeva, J. 1986. 'Word, dialogue and novel', in T. Moi (ed.), *The Kristeva Reader*. Oxford: Basil Blackwell.

Lash, S. and J. Urry 1987. *The End of Organized Capitalism*. Cambridge: Polity Press.
Laslett, P. 1965. *The World we Have Lost*. London: Methuen.
Laslett, P. 1977. *Family Life and Illicit Love in Earlier Generations*. Cambridge: Cambridge University Press.
Lasser, C. 1987. 'The domestic balance of power: relations between mistress and maid in nineteenth-century New England', *Labor History* 28 (1), 5–22.
Lee-Treweek, G. 1997. 'Women, resistance and care: an ethnographic study of nursing auxiliary work', *Work, Employment and Society* 11 (2).
Leslie, J. A. K. 1963. *A Survey of Dar es Salaam*. Oxford: Oxford University Press.
Lubeck, P. (ed.) 1987. *The African Bourgeoisie: Capitalist Development in Nigeria, Kenya and the Ivory Coast*. Boulder, Colorado: Lynne Reinner.

Mac an Ghaill, M. (ed.) 1996. *Understanding Masculinities*. Buckingham: Open University Press.
Mackintosh, M. 1989. *Gender, Class and Rural Transition: Agribusiness and the Food Crisis in Senegal*. London: Zed Press.
Maliyamkono, T. L. and M. S. D. Bagachwa 1990. *The Second Economy in Tanzania*. London: James Currey.
Mamdani, M. 1983. *Imperialism and Fascism in Uganda*. London: Heinemann.
Marx, K. 1930. *Capital* Vol. II. London: J. M. Dent.
Mascarenhas, O. and M. Mbilinyi 1983. *Women in Tanzania: an Analytical Bibliography*. Uppsala: Scandinavian Institute of African Studies.
Mbilinyi, M. 1985. 'The impact of the economic crisis on women's employment, wages and incomes in Tanzania'. Professorial inaugural lecture, University of Dar es Salaam, unpubd.
Mbilinyi, M. 1987. '"Women in Development" Ideology and the Marketplace', in V. Miner and H. Longino (eds), *Competition: A Feminist Taboo?* New York: The Feminist Press, 106–20.
Mbilinyi, M. 1989. '"I'd have been a man": Politics and the labour process in producing personal narratives', in Personal Narratives Group (ed.), qv.
Mbilinyi, M. 1991. *Big Slavery: Agribusiness and the Crisis in Women's Employment in Tanzania*. Dar es Salaam: Dar es Salaam University Press.

Mbughuni, P. with Bibi 1991. 'A life history of Bibi: a woman in urban Tanga', in M. Ngaiza and B. Koda (eds), qv.

Mbughuni, P. 1994. 'Gender and poverty alleviation in Tanzania', in M. Bagachwa (ed.), *Poverty Alleviation in Tanzania: Recent Research Issues*. Dar es Salaam: Dar es Salaam University Press.

McClintock, A. 1993. 'Family feuds: gender, nationalism and the family', *Feminist Review* 44.

McElhinny, B. 1994. 'An economy of effect: Objectivity, masculinity and the gendering of police work', in A. Cornwall and N. Lindisfarne (eds), qv.

Mgaya, M. H. 1976. *Study of Workers in a Factory in Tanzania*. MA thesis, University of Dar es Salaam.

Mihyo, P. 1983. *Industrial Conflict and Change in Tanzania*. Dar es Salaam: Tanzania Publishing House.

Mitchell, J. C. 1956. *The Kalela Dance: Aspects of Social Relationships among Urban Africans in Northern Rhodesia*. Rhodes Livingstone Paper No. 27.

Mitzlaff, U. von 1988. 'Women Farmers or Farmers' Wives? The Soil Erosion Control/ agriforestry project (SECAP) and the problem of the involvement of women'. Report for Deutsche Gesellschaft für Technische Zusammenarbeit, unpubd.

Mlagala, M. 1973. 'The traveller: Lulapangilo Zakaria Mhemedzi', in J. Iliffe (ed.), qv.

Mokake, S. 1997. 'Gender power relations'. Unpubd ms. Dar es Salaam.

Molohan, M. J. B. 1957. *Detribalisation*. Dar es Salaam: Government Printer.

Molyneux, M. 1979. 'Beyond the domestic labour debate', *New Left Review* 116, 3–28.

Musisi, N. B. 1992. 'Colonial and missionary education: women and domesticity in Uganda, 1900–1945', in K. T. Hansen (ed.), qv.

Mwingira, M. 1989. 'Day to day life in Tanzania', paper presented to Britain-Tanzania Society seminar, unpubd, London.

Myrdal, J. and G. Kessle 1970. *China: The Revolution Continues*. London: Penguin Books.

Nast, H. 1994. 'Women in the field: critical feminist methodologies and theoretical perspectives: Opening remarks', *Professional Geographer* 46 (1), 54–66.

Ngaiza, M. and B. Koda (eds) 1991. *Unsung Heroines*. Dar es Salaam: Women's Research and Documentation Project (WRDP) Publications.

Ngugi wa Thion'go 1983. *Barrel of a Pen: Resistance to Repression in Neo-colonial Kenya*. London: New Beacon Books.

Nichols, T. and P. Armstrong 1976. *Workers Divided*. Glasgow: Fontana/Collins.

Nkhoma-Wamunza, A. 1987. 'Women's studies in higher education: some experiences in Tanzania'. Unpubd paper delivered at the UNESCO/University of Zimbabwe seminar on Women's Studies, Sept.

Nyerere, J. 1968. *Ujamaa: Essays on Socialism*. Dar es Salaam: Oxford University Press.

Oakley, A. 1976. *Housewife*. London: Pelican books.

Oppong, C. 1974. *Marriage among a Matrilineal Elite: A Family Study of Ghanaian Senior Civil Servants*. Cambridge: Cambridge University Press.

Oyono, F. 1970. *The Houseboy*. London: Heinemann.

Palmer, P. 1989. *Domesticity and Dirt: Housewives and Domestic Servants in the United States 1920–1945*. Philadelphia: Temple University Press.

Pearson, R. 1988. 'Female workers in the First and Third Worlds: the greening of women's labour', in R. Pahl (ed.), *On Work*. Oxford: Basil Blackwell.

Pereira de Melo, H. 1989. 'Feminists and domestic workers in Rio de Janeiro', in E. Chaney and M. Castro (eds), qv.

Personal Narratives Group (eds) 1989. *Interpreting Women's Lives: Feminist Theory and Personal Narratives*. Bloomington:Indiana University Press.

Peter, C. and S. Mvungi 1985. 'The State and Student Struggles', in I. Shivji (ed.), *The State and the Working People in Tanzania*. Dakar: Codesria (157–98).

Phillips, A. and B. Taylor. 1980. 'Sex and Skill: Notes towards a Feminist Economics', *Feminist Review* 6.

Presnell, M. 1994. 'Postmodern ethnography: from representing the Other to co-producing a text', in K. Carter and M. Presnell (eds), *Interpretive Approaches to Interpersonal Communication*. New York: SUNY Press.

Ramazanoglu, C. (ed.) 1993. *Up Against Foucault: Explorations of Some Tensions between Foucault and Feminism*. London: Routledge.

Review of African Political Economy 8. 1977.

Review of African Political Economy 72. 1997. *Zaire, South Africa: Moving Forward?*

Rollins, J. 1985. *Between Women: Domestics and their Employers*. Philadelphia: Temple University Press.

Rollins, J. 1990. 'Ideology and Servitude', in R. Sanjek and S. Colen (eds), qv.

Rowbotham, S. 1974. *Hidden from History*. 2nd ed. London: Pluto Press.

Sabot, T. H. 1979. *Economic Development and Urban Migration: Tanzania 1900–1971*. Oxford: Clarendon Press.

Samuel, R. (ed.) 1975. *Village Life and Labour*. London: Routledge and Kegan Paul.

Sanjek, R. 1990. 'Maid servants and market women's apprentices in Adabraka', in R. Sanjek and S. Colen (eds), qv.

Sanjek, R. and S. Colen (eds) 1990. *At Work in Homes: Household Workers in World Perspective*. Washington DC: American Ethnological Society Monograph.

Sarros, A. H. and P. Tinios 1995. 'Consumption and Poverty in Tanzania in 1976 and 1991: a comparison using survey data', *World Development* 23 (8), 1401–19.

Saul, J. 1983. 'The state in post colonial societies: Tanzania', in D. Held (ed.), *States and Societies*. Oxford: Martin Robertson.

Sauti ya Siti. Dar es Salaam: Tanzania Media Women's Association (TAMWA).

Schildkrout, E. 1978. 'Roles of children in urban Kano', in J. S. La Fontaine (ed.), *Sex and Age as Principles of Social Differentiation*. London: Academic Press.

Scott, A. 1986. 'Industrialisation, Gender Segregation and Stratification Theory', in R. Crompton and M. Mann (eds), *Gender and Stratification*. Cambridge: Polity Press, 154–89.

Seccombe, W. 1974. 'The housewife and her labour under capitalism', *New Left Review* 94.

Seccombe, W. 1980. 'The extended reproduction cycle of labour power in twentieth-century capitalism', in B. Fox (ed.), *Hidden in the Household: Women's Domestic Labour under Capitalism*. Ontario: The Women's Press.

Sender, J. and S. Smith 1990. *Poverty, Class and Gender in Rural Africa: A Tanzanian Case Study*. London: Routledge.

Shaidi, L. 1984. 'Tanzania: the Human Resources Deployment Act 1983 – a desperate measure to contain a desperate situation', *Review of African Political Economy* 31.

Sharma, U. 1986. *Women's Work, Class and the Urban Household: A Study of Shimla, North India*. London: Tavistock.

Sheikh-Hashim, L. 1988. 'Housegirls: the dilemma', *Sauti ya Siti* 1.

Shindler, J. 1980. 'The effects of influx control and labour saving appliances on domestic service', *South African Labour Bulletin* 6 (1).

Shivji, I. 1976. *Class Struggles in Tanzania*. London: Heinemann.

Shivji, I. 1983. 'Working class struggles and organisations in Tanzania 1939–1976', *Mawazo* 5 (2). Dar es Salaam.

Shivji, I. 1986. *Law, State and the Working Class in Tanzania*. London: James Currey.

Shivji, I. 1991. 'The democracy debate in Africa: Tanzania', *Review of African Political Economy* 50.

Shivji, I. 1993. 'Press-gag or Shija-gate in the making'. Series of articles in *Family Mirror* 1 August–30 September.

Shivji, I. 1994. 'Electoral politics, liberalisation and democracy', in K. Mukandala and H. Othman (eds), *Liberalisation and Politics: the 1990 Elections in Tanzania*. Dar es Salaam: Dar es Salaam University Press.

Slater, D. 1993. 'The political meanings of development: in search of new horizons', in F. J. Schuurman (ed.), *Beyond the Impasse: New Directions in Development Theory*. London: Zed Press.

Smith, M. 1975. 'The female domestic servant and social change: Lima, Peru', in R. Rohrlich-Leavitt (ed.), *Women Cross-Culturally, Change and Challenge*. The Hague: Mouton.

Stanley, L. (ed.) 1984. *The Diaries of Hannah Cullwick*. London: Virago.

Stanley, L. 1992. *The Auto/biographical I: the Theory and Practice of Feminist Auto/biography*. Manchester: Manchester University Press.

Stichter, S. 1975. 'The formation of a working class in Kenya', in R. Sandbrook and R. Cohen (eds), *The Development of an African Working Class*. London: Longman.

Stichter, S. 1978. 'Trade unionism in Kenya, 1947–52: the militant phase', in P. Gutkind, R. Cohen and S. Copans (eds), *African Labour History*. London: Sage.

Stichter, S. 1988. 'The Middle Class Family in Kenya: Changes in Gender Relations', in S. Stichter and J. Parpart (eds), *Patriarchy and Class: African Women in the Home and the Workforce*. Boulder: Westview Press.

Strobel, M. 1984. 'Slavery and reproductive labour in Mombasa', in C. Robertson and M. Klein (eds), *Women and Slavery in Africa*. Madison: University of Wisconsin Press.

Strobel, M. 1991. *European Women and the Second British Empire*. Bloomington: Indiana University Press.

Sweetman, C. 1998. 'Men's work, masculinities and gender divisions of labour'. Paper presented to Men, Masculinities and Development Seminar. Bradford.

Szeftel, M. 1994. 'Ethnicity and democratisation in South Africa', *Review of African Political Economy* 60.

Tanga Integrated Rural Development Programme (TIRDEP) 1975. *Tanga Regional Development Plan 1975–80*. Tanga: Regional Development Director's Office.

Tanga Integrated Rural Development Programme (TIRDEP) 1985. *Tanga Integrated Rural Development Programme* (Update on implementation). Tanga: Regional Development Director's Office.

Taylor, P. 1979. 'Daughters and mothers – maids and mistresses: domestic service between the wars', in J. Clarke et al. (eds), *Working Class Culture*. London: Hutchinson.

Tellis-Nayak, V. 1983. 'Power and solidarity : clientage in domestic service', *Current Anthropology* 20 (1).

Thompson, E. P. 1978. *The Poverty of Theory and Other Essays*. London: Merlin Press.

Thompson, P. 1988. *The Voice of the Past*. 2nd ed. Oxford: Oxford University Press.

Thompson, P. and S. Ackroyd 1995. 'All quiet on the workplace front? A critique of recent trends in British industrial sociology', *Sociology* 29 (4).

Tripp, A-M. 1994. 'Deindustrialisation and the growth of women's economic associations and networks in urban Tanzania', in S. Rowbothan and S. Mitter (eds), *Dignity and Daily Bread*. London: Routledge.

Van Onselen, C. 1982. *New Ninevah*, Vol. 2 of Studies in the Social and Economic History of the Witwatersrand 1886–1914. Harlow: Longman.

Veblen, T. 1899. *The Theory of the Leisure Class*. London: George Allen and Unwin.

Von Freyhold, M. 1977. 'The Post-Colonial State and its Tanzanian Version', *Review of African Political Economy* 8.

Von Freyhold, M. 1979. *Ujamaa Villages in Tanzania: Analysis of a Social Experiment*. London: Heinemann.

Walby, S. (ed.) 1988. *Gender Segregation at Work*. Milton Keynes: Open University Press.

Watson, W. 1958. *Tribal Cohesion in a Money Economy*. Manchester: Manchester University Press.

Weinrich, A. K. H. 1976. *Mucheke: Race, Status and Politics in a Rhodesian Community*. UNESCO.

Werbner, R. 1991. *Tears of the Dead: The Social Biography of an African Family*. International African Institute. Edinburgh: Edinburgh University Press.

West, J. (ed.) 1982. *Work, Women and the Labour Market*. London: Routledge and Kegan Paul.

Whisson, M. and W. Weil 1971. *Domestic Service: A Microcosm of the 'Race Problem'*. Johannesburg: South African Institute of Race Relations.

Willis, P. 1979. 'Shop-floor culture, masculinity and the wage form', in J. Clarke, C. Critcher and R. Johnson (eds), *Working Class Culture: Studies in History and Theory*. London: Hutchinson.

Willott, S. and C. Griffin 1996. 'Men, masculinity and the challenge of long-term unemployment', in M. Mac an Ghaill (ed.), qv.

Women's Service League of Tanganyika 1947. *Notes for Newcomers to Tanganyika Territory*. Dar es Salaam: Government Printer.

Women's Service League of Tanganyika 1948. *Notes on African Domestic Labour in Dar es Salaam*. Dar es Salaam: Government Printer.

World Bank. 1979/1990/1994. *World Development Reports*. Washington.

Wright, M. 1993. *Strategies of Slaves and Women: Life stories from East/Central Africa*. New York: Lilian Barber Press.

Wrigley, J. 1991. 'Feminists and domestic workers', *Feminist Studies* 17 (2), 317–29.

Yeager, R. 1989. *Tanzania: An African Experiment*. 2nd. ed. Boulder: Westview.

INDEX